CONTENTS

IV IT'S SHOWTIME!

ACKNOWLEDGMENTS

First of all, I would like to thank my Father, John L. Hayes for his contributions in Chapter One. His help and recollections gave me the basis and framework for that chapter. With help from others whom I will thank individually, we were able to use his framework and fill in the blanks in the timeline so time periods would be relevant and historically correct. Thanks again for your help Dad.

Next, I would like to thank my Uncles: Gordon, Gilbert, Keith, Charlie and Patrick for blazing the trail carved out by their Father, Leander 'Lea' Hayes, my Grandfather who expanded the Las Vegas Entertainment Industry. I know it wasn't easy and there were probably more hardships and problems than rewards, but what you created is still standing and going strong nearly 80 years after its inception. You are all the true stars of Las Vegas.

A heartfelt thank you goes out to the true headliners of the Las Vegas Entertainment Industry: my Grandfather Leander and my Grandmother Emma. Now that I have read much more of their life stories, I appreciate the incredibly difficult times in which they lived and bear witness to the magnitude of the undertaking they engaged in. I am but one beneficiary, as are the thousands of others behind the scenes and their families. It truly saddens me to know my Grandparents did not benefit financially, to any degree, commensurate with their work and sacrifice. Thank you for working so hard and sacrificing so much.

A warm thank you goes out to my Mother Sharron and my Aunts Jeanette, Marge, Palma, Carole, Karen, Lois, and Bobbee for their supporting roles in this play we call Showbiz. Being married to my Uncles and supporting them whether they pursued their careers in or out of Showbiz set a wonderful example for the rest of the family. Thanks so very much.

I acknowledge with the deepest of gratitude my cousins Kathryn, Stacey, Palma, Gordon, Garry, Bryan, Krista, and Teresa for the information and research given to me concerning their fathers. My favorite part of this book has been reconnecting with all of you and sharing stories about our family. You are all awesome.

A huge thank you goes out to Victoria Hart @ Pink Kitty Creative for her mad skills at graphic design. I know this is the most complicated layout I have thrown at you thus far and you once again knocked it out of the park. Thank you again.

I am grateful to have such an incredible proofreading and editing team: My wife Linda, always the first to proofread and edit my books. Thank you for supporting me in yet another book which both requires time and money in order to complete. My Mother Sharron Leavitt for investing your time and skill in editing and improving my stories. You bring a great deal to the table. My dear friend, Kelli Draper Wolf, my occasional ghost writer, who threatens to never speak to me again, our Friendship teetering in question each time I tell her I have another Project in mind. I thought you would never work with me again after we completed, 'After Our Fall.' I am so glad you finally agreed to join me, again, on yet another one of my crazy adventures. This is my editing and proofreading super team, punctuated by the 'piece de resistance,' Christine M. Allen!!

To those who contributed all of their wonderful stories in Chapter Eight, I know it isn't easy to put yourself out there and share your life with the rest of the world. I deeply appreciate you for taking the time and not being shy with this project. Thank you again.

Applause, Applause, Applause! For each and every character that performed a role in this 'Production,' there were no small parts in this 'Play' and everyone's contribution made this book what it is. Thank You.

A final thank you goes out to Chuck Rounds for his eye in creating the cover photo.

DEDICATION

First and foremost I dedicate this book to my Grandfather Leander Fields Hayes and my Grandmother Lavenia Emma Casper-Hayes for everything they did in expanding the Las Vegas Entertainment Industry. This dedication also includes the true visionaries of what Las Vegas' potential could be. A massive hat tip goes out to Billy Wilkerson and Benjamin "Bugsy" Siegel.

Secondly, I dedicate this book to my Uncles; Gordon, Gilbert, Keith, Charlie, Patrick, and my Father John for all the work they did in the early days of Las Vegas entertainment. They established the standards, craft professionalism, and work ethic along with other like minded individuals throughout our industry.

Thirdly, I dedicate this book to each and every entertainer who came seeking fame and fortune on the stages in the Las Vegas hotels. Most of you never achieved what you sought but my hat is off to you for putting yourselves out there and taking your shot at grabbing the golden ring. For those of you who found success, regardless of its degree, you made Las Vegas what it is today; "The Entertainment Capitol of the World."

Last, but certainly not least, I dedicate this book to my Brothers and Sisters in I.A.T.S.E. Local 720. My fellow stagehands and wardrobe craftspeople are, for the most part, examples of what true professionals and craftspeople should be. I am proud of my 40 plus years working out of Local 720 and look forward to several more years of working in the greatest industry in the world. You are not only my co-workers, you are my friends.

FOREWORD

What can I say about someone who is one of my very best friends? Who is one of the nicest, kindest, most generous people that I know; *(no...he did not pay me to say this...)* someone who I have known, and worked next to in different capacities - for over 40 plus years; someone who has worked with professional and not-so-professional (lol), entertainers and technicians, on a wide variety of music-projects and other types of media-projects for decades...someone who has walked with me as my friend and a co-creative, through many of the ups and downs of life, from high-school years, to recent times, in Church activities, through music-projects, live-concerts, and beyond; someone who has taught me many of the pro-sound & pro-visual stage techniques that I have used throughout my career.

Craig is one of those guys who constantly thinks outside-the-box: highly creative, unafraid, and yet simultaneously knows how to work effectively within established teams and systems, but then can alter and even improve those system's dynamics where needed.

He is one of the hardest working people I know! I have always appreciated his down-to-earth, no-BS approach to life, and to getting the job done! He is well-respected within many Las Vegas Entertainment Industry circles; as well he should be, as he has worked consistently in the capacities of live and recorded sound, stage and music production.

We have enjoyed decades together, working in a multitude of interesting, often unexpected, even bizarre, and sometimes-hilarious situations: on stage and behind-the-scenes, 'on and behind' the camera, as the stories within this book demonstrate!

Whether dealing with a green-room (dressing-room) full of highly eccentric, and temperamental performers (5 minutes before showtime) or a busload full of smelly, scrapping, cheeky Boy Scouts, he always could, and did, and does, maintain his cool.

Show-Business / Entertainment is more than just a side-jaunt, more than simply a "fun idea," or a "fun ride." It is a multi-billion-dollar industry that employs millions, AND that entertains, educates, and inspires audiences around the world. In many ways, show-business represents a microcosm of the many, varied situations, and personalities, that one may come across in everyday life. Learning to confidently negotiate different challenges, which constantly pop-up on stage, on camera, or in the studio, refines those who are directly involved - both on and off stage.

Seeing that Craig has worked over 20,000 shows, across 40-plus years, serving in multiple roles - as Stagehand, Stage-Tech, Layout and Construction Carpenter, Head-Carpenter,

Stage Director, Technical Director, Cue Caller, Lounge-Tech, Audio-Engineer, Music-Producer, High Rigger, Laser Technician / Operator, Scenic Artist, Lighting-Designer, Welder, Job Steward, and 'Head-Problem-Solver,' it is safe to assume that he has seen virtually every kind of situation imaginable, while quietly evolving into a seasoned PRO and has been able to lend some of that experience to others around him.

It has been my great privilege to work with Craig on a variety of songs and artist projects - including one of our favorite album-projects, the independently-produced album "Contrary To Popular Belief." A Las Vegas-based, multi-artist, multi-genre, compilation-album / concept, that was years ahead of its time! Thirty years later, this collection of songs is still a pleasure to listen to and still garners compliments from others who have listened to it: a testament to its timelessness, and the TLC, engineering, and production skills incorporated into its creation and development.

Here we are, 40-plus years later, (from literally bumping into each other - "accidentally" in a chapel gymnasium; me with my boom-box, Craig with his basketball - all those years ago - in the early 80's) and here we are still - creating music and visuals together. In fact, we're making plans to work on the long-awaited sequel to "Contrary To Popular Belief."

As you read through the pages of this entertaining and informative book, you will be transported through a variety of wonderful stories and anecdotes centering around Craig's point-of-view, his connection with other entertainment-specialists, and his connection with the entertainment world within Las Vegas.

Chapter 1 - covers some of the early history (much of the last century) of showroom entertainment in Las Vegas, starting with Craig's Grand-Parents: Leander & Emma Hayes and their six sons, and the overall impact that they had in show business in the Entertainment Capital of the World.

Chapter 2 - recounts stories from Craig's earlier years, (ranging from age four to twenty years old) including his beginnings and evolution in the stagehands union, the International Alliance of Stage and Theatrical Employees, (I.A.T.S.E., Local 720), which naturally introduced and connected him to a wide variety of situations, shows, and entertainers.

Chapter 3 - shares his years at the Mint Hotel in Las Vegas and at the Merlin-Perth Hotel in Australia, along with the many up-and-downs of show-biz life and the ways in which it affected his family life as well.

Chapter 4 - reveals how Craig temporarily got out of Showbiz and tried his hand at building custom pools and waterfalls.

Chapter 5 - covers his years at the Riviera Hotel on the Strip. It was here that Craig was thrown into an endless array of different shows, formats, casts, and even new technology / equipment, of which he had to quickly adapt to, and navigate through - i.e. he never said *"No!"* His ability to acclimate to whatever situation came up, allowed him to maintain and progress through higher levels of stagecraft, and made him an ever more valuable Stage-Technician.

Chapter 6 - describes his time at the Las Vegas Hilton (now known as the Westgate Resort Las Vegas). It was there that all those years working at smaller venues paid off, in-as-much-as he was able to work the big stages with big names on a consistent basis from Barry Manilow to Smokey Robinson. From Brookes & Dunn to Styx. From Tony Bennett to ZZTop. From Earth, Wind and Fire, to Etta James. From Jamie Foxx to Damon Williams. The list goes on and on. 20,000 shows! *Holy crap!*

Chapter 7 - focuses on Craig's present situation in life, and what he thinks he might be doing over the next few years.

Chapter 8 - encompasses many colorful stories from friends, co-workers, and Stagehands whom Craig has associated with throughout his life in show business.

Epilogue - brings everything together, including Craig's final thoughts and feelings pertaining to show business.

Encore - Encore - is two parts. The first half covers an interview with Craig's Grandfather Leander Hayes recounting some of the history of entertainment in Las Vegas in an interview given to the University of Nevada Las Vegas Historical Project. The second half is the autobiography of Leander Hayes.

Recommendation: I thoroughly enjoyed reading through the pages of this book and you will too! It is informative and enlightening while simultaneously entertaining. Enjoy!

Talbot T. Snow

PREFACE

It's Opening Night!

You purchased your tickets months ago. This day has finally arrived! The line you are in slowly serpentines through the casino passing games of chance on its way into the Showroom. You couldn't help yourself. You tried out Lady Luck and she paid off, but the few dollars you won are not the reason you are here tonight.

You are now at the front of the line about to enter the showroom. An usher at the door takes your ticket and another usher steps up and guides you to your seats, but you are not ready to sit down, yet. They point out the way to the bar and you go to get your drinks. You return with drinks in hand and are sitting with your date waiting for the show to begin when a Cashman Photo photographer asks if you want to capture this moment! Now you will always remember this evening and can't help fidgeting in your seats anticipating the start of the show.

Everyone around you is excited and they all have similar stories regarding what it took for them to be here tonight.

Suddenly the pre-show music fades out and the house lights are dimmed to half intensity. This pause lasts for about 30 seconds, but it seems much longer. Then the lights gradually fade until they are completely out. You can't even see your date sitting next to you when out of the darkness you hear a voice boom out over the sound system introducing the entertainer you came to see tonight.

Music from the band begins playing, lights flash as they pan over the audience, your pulse quickens and the main curtain quickly flies up and out of view. The entire stage is open and comes to life as you watch the band carts filled with singers, musicians and their instruments, move into position. While all of this is taking place, scenic elements are displayed on giant video walls strategically located all over the stage. You are not sure where to look. There is only one thing missing.

From behind the curtain stage right, the star of the show enters, running to center stage. He is as close to the audience as he can get. He strikes a pose as five Lycian M-2 long throw spotlights simultaneously open up on him. Everyone jumps to their feet applauding and cheering. Electricity fills the air. The show has officially begun!

For the next 90-120 minutes, the length of a typical Las Vegas Show, the audience will be transported. Taken on a ride with lyrics, music, and storytelling, highlighted with lighting and video images, carefully prepared and packaged for them by the entertainer. If done right, strangers can become family if only for a couple hours. Their shared experience and memories can last a lifetime.

The audience never saw the invisible people working behind the scenes to make tonight's show happen. This would include the 21 stage technicians, the hotel's management team, and the artist's production team. Unless you are the type of person that likes to read all the credits at the end of a movie, none of those 35 people mean anything to you. All that mattered was that you saw a great show. The work that goes on behind the scenes in the shadows is where professional stage technicians thrive. We are Theatrical Stagehands.

Before you enjoyed the opening night festivities and performance, we had spent weeks loading in, setting up and preparing for technical 'tech' rehearsals. This is a fancy way of saying we are going to test every piece and every part over and over and over again to ensure everything works and functions flawlessly. Perfect every time. These tech rehearsals will include learning to operate new equipment such as upgraded robotic lights, high definition video wall / projection systems and new rigging automation controls.

Critical to the show's performance is the driving of the band carts. Band cart driving school will take time, prior to and after, tech rehearsals. The drivers must learn to steer their respective band carts from underneath, in the dark, with near zero visibility following a line taped on the floor, trying not to crash into one another with the singers and band members dancing above them.

All technical issues are resolved one at a time.

While all this is going on, the creative team has been working around the clock programming lighting looks that blend beautifully with the video elements.

The artist and his band are scheduled to arrive tonight and rehearsals are planned for tomorrow morning. If all goes well today, we will just make these deadlines.

Everyone on the crew has been working 12 hours a day for weeks without a day off and it shows. We are all tired and the real work and long days haven't even started yet. Opening night is in three weeks and there is still so much work to do. Those weeks will consist of work days lasting 8-12 hours each day. If anything breaks and needs repair or if there needs to be reprogramming of lighting or video content then these things will take place at night when everyone else has gone home.

Opening night is only a week away and everyone is exhausted. A day off would be the greatest gift ever, but it is not in the cards. We're in the final push and from here on out it will be 12-16 hour days. In the thick of it, you can't help but think of days off, and dream of what you might do if there was such a thing. It is your own personal light at the end of the tunnel.

If opening week goes well, there is that light, and your dream of a day off materializes. However, that hint of a dream is still seven days away. If there are issues you take a deep breath and hold onto the dream. Exhausted or not. You make it happen. Long after the sun has set, in the middle of your rehearsing 12-16 hours a day, you do eventually get to go home. By the time you do leave until your head hits the pillow you are on autopilot. You walk in the door and all you want is sleep but you force yourself to shower first. With a mere 8 hours between the time you leave and clock in again the next morning, you appear to your family a vaporous apparition but this schedule is nothing new to them. They have seen *'Ghost-Dad,'* or *'Ghost-Mom,'* many times before.

An hour before the talent arrives, the crew prepares the stage for rehearsal. There is much to do in that one hour. The stage needs to be swept, mopped, the band carts need to be cleaned and set at their 'top of show' positions, the flying Plexiglass stage needs to be checked and polished. The winches on the video walls need to be checked and calibrated. All burned out lamps and broken lighting instruments and video equipment needs to be changed out. All show changes from last night's rehearsal need to be implemented into our individual '*cue sheets*' (i.e. individual parts / tracks of the show.)

The show opens tomorrow night, come hell or high water. This final push has paid off and everyone is confident in their *show cues*. If everything goes well today, we will have a shorter day tomorrow with only two or three full dress rehearsals. No stops.

Opening Night is finally here! The full dress rehearsals went well and everyone just wants to do the show 'for real.' We're ready! In just over an hour doors open and the most pertinent part of the production arrives, the Audience! It's crunch time! A final check of all show systems is completed. Everything needs to be cleaned, polished, and prepped one final time. The crew cross-checks all systems ensuring everything *is* perfect.

It's 10 minutes 'til doors.' As Head Carpenter, I make one last check before I call the Head Flyman to bring in the Main Curtain. I then call for the Head of Lighting to bring up the walk-in look and to the Head Soundman to start the pre-show audio (walk-in-music) and inform the Head Usher the room is theirs. With flashlights in hand, the ushers begin greeting and guiding some 1,500 people who funnel in and circulate through the aisles bringing the Showroom to life! While they are coming in the front door, we head out the back door to take a meal break.

The crew arrives back on stage thirty minutes before the show to check everything again. As the band trickles in and are settling in '*to* (their) *places*' on the band carts, they greet the crew and the banter starts up. It is a much needed and more light-hearted break than the past few weeks. Everything will become serious in just a few minutes. At five minutes 'til, I start the roll call on headset. The crew is expected to be set and ready now, but occasionally there are one or two missing still wrapping up last minute pre-show checks and bio breaks and it's a last chance for a bit of banter to wiggle in, rearing its little head.

We are ready, to finally 'Do What We Do!' With a noticeable change in vocal tone, I send a silent nod understood by my crew for radio chatter to end, 'it's on,' as I confirm to the Stage Manager (cue caller), via headset, "the Stage is set and ready!" Now we wait.

The star of the show arrives on stage behind the Main Curtain and walks around to his band, backup singers, and Music Director to *joke around* with them and give a final note or two for the show. He takes his place stage right behind the curtain for his entrance and gives the signal for the show to start. The lights are going out and the music has stopped playing.

It's Showtime…!

You have just seen the best show of your life. You haven't noticed any of us or what goes on behind the scenes. Nor do you have any idea what it took to make tonight actually happen. This is not your concern; it is ours and we love it!

What you have just read is 100% accurate for some of the shows I have worked. Depending on the size and scale of the show, this same scenario plays out for every show in Las Vegas. All shows require a great deal of labor and time to perfect. The key to making it look simple is to rehearse, rehearse, and rehearse some more. This is what we do every day, {When… we are allowed to.} For, this is 'Our Lives Behind the Scenes on Las Vegas Showroom Stages.'

I truly hope you enjoy what you are about to read.

CHAPTER ONE: WHERE I CAME FROM

All books begin with their author choosing a subject he or she wants to explore and give their perspective on. Then he or she outlines and creates the story. I know this process very well. I usually start a story with a simple idea and know the end of the story before beginning the first chapter. The rest of the chapters are designed to connect the end with the beginning. Our lives are prime examples of this writing process. The real question is, how many chapters of a book do we have?

I believe I still have a few chapters left in my life and career in Showbiz. My personal journey started over 50 years ago.

It would be easy to jump right in and start telling story after story from my life working on stages in Las Vegas for over 40 years, but this would be an incomplete history. The story of my life on a stage both as a performer and as a stage technician begins in Menan, Idaho circa 1925.

I can already hear it from you. 'What in the world does a little backwoods town in the middle of Idaho some 600 miles from Las Vegas have to do with 'The Entertainment Capitol of the World?' The explanation requires our going back in time even further.

There are two very important years and two locations we will need to visit if for only a very short time. The first date is 1907 and the location is Salt Lake City, Utah. The second date is 1910 and the location is Lewisville, Idaho. The truly miraculous part of this story is how these obscure locations and times all tie up in a neat little bow as we work our way towards the early days of Las Vegas.

As we travel back to Salt Lake City, Utah in1907 we note the birth of a baby boy. There is nothing special, unique, or of great significance about this child. There are many children born during this year. None of those babies will have the experiences this baby will have during his life. His name is Leander Fields Hayes. He is my grandfather. I would like to say it was obvious his birth, upbringing, and early years showed what he was destined to become and accomplish, but it was not. He would spend the next 12 years growing up and acting like all other boys in Salt Lake City and Vernal, Utah.

When Lea was in his early teens, the family moved from Salt Lake City to Rigby, Idaho. In high school, Lea became quite the basketball player. In fact it was during his senior year that Lea was an all-state basketball player. You might think this to be no big deal but for me it is amazing. You see, Lea was only five feet-five inches tall. What he lacked in size he made up for in tenacity and skills.

Basketball in the early 1900's was played in a completely different way than what we see today. Back then, if you got a lead of say 4+ points you would stall or play keep away from the other team. There was no 24 second shot clock. You could also run all over the court during this stall time. There was no over and back rule for half court. Perhaps Lea's short stature and agility was a perfect fit for the style of basketball they played back then, and size really didn't matter.

We can now move onto the second date and location. It is now 1910 in Lewisville, Idaho. A baby girl is born to a family of potato farmers. Her official name is Lavenia Emma Casper, but she prefers to be called and will always be known as Emma. She is my grandmother. As she grows up she is found to have an exceptional talent for music. She will become a great piano and organ player. This skill will benefit her later after her marriage.

EMMA CASPER HAYES
AROUND 30 YEARS OLD.

LEANDER FIELDS HAYES
AROUND 20 YEARS OLD.

Sometime during 1927, a young man from Rigby, Idaho and a young lady from Lewisville, Idaho meet, date, fall in love, and get married. To earn a living, they would form a joint venture showing silent movies in churches and gymnasiums all over Idaho. Their home base of operations was Menan, Idaho. Lea would set up and run the projection for the movies and Emma would play the piano or organ for these films. She would sit facing the movie and play the mood music as the film played. If there was a chase scene, she would play fast dramatic music. If there was a love scene she would set the mood with soft music and so on. This was making them a living, but it was not a life.

By 1929, the Hayes family was living in Soda Springs, Idaho. They were still showing movies at night, but now Lea had become a Shell Oil dealer for a section of Idaho. It was a risky business but it had high earning potential. Purchasing supplies on credit for the gas stations in his area placed a great deal of financial pressure on the family. Then it seemed to have paid off. Lea received a $10,000 check from Shell Oil Company and went to the bank in Soda Springs to deposit it. In 1929 this check for $10,000 was a fortune.

Now Lea could pay off all the debts he had incurred and still have a sizable amount of money left over for the family and for future business expenses. It was on a Friday when Lea deposited the check. This was the Friday, (October 25) before the stock market crash on Tuesday October 29, 1929 the following week. When Lea went to the bank the week of the crash the bank informed him they had no record of any check being deposited by him. To put it plainly, the bank stole the money, probably to shore up their own balance sheets. The safeguards we have today did not exist then. Lea and Emma had no other recourse than to figure out what to do next about all their debt.

Times were about to get even more difficult. The economy was crashing and heading towards the depression and Lea had a great deal of debt. He could have done what so many others during that time did and file for bankruptcy but he didn't. He was a man of honor and integrity. He had borrowed money and promised to pay it back. This is what he did. It took a few years to do so but every loan he had taken out was paid back in full. It was time to leave Soda Springs.

There is some conflict in accuracy with the above story. I have presented it the way I was told by Lea and my father John over the years. In Lea's autobiography, which you can read at the end of this book, the above story is not mentioned. This may have been an oversight on Lea's part, but I wanted to mention it here for accuracy and for full disclosure so the reader can determine its validity.

The family moved back to Menan for a short time and Lea worked in the family store. He would only be there for a short time before moving to Logan, Utah. While in Menan, Charlie was born bringing the family to four sons.

The family moved to Logan, Utah. Lea and Emma were the parents of four sons, Gordon, Gilbert, Keith, and Charlie. Lea took a job as the projectionist at the city's movie theater and Emma played the mood music. She would soon be obsolete as a musician. A new invention for the movies was sweeping the nation. As "talkies" movies became the standard, (movies that had sound imbedded into the film and played simultaneously with the movie), theaters replaced their musicians with projectors and audio equipment. The onetime expense of the new equipment came with a human cost. As theaters were switched over to "talkies" films, musicians lost their jobs and were added to the unemployment rolls. The positive side of this new technology was once the new equipment was paid for, theaters became more profitable. Human cause and effects aside, theaters now showed the movies as the directors and screenwriters envisioned the story.

The 1933 film "King Kong" is of special interest to me. The movie's female lead was Fay Wray. She is the first cousin to Emma. Everywhere I look in the past with Lea and Emma I see 'Showbiz' intersecting their lives. If they could only see what their lives were about to become in Showbiz, they probably would not have believed their eyes.

The Great American Depression placed a great deal of stress and strain on the American people. With unemployment ranging from 10-25%, it seemed as if life in America would never improve. The people needed an escape from reality. They needed a short respite from the gloom. They needed…the movies.

As a child and into my early adult life, I could not understand why movie theaters thrived during the depression while other businesses failed. Until you are an adult and have had to struggle through a financial collapse or downturn, you really can't comprehend such a thing.

I have been through several such downturns and fully understand now.

The world in 1929 may have been collapsing all around them, but two hours in a movie theater gave the desperate and in despair the shot of joy they needed to endure the difficult times of the period. Theater owners were making a very good profit during these times. This became obvious to the employees of the theaters as they seek a raise in their pay. Some owners 'spread the wealth' with their employees. Others take a different path. Economic downturns mixed with greed and zero compassion brings out the worst in some people.

It was around 1940-1941 when the projectionists in Logan, Utah went on strike seeking better wages. Today, negotiators and arbitrators would work on behalf of both sides to avoid a strike or end one quickly. In 1940, the theater owners took a different tactic.

While Lea and his fellow projectionists walked the picket line in front of the movie theaters, cars pulled up in front of them and out climbed some of the biggest goons the theater owners could find. Their job was to bust up the strike and end it or bust up the strikers, or both. Almost immediately the goons began beating the strikers. The fight was on. I know my grandfather. I have never known him to be afraid of anyone. Additionally, he always liked a good fight. It was the Irish in him. I know he dished out some pain on the goons but in the end he took more of a beating than he dished out.

The writing was on the wall. Logan was no place to raise his sons. He also found that by striking at the theater and losing his job, no other businesses in Logan would give him work. He had to leave and seek work somewhere else.

The decision to leave may have been apparent, but where to go was the big question. A solution was given to Lea by the International Alliance of Theater and Stage Employees and Moving Picture Machine Operators of the United States and Canada. Herein we will refer to this union as the 'International' and the local union in Las Vegas as 'Local 720'. There was a need for qualified projectionists in Nevada, Arizona, and Southern California. It had become difficult due to World War II to supply personnel to cover days off for full time employees in those states.

LEA HAYES (SIXTH FROM LEFT SIDE, BOTTOM ROW) WORKING ON A WESTERN; MOVIE TITLE AND LOCATION UNKNOWN.

With no other viable option he made the decision to leave Emma and their five sons in Logan and become a 'nomadic' projectionist. Lea spent 1941 and 1942 doing three things: driving from town to town, showing movies, and missing his family in Logan. This was not the ideal life but with a depression still lingering on and a war being fought on two continents this was the life they had to make work.

As a side note here, I have discovered a little bit of history concerning two of my ancestors. In 1932, my great grandfather on my mother's side, Thomas Dudley Leavitt was hired as the projectionist at the Boulder Theater in Boulder City, Nevada. Boulder City was a "company town." It was established by the Six Companies Incorporated (the companies building Hoover Dam) as a place where the workers and their families could live. Thomas worked in Boulder City at the movie theater until 1937. He moved to the Moapa Valley or Logandale, Nevada for a year or two but returned to Boulder City around 1939.

He worked for the city for two years before working in the Earl Brothers Movie Theater as a projectionist for one year. The 1941-1942 time periods would fit perfectly with Lea traveling the Southwest as a relief projectionist. I am not sure if Lea and Thomas ever met or if Lea filled in for Thomas on one of his days off. I would think the likelihood is very strong they did.

I just thought how strange it would have been to have two of my ancestors meet and work with each other not knowing what their direct descendants would do or become. Mainly, I find it interesting that Showbiz runs through both sides of my family.

As stated before, World War II was in full swing during those years of endless travel for Lea. In 1943 a little town southeast of Las Vegas would change the present and future for the Hayes family. The name of the town was Basic, Nevada. It was a company town formed around the Basic Magnesium Incorporated factory or plant. The company's plant supplied metals to the U.S. Government for the war effort. The town was growing quickly and of course they needed a movie theater for the factory employees.

To help you visualize where this little town is located in the Las Vegas Valley, here is your clue. The town would years later change its name to Henderson, of course. Lea was offered the position of projectionist for the new theater and he gladly took it. There would be no more endless traveling for Lea. He had a full time position with a steady income. He could now send for Emma and their six sons to join him.

After arriving in Southern Nevada in 1943, the family moved into their new home in Basic (Henderson) but they would only be whole for one year. In 1944 Emma took their five youngest sons back to Logan, Utah. It was never made clear why Emma did this. I know the air quality in Basic was poor and it led to the youngest son Patrick getting poisoned and becoming very ill. It may have been for this reason or a plethora of other reasons Emma left the Las Vegas Valley. This separation from Lea only lasted for one year.

The first time Lea was Local 720's Business Representative occurred during this year. At a General Membership meeting, the current Business Representative resigned his position leaving a temporary vacancy needing to be filled until formal nominations and a vote could take place. Lea was asked by the President of Local 720 to fill in during this time. He accepted a temporary assignment but did not seek the position at the nomination meeting. He would, in less than eight years, seek the position and be elected by the membership to represent them.

In August of 1945, World War II ended and so did the split up of the Hayes family. Emma returned to the Las Vegas Valley with the five youngest sons and they moved into their new home in Las Vegas on 15th Street and Charleston Boulevard. She would remain in Las Vegas and in that very house until the day she passed away.

After Emma had settled into her new home, Lea took her for a drive towards Los Angeles, California. When he pulled off the road leading out of town about five miles from downtown Las Vegas, he showed her a large piece of land he wanted to buy. The land cost $850 and Lea had the money on him but wanted Emma's approval before concluding the transaction. Emma, being a potato farmer, could not see the value in any land you can't grow crops on so they didn't buy the land. Oh, if they had only known.

A few months later that very same land would be bought by a true visionary who wanted to change Las Vegas. His nickname was 'Bugsy,' or was it?

There is a misconception about Las Vegas, gambling, prostitution, and the mob. Some believe the mob brought gambling and all the vices that go with it to Las Vegas. Gambling was legalized in Nevada in 1931. The consumption of alcoholic beverages was legalized in 1933. Prostitution is still legal in Nevada but it was outlawed in (Clark County) Las Vegas since 1971. The mob may have had their fingers in the operations of saloons and houses of ill repute but what they had in Benjamin 'Bugsy' Siegel was a mob associate with Hollywood connections willing to change the future in Las Vegas.

While Bugsy was driving to Los Angeles from Las Vegas, he pulled over five miles south of Downtown Las Vegas and saw the potential of a resort being built on that spot. This is the Hollywood version of 'Bugsy' starring Warren Beatty and Annette Bening. The truth is much more interesting.

The design and construction of the Flamingo Hotel was the brainchild of Billy Wilkerson. He was the owner of the Hollywood Reporter magazine and of several nightclubs along the Sunset Strip. Billy loved to gamble and wanted to own a luxury hotel in Las Vegas with a showroom and top gourmet restaurants. His vision was what the Flamingo was designed to become. There was just one slight problem.

After World War II there was a shortage of building materials in the nation. The cost of the materials you could get was exorbitant. Soon, Billy ran out of money to build his dream. Low and behold, there was Ben Siegel willing to buy out Billy and take over the project. Billy had no options but to sell. Bugsy would finish the construction and open the hotel to great fanfare with some help from his Hollywood buddies.

We should also correct one more error in the movie, 'Bugsy.' It was depicted that the Flamingo Hotel was the first hotel and casino built on Las Vegas Boulevard or 'The Strip.' It wasn't. Two other hotels were operating prior to the Flamingo. The El Rancho Vegas and New Frontier hotels were more reminiscent of the Downtown Las Vegas saloons.

As far as their entertainment attractions in these hotels, they each had a small stage where a solo or small group could perform for the hotel's guests. The main offering of entertainment was country and western music. The Flamingo was designed and built to change everything in Las Vegas.

At the time, saloons or gambling halls were mainly located in Downtown Las Vegas. In fact, Ben Siegel was part owner of the El Cortez gambling hall in Downtown Las Vegas. The hotel is still operating today. About those gambling halls; if you were to picture in your mind any movie about a saloon in the Wild West with a bar, poker tables, and other games of chance, you would be close to what the saloons looked like in 1945. To make the picture complete, add slot machines and of course a few prostitutes. Welcome to 1945 gambling in Las Vegas!

When Nevada legalized gambling in 1931, the state didn't create a gaming control board to regulate and investigate the casinos. It was a wide open frontier for anyone to exploit. Members of the mobs came to town looking to expand their influence and tap a new source of revenue. The mobs were the people who had the necessary experience to operate the saloons and cat houses. They had been running these types of businesses illegally for years in the east and on the west coast. Money from Las Vegas had been trickling into mob coffers for a few years but what Bugsy envisioned would bring a torrent of cash to the mob bosses.

In 1946, Las Vegas was reborn. Bugsy opened the Flamingo Hotel and Casino and created a resort destination for people from southern California. The modern era of themed resorts had begun. Soon, the era of mega resorts would take over and transform the Las Vegas Valley. The Golden Nugget also opened their doors for business on Fremont Street in Downtown Las Vegas that year. By comparison, it was just another saloon. The new resort five miles south was the true future of this town and a trend setter.

The Flamingo was being built to be a resort. It had the usual casino with all the latest games of chance. There were bars and cocktail waitresses in order for you to wet your whistle with an adult beverage. Restaurants were strategically placed in the casino so you had to walk past gaming areas on your way to and from a good meal. A lounge with live

THE HAYES FAMILY CIRCA 1950. FRONT ROW: PATRICK, LEA, JOHN, AND EMMA. BACK ROW: GORDON, CHARLIE, KEITH, AND GILBERT.

music gave atmosphere and excitement to the casino floor. A headliner showroom was built into the hotel for an extra touch of entertainment panache. The hotel rooms were actually bungalows situated around the swimming pool. Nothing like this had ever been seen in Las Vegas and this would now be the standard for all resorts in this town.

While the Flamingo was being built, Lea was sent by the elected officers of Local 720 to meet with the owner and offer him the services of the union. When Lea met with Ben Siegel, he told the new owner how impressed he was with the resort he was building. Lea then went on to inform Ben that he was a member of a trade union and could supply Ben Siegel with stage technicians to operate the lounge and showroom. After some discussions, an agreement was reached between the Flamingo Hotel and Local 720. With a handshake between the two men, the union would supply technicians to operate the entertainment venues on the new property.

The handshake between Benjamin 'Bugsy' Siegel and Leander Fields Hayes did more than secure good paying jobs for stage technicians at a single hotel. It began the Las Vegas Entertainment Industry which would eventually create the title of 'The Entertainment Capitol of the World' as a trademark for Las Vegas. The handshake also transformed Local 720 from a movie projectionist union into a mixed local union. Local 720 was now a big player in all entertainment venues whether they were movie theaters, convention rooms, or hotels.

No one knew it at the time, but Las Vegas was about to go on a 70 year building boom as resorts were built, demolished, built bigger, demolished, and turned into the mega resorts we see today. In the early years of this building boom Lea and his sons would be involved in the installation and operation of almost every one of the new showrooms being built. Many of those showrooms owe a great deal of thanks to my Grandfather, Uncles, and my Father, John, for their work in those early years.

The next major resort to be built in Las Vegas was the Thunderbird in 1948. I have not been able to get any clear confirmation of Lea's work at this resort. Suffice it to say he was most likely involved with technical advice or at the least supplying qualified stage technicians to the resort. This pattern of his involvement would continue for many years into the future.

In 1950, with the opening of the Desert Inn Resort, Lea would begin nearly 30 years of working with his sons on stages throughout Las Vegas. Lea retired before I started working through Local 720. It would have been great to have worked on any stage with my Father, Uncles, and Grandfather all at the same time. There was one unique feature the Desert Inn had that no other resort had, an 18-hole golf course. Las Vegas resorts were changing to cater to a wider clientele. Uncle Gordon was made the head technician at the Desert Inn. This was quite an accomplishment considering he was only 22 years old at the time. Uncle Keith would run spotlight at night for the various shows. He was not looking for a full time stage job because he had other interests. He was attending school during the day on his way to becoming a lawyer and eventually a judge.

The same year the Desert Inn opened, another much smaller casino opened across the street. It was called the

Silver Slipper. The property was similar to the downtown saloons. It had a lounge and a small showroom for their customers' entertainment. Lea and Gordon were not involved with this property. The Flamingo was Lea's first concern as was the Desert Inn for Gordon.

It was during these early years of the 1950's when Lea was elected by the membership of Local 720 to be their Business Representative. He would be responsible for filling vacancies in the showrooms and lounges with qualified technicians. He would also need to represent an employee who was being disciplined by hotel management. Enforcing the contract was the most important duty of the Business Representative's Office. When I say contract, you might think of a long-winded document with conditions, pay, benefits, and requirements written into legal script. It was not. These were the early years of Las Vegas and the "contracts" were still verbal agreements sealed with a handshake.

Knowing my Grandfather like I do and having heard many a story about his time as Local 720 Business Representative, I can assure you of a few things. If you were a screw up and caused management to have a negative opinion of or lose confidence in Local 720, Lea would chew your a** out. He might even move to have you removed from the local. He expected every member to be a professional in our trade. He knew what we all know; bad members and problem children make it more difficult for the rest of us to earn a living.

In 1952 Lea would leave the Flamingo Hotel and take a position at the newly re-opened Sahara Hotel. During the day, Uncle Gordon worked with Lea on upgrades to the

Casbar Lounge and the Congo Showroom. Soon, Lea would be joined by his other sons working during the day on stages and working in their own showrooms at night.

When the Sands Hotel opened in 1952, Lea and Uncle Gordon did what was very common during those times. They worked during the day to install lights and sound in the showroom and lounge. They would then leave with time enough to go home, take a shower, grab a meal, and head off to their respective hotels to operate the shows. Most people would not undertake a lifestyle like this. In the Hayes family, this was the norm.

Three years later in 1955 my father, John, would run spotlight in the showroom at the Sands. It was his first stagehand job and he was only 17. Oh yeah, the star of the show was the 'Chairman of the Board,' Frank Sinatra. Lea now had five of his six sons working in the business at various hotels and in a variety of positions and capacities.

The Showboat Hotel opened its doors in 1954 near the corner of Fremont Street and Charleston Boulevard. The front of the hotel looked like a showboat with a turning paddle wheel set in water. The inside of the hotel was just another typical casino. It lacked a showroom or lounge and this gave Lea and sons a break from working double shifts that year.

Four new hotels opened their doors in 1955. The New Frontier Hotel and Casino was the first to open. Lea and sons had their fingerprints on this hotel's showroom and every other hotel showroom that opened during the year. There is a secondary reason why Lea and sons were so heavily involved in every showroom and lounge in the new hotels. It was not only because of their skills and work ethic. The opening of the Riviera Hotel and Casino brought another one of the Hayes boys into the business of stagecraft. Uncle Charlie worked on the Versailles Showroom stage from its opening until he was drafted into the U.S. Army after college.

The Dunes Hotel and Casino was the third to open their doors in 1955. Like the Desert Inn, the Dunes had an 18 hole-golf course on its back lot. The Moulin Rouge Hotel and Casino was the last of the four to open that year. Lea and sons were all involved with the consultation, installation, and checking the technical aspects of the sound and lighting systems in all of these hotel's showrooms and lounges.

There was a secondary reason why Lea and sons were so involved with the installation of every showroom's lighting and sound systems. With the rapid growth of the gambling and entertainment industries in Las Vegas, Lea saw an opportunity to not only secure employment for himself, his sons, and other technicians, he saw the building boom as a business opportunity.

Stage, Sound, and Equipment (henceforth known as SS&E), opened their doors in 1955. Lea and sons would not only work in the showrooms in Las Vegas but they would consult, supply, install, and quality check all needed equipment. Lea and Emma were the principle owners of this new company with their six sons all having shares in the business. Gordon, Gilbert, and John were the three sons who had the most involvement in the family business.

At its height, SS&E was the largest stage production company west of the Mississippi River. But just because one owns a successful stage production company doesn't mean he gets to sit back and enjoy life. Lea and his sons all worked the family business during the days and then went to their separate hotels at night and worked in the showrooms.

LEA HAYES OPERATING A LIGHTING CONSOLE IN A HOTEL SHOWROOM.

Showbiz is a very demanding mistress. If you allow her to, as many of us have, she will consume your life.

With the opening of the Fremont Hotel and Casino, Downtown Las Vegas, in 1956, SS&E was involved with the consultation, specifications, supplying, and installation of the hotel's showroom lighting and sound equipment. At the far south end of Las Vegas Boulevard in this same year the Hacienda Hotel and Casino opened for business. SS&E was heavily involved with their stage set up and Uncle Gilbert took the lead on the installation.

The Las Vegas Strip was now anchored on the north end by the Sahara Hotel and on the south end by the Hacienda Hotel. There was a lot of land in between these two hotels for additional resorts. To this point, the Tropicana Hotel and Casino opened their doors in 1957. SS&E was right in the middle of the showroom consultation, supplying of, and installation of their lighting and sound systems. This was also true during this year when a new downtown Las Vegas hotel opened for business. The Mint Hotel and Casino had a lounge that required the expertise of SS&E. It was very likely Gordon and Gilbert ran point on the consultation, recommendation of equipment, and supervised the installation of the lighting and sound systems in the Merrimint Lounge.

I have a point of interest here concerning the Mint Hotel, my Father, and myself. My father John worked in the Merrimint Lounge from 1960-1962. Sometime after I was born in 1962, Dad left the Mint to work elsewhere. Two decades later, I was working at the Mint Hotel in the

Merrimint Lounge when my three oldest children were born. History would not repeat itself again.

In 1958 the Stardust Hotel and Casino debuted on the Las Vegas Strip. SS&E was once again in the very thick of things concerning the Stardust's showroom and lounge. Lea and Uncle Gordon once again handled the consultation, design, supplying of equipment, and supervised the installation of the light and sound systems.

The showrooms and lounges had proven to be a lucrative source of revenue for SS&E but there were other aspects of a hotel and casino that were equally as lucrative. SS&E had moved into the design and installation of hotel and casino music and paging systems. They also did this type of work for smaller businesses around town. As new resorts opened or older resorts expanded, SS&E was there to handle those needs.

The larger resorts were not the only types of casinos opening up downtown and on the Las Vegas Strip. Smaller casinos more reminiscent to the early saloons were popping up all over town. They were no frills gambling joints. Slots, table games, bars, and a snack bar were the usual furnishings for these places. They were called 'grind joints' for a reason. They would focus their business model on smaller gambling limits and 'grind' out a profit from smaller bets. SS&E installed many of these 'grind joints' music and page systems.

Without looking ahead in this story, can you tell me what the 2nd and 3rd names of the Tally Ho Hotel and Casino were? If you said the Aladdin Hotel and Casino for the 2nd name and Planet Hollywood Hotel and Casino for the 3rd name, then you have lived in Las Vegas a long time. For bonus points, can you name the year the Tally Ho opened? It was 1963. SS&E did the usual consulting, supplying, and installation of equipment for the hotel showroom and lounge. None of the Hayes family worked at the property as far as I have been able to research.

Las Vegas has had a few hotels that could be called 'Icons.' In 1966 perhaps the most famous and world renowned resort opened. Caesars Palace Hotel and Casino became the newest resident on the Las Vegas Strip. SS&E had been very involved with its usual scope of work consulting, supplying, and installing the lighting and sound systems for the Circus Maximus showroom and Cleopatra's Barge, the hotel's lounge. Lea was hired to operate the stage elevators and John was hired to be the head flyman for the showroom.

Here is another three part quiz for you. Where was the Bonanza Hotel and Casino located? After its demolition, what hotel took its place? What is the name of the hotel there now? For a bonus point, when did the Bonanza Hotel open? The Bonanza Hotel was located on the southeast corner of the Las Vegas Strip and Flamingo Boulevard. After its demolition, the first MGM Grand Hotel and Casino opened in its place. The current name of the hotel and casino there now is Bally's Hotel and Casino. The answer to the bonus question is the Bonanza Hotel opened in 1967.

The Las Vegas casino market was growing and some new players were staking their claim to future fortunes. Kirk Kerkorian had bought the Flamingo Hotel a short time prior to 1967 and built the Bonanza as the newest jewel on the Las Vegas Strip. This would be the last hotel and stage SS&E would ever work in. SS&E would do their usual work in the showroom and John would become the Technical Director over entertainment for the Bonanza Hotel.

The acquisition of the Flamingo Resort and the opening of the Bonanza Hotel would not be the only investments in properties in Las Vegas for Kirk Kerkorian. He also bought 65 acres of land off the Las Vegas Strip and just north of the Las Vegas Convention Center. He had plans for that land, big plans. Earth moving machines were already clearing the land for what is to come.

It is 1967 and there needs to be some explanation about the demise of Stage, Sound, and Equipment or SS&E. Lea was 60 years old this year, and I am sure he was feeling the effects of a long life fighting for everything including his survival. He had lived through the Depression and kept his family alive and healthy. With every punch to the gut he doubled over but never fell to the ground. He eventually moved to Las Vegas and made a good living for Emma, his sons, a good number of stage technicians, and of course himself. He also created a prosperous business with SS&E. He had lived a life of honor, honesty, and integrity.

The hardest thing for a man like Lea Hayes to understand is people who do not share the same values and qualities that he holds dear.

Lea had entered into hundreds of agreements with the mob run hotels and casinos, schools, and convention centers with only a handshake. His word and his handshake were the only contracts Lea believed in. The times and people of Las Vegas were changing. His sons were having less to do with the family business and going their own way in the hotels. Lea was looking for a way out. When he made it known he was looking to sell SS&E, an investor from a Texas stage production company made the trip to Las Vegas and offered Lea $2.1 million for the entirety of SS&E.

This was what Lea was looking for. He could walk away from the business and have plenty of money to enjoy the rest of his and Emma's lives. His sons would get a share of the profits according to their stake in the company. This would help set them up for a comfortable future. It was almost too good to be true.

Over the objections of his sons, especially Keith who was now a lawyer and could see there was something wrong with this deal, Lea sold SS&E on a handshake and went home to pack for a long overdue vacation to the South Pacific with Emma. After a couple weeks, the agreed upon payment for the business was not made to Lea's account. When the sons went to the company building, it was obvious a theft had taken place. The building had been cleaned out of all the most expensive equipment.

This was not a random breaking in and burglary. This was done by fellow stage technicians who were in cahoots with the Texas investor and wanted to put SS&E out of business so they could start and grow their own businesses without competition from Lea and sons. To try and cover their tracks in the crime and assuage their guilt, once they (the fellow stage technicians) had taken their final load of gear from the premises they called the sons to tell them of something being amiss at SS&E.

Lea and Emma were contacted in New Zealand and told to come home. The business was gone and there was no money for their vacation. As Lea and Emma made their way back home to Las Vegas from Australia and New Zealand, the Hayes boys and some of the wives went to the SS&E shop and loaded up all the company vehicles with anything that was left of value. Keith then had them take the vehicles to his house and park them in his backyard.

Lea had been swindled. It would have been a far better feeling had it been done by professional business robbers. This was an inside job done by fellow stage technicians in his own union who owed their livelihood to Lea for all the work he had done on their behalf. Lea had created from scratch (with the handshake from Benjamin 'Bugsy' Siegel) a new division within Local 720's projection charter. Hundreds of technicians and their families including those who just organized the theft of SS&E benefitted from his work. This was a theft, but more disgustingly, it was a betrayal to the man who should have been revered. All I can hear in my head are the immortal words from Julius Caesar: "Et tu, Brute?"

Lea and Emma were now back in town and have witnessed the end results of the demise of SS&E. There would be no legal action taken by Lea against those who crafted this destruction; it would have been cost prohibitive. There would not be a call to rebuild the business. Starting over at

60 years old seemed daunting and Lea just didn't have the drive to do it again. Lea and Emma only had one option, get back to work. Lea found employment operating a spotlight at the Dunes hotel in the lounge. Emma found employment working at a home for un-wed mothers. She worked there until her death in 1974. Lea would retire from Local 720 after Emma's death and would pass away in 1983.

It's 1968 and we are going to bake a new casino cake. Mix a casino with all the usual games found in them with a hotel, a stage above the main casino floor with acts performing on it and above the heads of your gamblers. Add in a carnival midway with all the usual games of chance, and then throw in a bumper car track and a showroom. What do you have? Why, Circus Circus Hotel and Casino of course. Oh yeah, you will need to build your casino in the shape of a circus tent and paint everything in pink and white stripes. John was hired as Technical Director for all the entertainment venues at this hotel.

In 1968 this combination or collection of ideas under one roof was not only audacious but some critics thought it would never work. Fifty years and billions of dollars in revenue have proven those critics wrong. In fact, this one property generated enough revenue for it to build another copy of itself in Reno, Nevada for cash. The two properties then went on to build the Excalibur Hotel and Casino, the Luxor Hotel and Casino, and the Mandalay Bay Hotel and Casino purely out of cash flow.

Modeled after the Seattle Space Needle which opened in 1962, the Landmark Hotel and Casino opened in 1969. It had taken eight years to complete the futuristic hotel due to financing issues. Once Howard Hughes purchased the troubled property and put his wealth behind its completion, the opening was all but guaranteed. John worked on the installation crew in the showroom but didn't work any shows there. He was going across the street to another property that was about to open.

The Landmark would eventually close its doors and be destroyed by Martians in Tim Burton's movie 'Mars Attacks.' This was after it was purchased by the Las Vegas Convention Center and turned into a parking lot. It is now a massive convention hall across the street from the main convention center.

Kirk Kerkorian's newest project was called the International Hotel and Casino when it opened on July 31, 1969. I only know this date because I was hired on this exact date 25 years later to run the showroom. In its 50+ years of existence it has been through a few name changes. After the International Hotel was bought by Hilton Hotels it became the Las Vegas Hilton, then the LVH, and now it is called the Westgate Resort Las Vegas.

Kirk Kerkorian is an innovator. He put two main showrooms along with a lounge in his newest property. One showroom was for headline stars and the other was for production shows. This elevated entertainment policy would be his trademark as he built other hotels in Las Vegas. If you claim to be the 'Entertainment Capitol of the World' then you need to always be raising the bar and proving to the world that your claim is legitimate. This is the genius of Kirk Kerkorian.

Lea and Uncle Gilbert worked during the days of the installation process of stage, sound, and lighting equipment. SS&E was gone but the experience and knowhow of Lea and his sons was invaluable. At night, Lea and Uncle Gilbert would return to their respective showrooms and work the shows. Neither of them worked the International Showroom's opening night show of Barbara Streisand. The following day John was called in to help correct some issues that had arisen the night before. John took a position at the Sahara Hotel and Casino during the day and worked the shows in the International Showroom at night.

Kirk Kerkorian had not only raised the bar on what Las Vegas entertainment meant to the town he also set the bar much higher when it came to the hotel adjoining the casino.

LEA HAYES AND SONS AT EMMA'S FUNERAL IN 1974. L-R CHARLIE, PATRICK, GORDON, LEA, KEITH, JOHN, AND GILBERT.

From 1969 forward the theme in Las Vegas resorts was 'GO BIG, or GO EVEN BIGGER.' The dawn of the Las Vegas mega resorts was here.

During the 70's, Lea, Gordon, Gilbert, and John all worked at various hotels up and down the Las Vegas Strip. Thus far, none of the grandchildren of Lea and Emma had followed in Lea's footsteps and become stage technicians. As the 80's drew near, the next generation of Hayes family stage technicians would emerge.

Thus far I have covered a great deal of history and the work of Lea Hayes. It would be unfair not to give Emma a little space and a lot of appreciation for her contributions during those times. Lea may have been out fighting for meaningful employment but it was Emma who had to maintain the house and raise six sons. I am a firm believer she had the more difficult of the jobs.

Emma may have been a small woman in stature, but she was a giant when it came to working hard and enduring to the end. One thing is for sure concerning the life of Emma Hayes; she was a strong woman and only a strong woman could have endured these times.

I would like to share a story or two about Emma given to me by her youngest son Patrick.

EMMA'S BOBCAT STORY

It was a Sunday like most any Sunday at the Hayes' home.

I was home from college in 1962. Being the youngest of six boys, I was home by myself with only mom and dad to keep me company. I had decided to go to Sunday Service and mom decided to stay home to be there when dad woke up. When I came home I learned of a most interesting event that took place while I was gone.

Dad only had one day off a week and that day was Sunday. He worked six days a week at our family business, Stage Sound and Equipment and six nights a week operating the lighting console at one of the hotel showrooms in town. Saturday night's second show had ended at 2AM and dad came home to enjoy a good night's rest not having to work in the morning.

When he woke up, mom fixed him a good breakfast. After their meal, dad went into the living room and sat in his favorite chair by the entrance to the kitchen. If he desired, he could look to his right and look out the sliding glass door into the back yard. He usually just sat there quietly with his eyes shut and relaxed. He just needed to de-compress from another long week of work.

On this particular Sunday morning mom went to the sliding glass door to look at the birds, her yard, grapevines, fruit trees, and the large cat lying underneath the apricot tree. As mom described everything in the back yard she was looking at to dad, he kept his eyes shut and just listened, sort of. He would give a few vocal sounds to let her know he was still awake.

When mom described the cat as very large with brown fur, large paws, no tail, and pointed ears, dad heard every word she said but it wasn't registering with him. By this time, mom had gone to the kitchen, thinking the cat might be hungry, and found some food to give it. She went outside across the grass and dropped the food near the cat and it ate everything immediately. By the time mom dropped the food; dad had finally come to his senses and realized what she had described a moment earlier. It wasn't a cat. It was a Bobcat. Dad opened the door to go outside and he was stage whispering, "Emma, that's a Bobcat!" Mom rushed quickly into the house.

Once inside, dad called the Police and animal control to remove the Bobcat as soon as possible. All of the excitement was over before I returned home from Sunday Service. Mom told me about her adventure with a smile on her face and a glow in her countenance. Mom always had a way with animals and to her all she had done was feed one of God's great creations.

JOYRIDE / DRIVER TRAINING?

I want to tell you one more short story about my mom. She was a small woman but she stood head and shoulders above many of the women and men I have known in my life. She was tough as nails, (she had to be), she had six sons and a very stubborn husband to contend with every day. She was the kindest and most caring women I know.

In November 1958 I was 15 years old and only two months from turning 16. I was looking forward to getting my driver's license but there was a problem. I didn't take any of the driver's education classes in high school opting instead to take college prep classes. I was in desperate need of more behind the wheel driving time. My brothers John and Charlie had helped out a little with this need but they both had careers and families they needed to focus on. I should have asked my mom for help but she didn't drive at that time and I wasn't going to ask my very busy dad for driving lessons.

My solution was simple. It would work perfectly as long as nobody found out what I was up to. This is how a brilliant idea develops inside the head of a 15 year old Hayes boy.

Dad usually came home from Stage Sound and Equipment around 5PM, and would take an hour nap before having some supper. He would then head off to run lights in one of the showrooms. This was my chance. I would sneak into the bedroom and take his keys off the dresser and quietly slip outside. I would hop in his car and drive it around the neighborhood for about a half hour. This gave me plenty of time to get home and put everything back in its place before dad woke up. I had done this several times and gotten away with it, until now!

When I turned the corner heading home I saw my mom standing in the front yard with something in her hand. I was busted! Getting closer, I could see the object in her hand was a size thirteen sneaker. I knew what was coming!! As soon as I got out of the car she smacked my bottom with that shoe. It didn't really hurt, I just hoped no one in the neighborhood was watching and getting a good laugh at my expense. Then I got 'the lecture.'

I was informed about how dangerous a thing I had just done. If I had been in a wreck and didn't have a license or insurance, she and dad could have lost everything including the house and business. She was right of course. So much for my brilliant plan. I promised her to not do it again and that was that.

A couple of months later she went with me for my driver's test and I passed. As I dove home with mom in the car and my license in my pocket, I gave mom one last thrill. I had to cross Charleston Blvd to get home. It was a very busy street even back then. I stomped on the gas pedal and sped across the street with horns blaring at me from other drivers. I had just given mom a few more grey hairs.

These are just a couple short stories about mom. She was such an incredible woman. I am thankful for the opportunity to tell you a little about her.

Thank you Uncle Pat. I wish to second your motion on what an incredible woman grandma was. Thank you for those stories. I had never heard them until now.

We need to make one more pit stop before we move onto my life on Las Vegas showroom stages. I have mentioned some of the sons of Lea and Emma several times while traveling through time and the history of Las Vegas. I will now take a little time and speak briefly about each of them and what they accomplished in their lives. I promise to keep this part short. I will start with the oldest son and work my way down to the youngest.

GORDON

September 30, 1928-December 8, 2017

We have seen his name quite extensively as we voyaged through the years in Las Vegas. Gordon went to Las Vegas High School and while there he wrote the school's fight song. He was also in the Army Reserve Officer Training Corps or ROTC program which he enjoyed. He won several awards for his leadership while in the program. This would be a benefit when he went to college.

Gordon went to the University of Nevada, Reno (UNR) for three years. He continued his Army ROTC and rose to the rank of 2nd Lieutenant. During those years he was awarded several prestigious awards for performance and leadership. Those who earned these awards in previous classes went on to high ranking military careers. He was on his way to a possible career in the military. In his junior year, his unit at UNR was called out on maneuvers to Washington State for six weeks. During these maneuvers, it was discovered he had terrible allergies that caused him to be medically discharged from the Army and placed on the ineligible list for any future draft. He was extremely disappointed at the time but later realized his allergies may have saved his life. Had he continued in the service he would have been sent to Korea and been a prime target for North Korean snipers.

While at UNR, he first majored in pre-law and then changed his major to electronics. He also joined the Thespians and performed several roles in their plays. His last role was that of a villain, and he played it so well that he scared himself on how he could transform into a 'monster' so easily on stage. This ended his acting performances at UNR. He married Jeanette who was a card dealer at one of the casinos in Reno in 1950. When he was discharged from the Army the following year, he ended his time at UNR and they moved to Las Vegas in 1951 for employment opportunities.

It was apparent during his teenage years that Gordon had a gift or good understanding of electronics. With his college education in electronics, he would put his knowledge to work for him. Once again he began working out of Local 720 in the showrooms, his abilities and aptitude for all things that passed electrical current helped him excel in his career. There was a time in the early 50's that Gordon was the only Master Electrician in State of Nevada. In fact his Master Electrician License is number 'one.'

An interesting piece of history was to learn that both Gordon and my grandfather Leander were camera men on several Western Movies filmed in Southern Nevada and in Southern Utah. I now have to wonder if I ever saw one of those movies since I enjoyed western movies so much as a youngster.

I only knew my Uncle Gordon as an audio technician/ engineer extraordinaire. He loved audio, the equipment, the new inventions that made audio, and the even newer equipment that made audio sound better. He was my main mentor during my career as an audio engineer. I couldn't have asked for anyone better to teach me the ropes.

His blossoming expertise was put to work very early in his career. After his college and ROTC years were behind him, he came back to Las Vegas and was placed in charge of everything audio at the new Desert Inn Hotel and Casino. He was only 22 years old. His age was never a negative during his career. Four years earlier he had gone to Chicago, Illinois with his Father Lea to a union convention to secure a change in Local 720 from a projectionist's local to a mixed local. They were successful and Local 720 now had a Stage Technician Craft or Division.

Here is a piece of nostalgia. For those who went to Fremont Street during the 50's through the early 70's you might remember 'Vegas Vic' as the 25 foot tall automated cowboy on the outside of the Pioneer Club. He would move his arms and say, "Howdy Partner" every 15 minutes, 24 hours a day, seven days a week. The original voice of Vegas Vic was my Grandfather Lea. The next voice of Vegas Vic for many years was my Uncle Gordon. Vegas Vic was silenced in the mid 70's due to noise complaints.

Gordon spent much of his career as a trouble shooter for many of the showrooms in Las Vegas. When Caesar's Palace opened their doors, they had the famous fountains in front of the hotel (the ones that Evel Knievel tried to jump over on his motorcycle), Gordon was tasked with lighting them. With the adding of dancing waters around the fountains he had to light them to music and create a 'show' for those who passed by.

While at the Desert Inn, he operated the dancing waters for the shows. This meant being right next to the water tanks, fountains, and controls every show. The result of that was to be soaked by the overspray every show, every night. He loved it. Nothing like being right in the middle of a show and having proof you were there.

In 1955 when Stage Sound and Equipment opened for business, Gordon was very involved in the electrical and audio specifications and installation process. This meant working all day at the shop or on the jobsite then going home to catch a nap before going to work in the showrooms all night. This was the pattern all the brothers who stayed in Showbiz would follow during their careers in Las Vegas.

With all his expertise in audio as a technician and trouble shooter, one should not dismiss his audio engineering or mixing abilities. When a new group from England came to America on tour in 1964, it was Gordon who engineered the sound for them at the Las Vegas Convention Center. The name of the group was 'The Beatles.' He told me the girls were screaming so loud the entire show you couldn't hear the singing. Only when the singing stopped and they spoke to the audience could you hear the sound from stage. Well, that was Beatlemania.

There were many hotel showrooms that benefitted from Gordon's expertise. He would stay at a hotel for a few years then move on to another place just for a change of scenery. In 1977 he managed a new audio company in town called Design Sound. It was a return to many years in the past at Stage Sound and Equipment. The only difference was he didn't work around the clock this time. When the business closed, Gordon went back to work in the showrooms and convention areas in the hotels.

He wrapped up his career at a couple places as far as I can remember. The next to last place he worked was at Circus Circus Hotel and Casino as a sound and light technician for the shows on the Mezzanine. Prior to its opening, he had been the lead technician on the installation of sound and lighting equipment for the 'Big Top' shows and in the showroom. The last place I can remember him working before he retired was at the Sahara Hotel and Casino as a convention technician.

When I started my career in 'Showbiz' and ran into an audio problem, I always knew I could call my Uncle Gordon, explain the issue, and he would walk me through the troubleshooting process until I found and fixed the malfunction. Not every audio technician or engineer had what I did: the best audio technician at my beck and call. I owe him so much.

Gordon's favorite pastime was to go sailing his boat named the Sea Sir Pil on Lake Meade. When his time to retire drew near, he bought a place on Orcus Island off the coast of Washington State. He planned to retire there with his second wife Marge. He took his sailboat there only to find out you can't sail a 'lake' boat on the ocean. It would be dangerous to do so because of how they build the different types of boats. He then sold his boat and his sailing days were now concluded.

While on Orcus Island, Gordon discovered there was a community theater. He did what he knows best. He rewired and upgraded their lighting and sound systems. I wonder if they knew how lucky they were to have someone like him in their community and willing to work for free. They probably never knew who he really was. Gordon was not one for bragging or talking much about himself.

Gordon fully retired in the mid 90's. For a short time after he retired, he had some health issues and was able to return with Marge and live in the state of his birth, Idaho. They lived with his stepdaughter Sandy and her husband until a house nearby could be found for them. After the death of Marge he moved to the warmer climate of southern Utah.

He lived out the rest of his years under the care of his stepson Phil outside of Saint George, Utah. Gordon passed in 2017.

GILBERT

August 3, 1930-November 22, 2002

Gilbert was born a right brained child meaning he was a southpaw or left handed. In the early 20th century this was thought of as abnormal and it was predicted those who were left handed would not be as successful in life as those who were right handed. To this end, Gilbert was restrained from using his natural dominant hand and forced to do everything right handed. He often said this retraining had consequences that were very negative as he grew up.

He had thought as a teenager he was less intelligent than his peers and was not sure he would amount to much. When he was drafted into the U.S. Navy he took the ASVAB Test to determine what job classification he would be assigned. He knew if he didn't score high on the test he would be peeling potatoes and scrubbing pans on the ships. He wanted more. When the results came back from his test, the commanding officer interviewed him in depth for an extended period of time. Finally the officer explained why the interview was taking so long. Gilbert had scored so high on the test the examiners thought he had cheated. This was the boost to his self confidence he needed and put to rest his concerns of not being smart or capable of a prosperous future.

The Navy assigned Gilbert as a gyroscope specialist on their ships. Did you ever wonder how a Navy ship could land a shell from many miles away and hit a target within the size of a tennis court on an ocean rolling with waves? The answer is gyroscopes. If not perfectly maintained, gyroscopes could send an explosive shell hundreds of yards or miles off target.

After his service in the Navy concluded, Gilbert came back to Las Vegas and continued his career as a stagehand in the showrooms. He worked at most of the hotels during his career. He spent the bulk of his employment at the Tropicana Hotel and Casino working several positions on the Follies Bergere Show. He would climb to the 'crow's nest' every night and run the buttons for the automation part of the performance. This means anything that moved using a winch or motor system was controlled by him. He eventually became the Head Props-man for many of his 25 years working the 'Follies.'

Gilbert, like his brothers and so many other stagehands worked all the time. During the days of Stage Sound and Equipment he would work all day at the shop or on installs and then catch a nap and head off to the hotels for the 8PM and 12:15AM shows. This didn't include the time spent on show changes which were often 24 plus hour shifts in those days.

I know he worked at the Dunes Hotel and Casino for a period of time both in the lounge and in the main showroom. This is where he met his wife Carole. She worked for the bar manager and in PBX as an operator. They were married in 1959 at the New Frontier Wedding Chapel. In the early 1970's he worked at the Desert Inn Hotel and Casino in the 'main room' as one of the audio technicians. At the end of the 1970's he worked as a sound technician at the MGM Grand Hotel and Casino on the Hallelujah Hollywood show.

While working at the MGM Grand, Gilbert would retire from showbiz in 1980 and leave Las Vegas permanently. A few months after he retired, the famous MGM Grand fire happened in November of that year. Gilbert had left at the right time and spent the rest of his days in southern Utah.

Moving out of Las Vegas and retiring from Showbiz meant he would probably never have the experiences he had while in the Entertainment Capitol of the World. Life on a stage is sometimes the most bizarre one can imagine. Having an African wild animal tied up in your backyard sounds preposterous, but in Showbiz life, it really isn't that peculiar. As an example, he would never again get to babysit a cheetah that was part of the show and owned by one of the entertainers.

When Gilbert retired to St George, Utah, he took a position as a phone systems installer with Executone Phone Systems of Southern Utah. His son Gordon worked with him for several years as a team installing phone systems all over the southern part of the state. Gordon left the company to work for the electric company but would work with Gilbert on big jobs. It was during this time that Gilbert had become an independent contractor for Executone. The job wasn't Showbiz but it was good physical labor and for someone who had always worked hard it was meaningful employment. Besides, when you are retired, having some extra income is always a good thing.

Gilbert thoroughly enjoyed being in Showbiz and being a stage technician. One of his favorite hobbies was being a Ham Radio operator. He enjoyed talking with friends all over the nation and the world. He also enjoyed being a pilot. He would sometimes fly his plane from Las Vegas to St. George, Utah and drive to his home in Gunlock, Utah. It took the same amount of time to drive back and forth and was cheaper but once in a while he had to scratch the itch and fly.

He returned to Logan, Utah several times with his brother Charlie just to visit and re-spark the good memories. He truly loved living in Logan for the years he had. The remainder of his life was spent in St. George, Utah until he passed in 2002.

KEITH

January 11, 1932-November 27, 1979

Growing up in a church where there were several prominent attorneys, Keith had the opportunity to query these men and learn the one thing early in life that others never do. He had a fascination with the law and politics and he decided from his youth to pursue those vocations.

There is one story about my Uncle Keith I especially like. While he was a teenager in Las Vegas he had a motorcycle he loved to ride. One day he was having motor problems and the only way to keep the motorcycle running was to continually gun the engine at high rpm's. This is not a problem if you know the situation. Perception is very important here. When Keith pulled up to a stop light, he had to rev the engine hoping to keep the bike running until he could get it home.

Unfortunately for Keith there was a Las Vegas Police Officer nearby and perceived Keith's revving of the motor as a desire to race others at the light. His explanation to the police officer fell on deaf ears. Keith was arrested for 'exhibition of power.' When he got his phone call, he dialed their home number and Emma picked up the phone.

Keith explained the situation to his Mother and asked her what he should do. Emma told him when he got out of jail he should come home. I am sure he was hoping for a rescue but instead he learned a lesson. I am not sure this experience had any impact on his future as an attorney and eventually a judge but I would like to think it did.

During high school, Keith worked as a projectionist at local movie theaters. He also worked on the Las Vegas Strip in some of the hotels as a stagehand. These two types of employment did two things for him. The first was the money he would need for college to pursue his law degree. The second was to firmly fix in his mind he didn't want to be a stagehand for the rest of his life. Many times it is just as important to know what you don't want in life as it to know what you do want.

The skills and experience Keith gained as a stage technician would never be lost. Drawing on those skills later was always in his future. For now, his graduation from high school meant a trip to Brigham Young University (B.Y.U.) to begin his tertiary education.

While at B.Y.U., Keith joined the U.S. Air Force Reserve Officers Training Corps. Once he graduated from college, he would need to serve for three years in the Air Force. At that point he would be an officer and he would be able to apply for flight school if he desired, and he did.

During a break from school, Keith returned to Las Vegas to pick up some work and it was while he was there he met his future wife Karen. Marriage would have to wait for its proper time. In the meantime, he worked on graduating with a major in political science. Once married and graduated from college, it was time to serve his three years in the Air Force. Keith and Karen moved their lives from Las Vegas and Provo, Utah to Harlington, Texas for the next three years.

Keith and Karen had plans for a large family and the Air Force did their part in supplying doctors to grow the family. Paying for the birth of children is one benefit while you serve in the armed forces. The other benefit is the G.I. Bill. It pays for college for those who have completed their service in the armed forces. This was part of Keith's plan. Go to law school after his service had concluded and use his G.I. Bill to pay for it.

Keith loved to fly and that is exactly what he did in the Air Force. He flew C-119 cargo planes and advanced to the rank of Captain. Jet powered aircraft were becoming more and more prevalent in the US Air Force and Keith was offered the opportunity to take jet training and move up in rank. This was not part of his plan and he turned this opportunity and promotion down. His time in the air force was coming to a close and it was time to make his move to law school. He may have stayed in the air force longer and made it a career, but both he and Karen wanted a big family. The air force life might have made that difficult.

Keith and Karen moved to Salt Lake City, Utah where he attended law school at the University of Utah. While at law school Keith remained in the air force reserves. This gave him some extra income and benefits during those years. As graduation neared, they had to decide where they would like to live. Once he graduated, Keith took the BAR exam for the State of Nevada and they moved and set up home in Las Vegas.

Keith could have gone to work for a slew of other law firms in Las Vegas. After a short partnership with Ted Marshall, he decided to open his own practice. He wanted to be his own boss and not rely on a paycheck from others. This was risky but it could be far more rewarding in the long run. He had a general practice but he specialized in mining law. During the early years of his practice, he served as the part time District Attorney for Esmeralda County, (Goldfield Nevada).

Circa 1968, Keith ran for public office in the Nevada Assembly and won. He would serve one term in that legislative body. He was then appointed by the Governor to fill a vacant seat as a District Court Judge. Karen would run for Keith's former Assembly seat and win four terms in their district. She always had Keith's full support in these endeavors because there were problems on the horizon, and he knew she had to be self reliant in the very near future. To this end, she ran for the office of Clark County Commissioner and won three terms of four years each.

In 1973 Keith was diagnosed with melanoma cancer. He would travel the nation and parts of the world looking for a silver bullet to slay this monster. He had a wife and six children to look out for and his last daughter had just been born. The outlook was not good and the clock was ticking. Keith passed away in 1979.

Keith had known for many years he would not have a long life but this didn't stop him from having a full life. The most important thing to him was having a family. He never wanted to pursue a career in showbiz like his father and some of his brothers had because he wanted to be home at nights and be part of his children's lives.

After leaving the air force, Keith would fly his Father-in-Law's plane on some occasions but only with another pilot riding along. His skills as a stagehand were put to use over the years whenever there was a play or production at church. He would pick up a spotlight and could be found running it for the show.

Perhaps he will be known throughout history as being the judge on the Howard Hughes will court case. Part of his legacy will be his children. Two went on to be attorneys like him. Others pursued careers in computer technologies and journalism. There is now a school named after both him and Karen in Las Vegas. It is called the Keith and Karen Hayes Elementary School.

Over the years I have spoken to many people who knew him during his time as a judge. They all say Keith was a very fair judge who followed the law and the Nevada and Federal Constitutions to the very best of his abilities and judgments. This is some very high praise from many of his contemporaries. Had he not been taken away from us in 1979, there was no limit on how far his political and/or judicial career could have taken him.

CHARLIE

April 12, 1934-February 5, 2019

Charlie was born in Menan, Idaho in 1934. He was the fourth son in a family of seven boys. By the time he was five years old, the family was living in Logan, Utah. The fondest of memories were imbedded into his mind during this time. He loved living in Logan. With a canal behind their house and a river just a few blocks away, Charlie was ready for his adventures to begin. I envision him as a boy right out of a Norman Rockwell painting. I can see him with his fishing pole in one hand and his slingshot sticking out of his back pocket heading off to the river for some fishing and target practice. A childhood in Logan might very well be the perfect place to start a life. Summers spent fishing and playing and winters spent at school and playing in the snow all made this time in his life perfect. This picturesque setting would not last for long.

The Great American Depression was in full bloom during this time and Charlie's Father Lea was looking for work and getting it all over Arizona, Southern California, and Southern Nevada. Once Lea was given full time employment as a projectionist in Basic, Nevada, (now called Henderson, Nevada), the family joined him there. This was very distressing to Charlie. He had come to love living in Logan and his father, whom he had a very rocky relationship with, was away from home for months at a time. He had found some peace with the extended absence of his father. Now they would all be together again and living in the desert.

Growing up in Las Vegas was very different from living in Logan, Utah. Charlie loved playing outside and enjoying the natural beauty surrounding his home. The green fields, mountains, and river flowing through the town allowed his imagination to run free and create an endless stream of adventures.

The desert of southern Nevada has its beauty but it was not the landscape of his early years. Walking around the desert and hunting jackrabbits became a favorite pastime. When home, he would play catch by himself. He would throw a baseball high up in the air while in either the front or back yard and run around the house and catch the ball before it hit the ground. This game developed a strong arm and fast legs. Playing and hunting were not the only things he was good at. During this time in school, it was obvious to anyone who paid attention he had a real gift for mathematics. This would serve him well in the future.

Charlie graduated from Las Vegas High School in 1952 and as quickly as he could, he left the Las Vegas Valley for the mountains of Utah. He would return to Las Vegas during the summers and holidays to earn money for school. Like his brother Keith had done, working in the showrooms in Las Vegas maximized their time and earnings potential. He attended Brigham Young University for four years and earned his Bachelor's degree in Science for mechanical engineering. Before he would earn his Master's degree in Science for mechanical engineering from U.S.C. or the University of Southern California, (in 1967), he was drafted into the U.S. Army in 1956.

Charlie was never going to be a career military man. He would only serve his necessary time and leave as soon as he could. Two things did happen to him while he was stationed at Redstone Arsenal Army Base in Huntsville, Alabama. He was able to play a lot of his favorite sport, baseball. The other thing was he met the love of his life. Her name was Lois Swindal. They would marry in 1958 and as soon as Charlie was discharged from the army, they moved to Southern California and began their lives as a married couple.

While in the army, it was discovered Charlie had varicose veins in his legs. This would prohibit him from ever being a pilot like his brother Keith but it didn't stop him from being a foot soldier. The army doctors decided to remove his varicose veins not in a hospital setting, but in the field. Charlie said it was quite barbaric what they did to him and the condition they did it in. The army life was now behind him. A career, USC, and life in California were in front of him now.

I had pointed out earlier Charlie's gift in mathematics. A story I remember about this topic came from his time in college. While in an advanced mathematics class the professor had written out an equation on the blackboard. Charlie saw it was incorrect and pointed it out to the professor. To say the least, this did not endear him with this professor.

Now in southern California in 1958, Charlie went to work for McDonnell Douglas Aircraft Corporation. As a member of the technical team, his duties were the shock, vibration, and acoustic testing of aircraft and missile subsystems and components. He would work there for two years before leaving to join another aircraft company.

For one year from 1960-1961, Charlie worked for North American Aviation Corporation. His sole job was to test and recommend improvements to the antenna system for the XB-70 supersonic bomber. The bomber was eventually placed into service as the B-70 Valkyrie Bomber. It was a deep penetration nuclear bomber designed for the Cold War with the Soviet Union.

The years from 1961-1968 Charlie worked for Jet Propulsion Laboratory's (JPL) in Pasadena, California. He also went back to school and earned his Masters in Science in mechanical engineering from USC. I didn't realize what I had written down in my notes for a few minutes and then it hit me. The years 1961-1968 was right in the middle of the space race and fulfilling President Kennedy's goal to land on the moon. My uncle was part of the effort that saw man walk on the moon for the first time. How cool is that?

In 1968, Charlie went to work for Singer-Librascope in Glendale California. This was a company that manufactured early digital computer systems for business and the military. I believe he worked on some of the projects listed below while employed there. It is difficult to determine some of his work and where and when he did it, but it seems logical he would have done this work while at Singer-Librascope.

A few of the projects I find most interesting are as follows:

The developement and coding of algorithms of anti-submarine warfare (ASW) for the U.S. Navy.

The development of software that was used to test and evaluate the U.S. Navy's Mark 48 Mod 0 torpedo system.

Development and evaluation of Cathode Ray Tube (CRT) aka television or displays for sonar data, submarine tracking, and evaluation information for the U.S. Navy.

There are other projects and developments he worked on, but I believe this is sufficient to demonstrate his math skills being fully utilized in the field of computer programming, systems testing and evaluation.

After eight years with Singer-Librascope, he moved his family to Birmingham, Alabama.

In 1977, it was time for Lois to return home if only for a while. Charlie went into business with a company that installed and removed fencing for construction sites and other properties in need of cordoning off from the public. When the business failed to thrive, Charlie looked for work in the area, but it was apparent he was overqualified for almost any position he applied for. There was only one answer for him. He had to return to California and work in the fields he had specialized in.

Upon returning to California, he went back to work for Singer-Librascope doing what he did best. Lois and his daughters, Krista and Teresa, would remain in Alabama for a little longer then follow Charlie back to California. He would only stay with Singer-Librascope for one year until he was offered the job he would remain at until his retirement in 1993.

In January of 1979 Charlie joined JPL/Section 521 as member of the technical staff. His job was to shock test, vibrate, and acoustically test all payloads going into space for NASA. I was now able to call my Uncle a "Rocket Scientist." I was fortunate enough to tour the facility one time and saw one of the Voyager space probes being tested in Charlie's lab. I was amazed at how big it was. It was almost the size of a bus. It was one of the most memorable times of my life seeing the test facility and gaining a better understanding of what he did for our nation's space program.

The husband, father, and grandfather Lois, Krista, and Teresa knew was the man who spoke little of what he was doing at work and concentrated much of his energies on being involved with his family. My cousins told me he would ask them daily what was going on in their lives and wanted to be a part of every aspect of their lives. He encouraged his daughters to be involved in athletics and showed up at every game and practice he could to support them. This same energy was spent on his grandchildren as well. They were very fortunate to have such a person in their lives.

As a youngster, I loved going to California and seeing my Uncle Charlie, Aunt Lois, and Cousins Krista and Teresa. There was usually a Dodgers game, Disneyland, Griffith Observatory, Natural History Museum, La Brea Tar pits, or the ocean involved during our visits. My favorite part was to go to the park with our gloves, bats, and baseballs and play catch with my uncle. It was the best of times.

Charlie was smart enough to maintain his connection to Local 720 over the years. When work slowed down in the defense or space industries, he would come to Las Vegas and work in one of the showrooms until things picked back up in California. He always seemed to work in August at the Sahara Hotel and Casino installing and working on the Jerry Lewis Labor Day Telethon.

During other visits to Las Vegas, he would often come to one of my basketball or softball games and cheer us on. At the end of the game, he would play coach and teach me something to improve my game. The last time I played catch with him was in April of 1981. It took me 19 years to do it, but I finally was able to throw a baseball further than he could. It was probably due to his superior coaching.

After Charlie retired, he spent some of his time tutoring math students at the local community college. Algebra, geometry, trigonometry, and calculus were easy for him and he passed on that knowledge to others. Using his knowledge and experience paid off. He used his skills in audio from his showroom days to install and wire the sound system for his church's meeting house. Knowing how to run a spotlight, setting up a sound system, or hooking up a lighting system is never forgotten. It is in our blood I believe.

One of Charlie's favorite past times was to play on his senior softball team. He participated from his mid 50's through his mid 70's. When he didn't play competitive anymore, he and a few of his other seasoned players would meet in the park to play catch and hit the ball around.

He lived a full life mainly from Showbiz and Las Vegas. Spending the most valuable commodity in the world, time with his family was more important to him than living a life in entertainment. That is exactly the way he wanted it.

Charlie passed on in 2019 at the age of 84.

GEORGE

He was born July 12, 1935 and died shortly after birth. Had he lived, there would have been seven sons in a town that puts high value on the 'Lucky Number 7.'

JOHN

December 9, 1938

Of all the sons of Lea and Emma Hayes, this is the one I know the most and in some ways the least about. He is my Father, John. Being in a family of stagehands and knowing from your youth that in 'Showbiz,' the show MUST go on, it is of no surprise to me when you must cover the jurisdiction and position at an early age. When an illness prior to a show at a major resort occurs, you grab one of your kids to fill in. This is exactly what happened with my grandfather and my dad. It didn't matter that John was only 15 and not signed into Local 720, you did what it takes to make the show happen. Today, this would not be allowed.

When Stage Sound and Equipment opened its doors in 1955, John was in high school at Las Vegas High and would work there after school and on the weekends. This put a little coin, or more accurately, very little coin in his pocket but it was laying the groundwork for a long career in 'Showbiz.' By his senior year, it was not uncommon for him to run a follow spotlight in the showrooms at night and attend class during the day. This greatly improved the amount of money in his pocket. His favorite entertainer to operate a follow spotlight for was Frank Sinatra. John worked many a night at the Sands Hotel and Casino when the 'Rat Pack' was the must-see show in Las Vegas.

After high school, John went to Brigham Young University for a very short time then it was back to Las Vegas and into the showrooms, lounges, convention centers, and of course Stage Sound and Equipment. The Casbar Lounge in the Sahara Hotel and Casino was one of his first pit stops. The Casbar Lounge was 'the' place to be late nights in Las Vegas. Don Rickles and Louie Prima were just a couple of the top entertainers in the "Swingin'est Town on Earth."

In 1960 he took employment at the Mint Hotel and Casino on Fremont Street in Downtown Las Vegas. After I was born in 1962, he left the Mint and worked at several of the hotels for about three years. He then went to Caesar's Palace Hotel and Casino and worked as the Head Flyman (the person that pulls on ropes to move counterweighted pipes for scenery and curtains on a stage) from the opening night until he left to open the Bonanza Hotel and Casino about a year later. After a few years, he went back to the Sahara Hotel and Casino.

John worked in the Space Center convention area of the hotel. The new 40,000 square feet convention area was one of the largest privately owned spaces in the world. Today, it would be considered just another small to medium sized meeting room. The age of conventions and mega conventions was just around the corner for the "Entertainment Capitol of the World."

Working in the Space Center during the day gave John his nights open and like all good stagehands, he found another job to do at night. The newly opened International Hotel and Casino had an impressive lineup of star power. Elvis, Barbara Streisand, and Liberace were just a few of their headliners. He would be offered the management position of Technical Director over entertainment and conventions at the Sahara Hotel around 1977. He would work in that position for about five years and then take the same position at the Riviera Hotel and Casino. After three years his career in management with hotels and showrooms came to a close.

John would wrap up his career in Las Vegas by working at Circus Circus Hotel and Casino and at Caesar's Palace. He retired in 1994 and moved to Cedar City, Utah where he took a position with Southern Utah University (S.U.U.) for 10 years managing their 5,000 seat auditorium. He fully retired in 2004 and has lived in many small towns during his retirement. He even returned to Las Vegas and lived there for three years. These days, he can be found living in St. George, Utah.

My Dad often said he was born under a wandering star. I believe he is correct. Not only does his work history show this to be true but his personal life also verifies this belief.

PATRICK

January 27, 1943-

Patrick is the youngest of the Hayes brothers. By the time he came along, he had older brothers four to fourteen years older than he was. As he got older, he would follow his father and brothers into the business of entertainment. He would not live his life as a stage technician like some of his other brothers though. He had other plans for his life and would follow them 400 miles from the Las Vegas Strip.

Once in high school, Pat found employment as a box boy (today we call them courtesy clerks) at a Safeway supermarket. This may have placed some coins in his pockets but it didn't alleviate his responsibilities at the family business. Pat and his Father would take inventory once a month on all the equipment and supplies at Stage Sound and Equipment. Once a quarter, they would take inventory of the General Electric theatrical light bulbs. These bulbs were on consignment from G.E. and an exact count was critical so they wouldn't underpay or overpay G.E.

One of Pat's jobs at SS&E was to make up electrical connectors for stage equipment. Stage equipment may use the same electricity as we use in our homes but the connectors are unique to the industry. He would spend many a weekend making these connectors and extension cords and became very efficient and quick at the task. Working in the family stage business was not the only exposure to showbiz for Pat.

Pat joined the Las Vegas High School's Thespian Club and worked in many positions during the plays. He was a stagehand, spot light operator, audio technician, and sometimes he was one of the performers. When the club decided to put on the play of Hansel and Gretel, Pat was chosen by the instructor, Fritz Bell, to play the role of Hansel. A star was born. Fame, like high school, doesn't last forever. After graduation, he was off to college at Brigham Young University for summer school.

Between semesters and during holidays and summers Pat would return to Las Vegas and work as a stage technician in one of the showrooms in order to pay for his college tuition. Two of his older brothers did this very same thing. Keith and Charlie both used their skills in showbiz to pay for a life outside of the business. Pat would do the same.

Emma always wanted her sons to go on a proselytizing mission for their church. Lea never supported this idea or was willing to financially support his sons in this endeavor because he was not a member of the Church of Jesus Christ of Latter-day Saints as was Emma and their boys. Emma demanded Lea support their last son on a mission and Lea finally agreed to do so.

At the end of Pat's first semester of his sophomore year, he was called to go on a mission for two years to Scotland. After serving his two years, Pat returned to Las Vegas. He had been given notice to appear before the military draft board in two days after completing his mission. If he was not in school, he would be drafted into the Vietnam War. Pat had to act quickly.

Pat did two things to aid him in his deferment. He signed up for the B.Y.U. block plan and could double up on his credits to finish his sophomore year by end of summer 1965. He also took his physical exam for the draft and failed. His poor vision prevented him from being inducted into the U. S. Military. His 1Y status for the draft ensured he would only be drafted during a national emergency. It was now time to get back to college and continue his life in other ways.

He would eventually graduate from B.Y.U. with a degree in political science. Completing his degree was not his only focus. He joined the B.Y.U. Folk Dancers and toured Europe for10 weeks from May to July of 1967. During this time as a folk dancer, Pat met his future wife. Her name was Barbara Anne Bitner. We all know her now as Aunt Bobbee.

August 1967 found Pat back in Las Vegas earning money for school by working in the showrooms. Back at B.Y.U., it was time to hit the books and plan a January 1968 wedding. With the conclusion of the spring semester, Pat returned to work in Las Vegas at the Flamingo lounge. It was time for graduate school. Tuition could be paid for with a summer's worth of work.

While working on his Master's Degree, Pat also worked on the Special events crew as a stage technician. This crew handled all events other than the theater events on campus. Four hundred miles from Las Vegas and he still finds work as a stagehand. Sometimes you can't escape what is in your DNA.

Between his two years in the master's program, Pat worked in Las Vegas at the Riviera Hotel in the showroom. Then it was back to school to finish his last year. At the end of his time at B.Y.U. he earned his Master's Degree in Public Administration in August of 1970. He would return to Las Vegas and work in the showrooms for two months after his graduation while he searched for employment using his degree. This would be the last time Pat worked as a stagehand in Las Vegas. His degree would now take him away from any remnants of his life in showbiz in Las Vegas.

In October of 1970, Pat returned to B.Y.U. not as a student this time but as an employee of the university. He put his degree to work in the personnel department of the university as the assistant trainer of new employees. He would spend two years in this position before taking another position even further away from Las Vegas.

From 1972 to 1974 Pat worked for the Governor's Office of Management and Budget in Wisconsin. When an offer was made to Pat and Bobbee to return to Utah, they took it. Pat would work for the Utah State Legislature in the Fiscal Analysis Office for nine years. He would leave that position in 1983 and work for the Utah Department of Transportation until he retired in 2009.

Pat and Bobbee still live in Orem, Utah today. They are only a couple miles from B.Y.U. They only travel to Las Vegas to see family and Pat has still not ventured back on a stage to work since 1970.

These are the men who in many ways, both directly and indirectly, helped me to become the person I am today. I give them all my deepest and most sincere appreciation for having them in my life. My story is in many ways their story.

CHAPTER TWO: THE EARLY YEARS

Being born into a showbiz family doesn't necessarily mean you are destined to spend your life, in one way or another, on a stage. For me, this is exactly what it meant. I was born in Las Vegas, Nevada at the Las Vegas Hospital. The hospital was located near Downtown Las Vegas and no longer exists. I am the second son of a second generation stagehand. I would later in life become a third generation stagehand. The doctor who delivered me was supposedly the brother of comedy legend Oliver Hardy from the Laurel and Hardy duo. I can't say this is absolutely true but it does add a little more showbiz flair to my story.

My first introduction to showbiz and the stagehand way of life was when I went with my father to Stage Sound and Equipment to visit my grandfather. I was taken into the shop area and asked to help them move some lights and cables. Being an obedient child, I did what was asked of me without hesitation. The lights and cables were very heavy but I worked with them until the job was done. Looking back at it is easy to understand why the lights and cables were so heavy for me; I was only five years old at that time.

No matter our age, we were expected to help when asked. Work was never a curse; it was important and even more important to do the job right.

From the age of five and moving forward, every church play or musical had one thing in common: I was in it. Whether performing or running the lights, you could always find me and sometimes my brother John involved in some way.

I loved being a Scout. While in the Cub Scouts, around the age of ten, the Boy Scouts of America Boulder Dam Area Council, (now the Las Vegas Area Council) had a city wide scout gathering at the Las Vegas Convention Center. The Rotunda had a good deal of lighting and sound equipment in it which was donated by several hotels for the function. Someone had to haul the gear all over the Rotunda and help set it up and you guessed it, that someone was me. Wait, this gets even better.

All the other scouts were walking around the convention center looking at the different booths and going into the Rotunda to watch the show about scouting. It was the same for me for a very short time. Looking back on this event I must think someone like my father should have known better than to put a headset on a ten year old kid and conscript him into running the light board for the show. He had been running the lights for the show but something went wrong and he had to leave his post and fix it.

It is amazing how much you can learn and how fast you can learn it when the pressure valve is opened up. A five minute course on what to do and I was abandoned for 20 or more minutes. I was told what to do and when to do it and that is exactly what I did. Soon my dad returned and took back his headset and control of the lighting console. I was now free to roam the convention floor until the show was over. Once the show ended, it was back to the Rotunda to haul gear to the trucks.

In 1972 everything concerning liability and OSHA safety protocols was different. Today, if an OSHA official or a corporate lawyer or loss prevention manager would have seen a ten year old boy crawling around the high steel in the Rotunda there would be fines, disciplinary action, and conniption fits being thrown. Like I said, things were different in 1972. Nobody seemed to care about such things and having another set of helping hands was always appreciated.

Being ten years old meant being the oldest kids in school at Robert E. Lake Elementary School. Our teacher, Mrs. Dennis asked the class if anyone would like to learn and put on a play for the kindergarten and first grade classes. My hand went up immediately and with a little coaxing from me, some of my friends also 'volunteered' to participate. I was selected to play one of the lead roles for this performance.

The play was Hansel and Gretel and no I wasn't selected to play Hansel. I was selected to play the evil witch. Go ahead, laugh a little and get it out of your system. It was also my first and only time in drag. If only there was a way for me to look 13 years into the future I would have seen this time in drag was but an omen for future events and shows. Anyway, I believe I pulled off being a wicked witch quite convincingly. Of course this was done with a comical flair.

While in 5th grade, I decided to learn something new and quite difficult. I was going to ride a unicycle. It was almost Christmas and I knew exactly what I wanted Santa to bring me. I had found what I was looking for in the Sears Christmas catalogue and it was not expensive to buy or to have elves make. Now I just had to learn to ride it. I don't know why everyone thinks learning to ride a unicycle is so difficult. It's much harder than *merely* difficult to ride a one wheeler.

On a bicycle, motion equals balance and stability. On a unicycle, balance and stability equals resistance. You might be peddling forward on a unicycle but as your front legs gives you forward motion, your rear leg is resisting the forward motion slightly and this makes it so you stay upright. It is the tension between the pedals and the seat that makes you able to ride a unicycle.

After weeks and weeks of trying to ride this one wheeled beast of frustration, you suddenly realize what you have been doing wrong. Your first true ride is not very long but now you know what to work on. Each attempt is getting longer and longer and covering more distance. Then it happens. You just start riding it like it is no big deal and soon you can't understand why this was so hard to do for so long. Within the hour you are riding it up and down the street and your friends are following you in amazement.

Next you will need to learn how to ride it backwards. You now have to reverse your thinking on riding forward. It is difficult at first, but in a few hours you can do it fairly well. I never thought I was good on a unicycle until I could ride

ME AT 59 YEARS OLD.

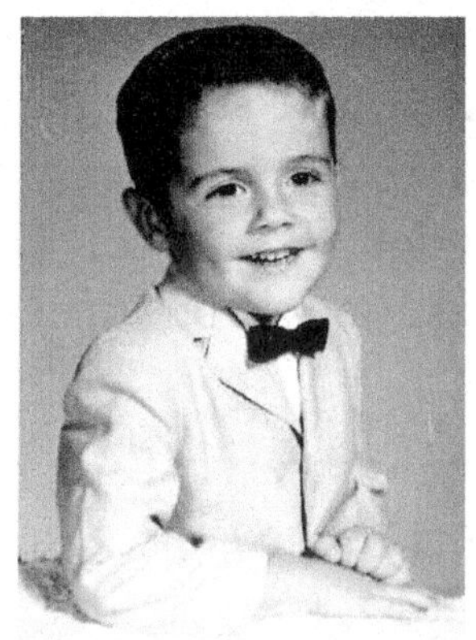

ME AT 5 YEARS OLD.

ME AT 8 YEARS OLD.

ME AT 59 YEARS OLD.

up and down our street backwards several times without stopping. Your training in the mystic arts of unicycle riding is almost complete.

To complete your training and become a master of the unicycle, you need two more things. You need to learn trick riding and practice every day to get better on your one wheeler. Ride your unicycle on the sidewalk and go off the curb onto the street. Now do this same thing backwards. Good. Do this over and over until you can do it without a single thought of doubt in your head. Now find an outside set of stairs and ride your unicycle up and down them multiple times until you can do it in your sleep. Now do it backwards. Good. You need to practice these things every day for an hour or more to maintain your edge. I know this all seems like a lot of information but there is a reason for it.

I rode that unicycle everywhere and rarely rode my bike unless it was long distance or I had to go somewhere quickly. By the end of my 6th grade year at Kit Carson Sixth Grade Center, I was very proficient on one wheel. It was while I attended Kit Carson that I decided to try out for the choir. The choir teacher, Bonnie Gaston, opened up the world of music to me and set me on a course to find my musical talents. I enjoy singing, and being a ham while performing, it comes naturally to me. One might think I would become a singing unicyclist. That would be silly. But, wait a minute.

As 6th grade came to an end it was time to prepare for junior high school at John C. Fremont Junior High School. I had one elective as a seventh grader and I chose to be in the choir. This is when I met James Sherman who was the music instructor at the school. The audition for him went well and the following September I was sitting in the choir room singing to my heart's content. While in choir, I met Eugene 'Butch' Balmain. My years at Fremont were about to get very interesting.

Upon the discovery that we both were unicycle enthusiasts, it was apparent we should form an act and enter the Fremont Talent Show. Our act was simple but effective. We rehearsed every day after school for weeks to perfect the act. It was presented along the lines of a Laurel and Hardy slapstick skit, but on unicycles. On the day we performed the routine in front of the entire student body and won the contest, I went from just another seventh grader to being the best known student on campus. I have to admit this was pretty cool.

The remainder of this year was spent adding elements to the act and rehearsing them into the ground. When not rehearsing, we were performing all over town at schools and other variety shows. Speaking of added elements, what we added were these: a four foot, a six foot, an eight foot, and a 15 foot tall unicycle. We also made up the front wheel and handle bars of a bicycle so that from a distance it looked like you were riding a bike until you dropped the front wheel and rode your one wheeler. The act was basically one of 'who can ride the taller unicycle.' I never rode the 15 footer. It freaked me out way too much.

My seventh grade year at Fremont was a busy one. Between performing in choir and rehearsing and performing our act all over town, the year went by in a flash. The following year would prove to be more interesting. Butch was a sophomore at Las Vegas High School and playing tuba in the marching band. I was only involved and performing in choir my eighth grade year at Fremont. Butch had an idea that any sane band director would have said "NO" to immediately upon hearing his proposal. Thank Heaven musicians and music directors are all a little odd.

Butch's twist on our act was for us to be the only unicycle riding tuba players in any Las Vegas high school. Carrying a tuba and playing it while riding in band formations sounds like a great idea. What could possibly go wrong? Picture this. I am in eighth grade at Fremont and would have to ride over to Las Vegas High School in the morning to learn their marching band routine and then ride back to finish my day at Fremont. Did I mention I don't know how to play tuba? I would ride around in formation and just act like I was playing.

The desired effect of having the only unicycle riding tuba players in a marching band worked. Every band in town heard about us and it was not uncommon for us to be on the TV news for the sports highlight reels. When the Clark County School District decided to have a battle of the high school marching bands and to broadcast it on TV, which of the bands do you think every band wanted to see? If you said Las Vegas High's marching band you would be correct. I am not sure if we won the contest, but I do know we made the biggest splash at the show!

Butch and I had been riding and performing our act for three years. We had the time of our lives doing these shows but I was about to go in another direction. I was about to start my sophomore year at Valley High School. It was clear to me the time had come to end my unicycle riding in a performance setting. I saw no future in the act other than performing at Circus Circus and I never wanted to work there. I had had enough. We went our separate ways and I don't think I ever saw Butch again.

In my sophomore year at Valley High the elective I chose was to take a drafting class instead of continuing in choir. Looking back on it, I can see when I broke up our unicycle act and left Fremont Junior High, for some reason I decided to make a total break from any type of performing. To this day and I have no clue why I walked away from any and all performing.

Choosing a drafting class in high school was an incredibly smart thing to do as I would learn later in life. For now, my high school sophomore year presented me with an opportunity that piqued my interest. The MGM Grand Hotel in Reno, Nevada was putting a new show in their showroom called Hallelujah Hollywood Hello. It was another Don Arden stage spectacular and it would be built in Las Vegas at a couple scenic shops. I was hired by one of them to work after school as a shop boy. The company's name was Design Concepts. Its owner was Fred Josephs.

I know my title is inspiring but all it means is I was to sweep the shop floors, clean and stack the tube steel, load trucks, clear areas for layout and construction purposes, and keep the journeymen stocked with materials while they built the new show. I think the real work was tolerating the verbal abuse from the journeymen building the show. While I worked I watched everything being built and asked the journeymen questions about how and why they were building certain set pieces. I wanted to learn everything possible from the welders, carpenters, electricians, and painters. I knew I would enjoy working in a scenery shop one day and building scenery for shows. I didn't know it but this wish would come true in just two years.

The work at Design Concepts ended after nine months and with summer approaching, I needed to find a summer job. The first hotel I worked at full time was Circus Circus. I had to laugh a little because a year or so earlier I had said I didn't want to work at Circus Circus and yet here I was. No, I was not on the stage riding my unicycle; I was working the games on the midway or mezzanine as a carnie. I only did the job for a month and was offered a job in the gift shop as a stockman. I worked there the rest of the summer and left when school started again.

In my junior year at Valley High I took advanced drafting and architecture for my electives. I was also getting the itch to perform again but didn't want to ride a unicycle or go back to a chorus setting. I found a way to scratch that itch by joining a ballroom dance team. Everyone on the team was between the ages of 14 and 18. It was necessary for anyone who auditioned and joined the team to take it seriously. The commitment in time for rehearsals and performing took precedent over anything else in my life.

If practice makes perfect then we would soon reach perfection. Tuesday nights from 4PM until 9PM were spent in a school multi-purpose room. Saturday mornings from 7AM until 12 PM were spent in a church gymnasium. I had spent the last 16 months on hiatus and not rehearsing or performing in any fashion. To be back in the groove was really quite nice.

Our instructor was Judy Peterson and she loved everything about dance. She expected us to be as perfect in our routines as humanly possible. We tried really hard to not let her down. Do you think it is strange to have about 24 teenagers from 14-18 years old dedicated to dancing the following numbers? We learned the International Waltz, which is a medley of four different waltzes. We also learned a square dance, the Polka, a Samba, a Cha-Cha, a Vaudeville number, the Charleston, a Disco dance, and a 50's Swing number. There may have been other routines but 40 years later I am grateful to remember this many. I still think we were a unique group of kids back then.

How does a person keep 24 teenagers interested in and committed to such a time consuming venture? I am not sure how Judy did everything she did but one thing was certain. We kept competitions going on within the team. I had learned long before this that the best way to obtain perfection is to rehearse and compete. The race was on. Who would be the best individual, duo, or sub group, on the team? I don't think we ever came up with an answer to this, but it kept everyone focused and committed.

We performed all over town for church groups, community groups, conventions, and any other group who wanted us to be their gathering's entertainment. We even traveled to San Diego to perform for a large church youth conference. It was now my senior year of high school and it would be my last year of performing with the Paradise Dance Team. There would be one more highlight to add to my time on dance team. After a year of doing shows we were asked to perform in Disneyland at the Carnation entertainment area next to Cinderella's castle. It was our best performance to date and we drew a sizable crowd who showed their appreciation for our efforts.

It is a little known fact in Showbiz that the main reason for performing is not always the money, it is the applause and cheers from the crowd. In many ways, the reaction from your audience is more of a drug than actual chemicals. I have experienced this many times in my performing life and the crowd at Disneyland gave us another 'fix' of the appreciation drug.

My graduation from high school also ended my time on dance team. The experiences I had will always be cherished but it was time to move on. My future in the entertainment industry or getting an education was in front of me and I usually don't like looking backwards.

One more event took place in December during my senior year. A play was written about Santa's workshop and I was cast in the role of Santa. OK, I was 17 and stood five feet 10 inches tall and weighed in at 150 pounds. This frame size doesn't exactly scream here's the jolly fat man. Crazier still is the fact I never auditioned for the part. I agreed to play the role only if I could do it my way. I got what I wanted a little too quickly from the director. During rehearsals I never went on stage and played my role. I sat in the audience and spoke my lines not knowing how I would pull this off. Then it hit me.

On the night of the performance I put on a make-shift fat suit, fake white hair, a white beard, and glued white eyebrows on over my natural eyebrows. Once I put on the red suit, a quick look in the mirror told me I succeeded. Now I had to pull off a show having never rehearsed it or memorized a single line from the script. Mrs. Santa Clause, Paula Borne, had a worried look on her face as curtain time drew near. My revelation a few days earlier was quite simple. I took a clipboard and put my script on it. With a pen in hand I would read along with the play and deliver my lines while pretending to check off inventory and all other matters in the workshop. It worked just as I had envisioned it. The director was even more amazed than I that I pulled this trick out of my hat. I don't know if I could ever do something like that again.

On the first Friday of June 1980 I graduated (by the skin of my teeth) from high school. My fellow graduates went out and partied like it was 1999. My celebration consisted of going to dinner and then a movie on my own. The next day I arose and went to Whitney's Texaco to do my usual Saturday work routine. Having been released from the prison of high school one might wonder why I had such a subdued weekend. No reason would be found. I had just finished one objective and on the following Monday morning I would begin a new job in the entertainment industry.

My first call out of Local 720 was to work as an apprentice in the MGM Grand Hotel's scenery shop. Don Arden was changing out his show called Hallelujah Hollywood with the one we would build called Hollywood Jubilee. Work in the shop started at 8AM and ended at 4:30 PM. I would then go to work the night shift to clean and close Whitney's Texaco gas station until 10PM. I enjoyed being busy and getting to work alone on most nights.

Almost three years before walking into the MGM Scenic Studio, I had worked at Design Concepts. There, I was a shop boy doing menial but necessary labor for the journeymen. Now here at the MGM shop I was an apprentice stagehand once again doing menial but necessary labor for the journeymen. The differences between then and now are the higher pay and now being allowed to actually work on the scenery.

To this day I still love working or just visiting a scenery shop. The smell of welded metal, wood being cut, fiberglass being applied, and paint drying are smells that please my olfactory senses. The other thing that makes working in a scenery shop is the atmosphere between craftsmen. There is a special form of communication between the trades, (usually using every swear word known to man) that is the icing on the cake when building a show for a Las Vegas stage.

After working in the shop for a couple months, I had been talking with older men about my future. They all recommended going to college and obtaining a career outside of showbiz. I listened to their advice and enrolled in community college for the fall semester. Within three weeks, I had had enough and went back to the shop to work full time. By the time I was 18 years old, I was not just a college dropout but a junior college dropout. Just want to be accurate here.

While returning to the shop after my extremely short college days, I made one of the biggest decisions of my life. I would from this time forward save every dollar possible in order to go out into the world and serve a proselytizing mission for my church. I didn't know it then but in nine months I would be walking the streets of Perth, Australia doing what I had just committed myself to do.

One of my closest friends growing up was Bobby Pool. We went to the same church, worked at Whitney's Texaco, been on dance team, and did just about everything together. This would include being good and getting into mischief together. One evening while the two of us were operating the sound for a large church talent show, this guy brings in a bunch of his own sound gear and starts making noise. We went over to speak with him and to find out who he was with. He had been asked to provide music by one of the groups who would be performing that night. Great, this means I get to take a break for one of the acts.

His name was Talbot Snow and he and his family had just moved to Las Vegas from New Zealand. He had met a few other teenagers but Bobby and I were the first people he had met who had the same interest in high end audio gear. A few meetings later the three of us formed KAZZ. It was a mobile sound and DJ service. Talbot had done something similar in New Zealand but now we wanted to take this to a new level. For the next six months before I left for Australia, we would play music for church dances, birthdays, weddings, anniversaries, and any other function willing to pay our fee. These were really good times.

On June 10, 1981, I arrived in Perth, Australia to begin my two year mission serving the Lord. Believe it or not, while there I didn't fully escape showbiz. It was while speaking to some business owners in Bunbury, a town of about 25,000 south of Perth by about a hundred miles, I was asked to be the voice for a few of their commercials. They liked my American accent and thought people would listen to their commercials hearing a unique voice. It was enjoyable to hear my voice on commercials around town and when people recognized my voice they would talk with us a little longer.

I was also given the opportunity to put my DJ experience to work a few times. One of the local roller skating rinks had a battle of the DJs and I was invited to participate. This is not something you would usually do on a mission but I gave it a whirl and had a good response from the youth. These two things changed the atmosphere a little in Bunbury. Those guys who ride around town on their bikes wearing suits really weren't anything to be afraid of. Many doors opened to us from basically having fun, maybe a little too much fun.

My time in Australia flew by and was over much sooner than I could grasp. I had served honorably and now it was time to go home. When I arrived back in Las Vegas the first employment I found was back in one of the scenery shops. The next chapter of my life in entertainment was about to begin.

THE ORIGINAL KAZZ MOBILE DJ SYSTEM IN 1981.

HE ORIGINAL KAZZ *CEO'S* FROM L-R, CRAIG HAYES @18, TALBOT SNOW @16 AND BOBBY POOL @16.

CHAPTER THREE: IS THIS GOING TO BE MY CAREER?

When I returned from Australia, I would have never guessed in a million years everything I would do over the next six years. Here is a synopsis. I would work in a scenery shop for a few months, go back to Australia and get married, take a management position at the Mint Hotel and Casino for two years, have three children, return to Australia and work there for almost a year, return to working as a technician at the Mint again, get fired, work out of Local 720 some more, and then switch careers completely; well sort of. Whew, that was exciting. Now we can take them a little slower and one at a time.

When I arrived back home in Las Vegas, the first thing to do was nothing. A couple days were needed to get over the jet lag of 15 hours time difference. A little decompression time was quite enjoyable too. Then I signed in with Local 720 and waited for the phone to ring. The first call I receivedwas as a welder at Las Vegas Scenery Shop for the Broadway show of Porgy and Bess. If memory serves me, there was about six or more week's worth of work. I enjoyed every day and especially enjoyed the paychecks. I was back in my element. When the show was finished being built, I was done working there for now. I signed back into Local 720 and waited for the phone to ring. I waited a lot.

With the country still in a recession, business was pretty slow in Vegas. I took any and every call no matter the length of time the call was scheduled for. Calls to change out shows were usually four to eight hours in length. I liked doing show changes. My favorite hotels to work show changes were Caesar's Palace and the Las Vegas Hilton.

In January of 1983, I returned to Australia to answer the question if my long distance romance was going to move forward. It was. On April 23, 1983, I married Lillian Thompson. We then spent the next six weeks obtaining her Green card or resident alien card. When we arrived in Las Vegas, I signed back in with Local 720 and waited for the phone to ring. I didn't have long to wait.

The economy was starting to come out of the recession but work in Las Vegas was still slow. The call to go back and work at Las Vegas Scenery Studios was heaven sent. They were building the set for the Jerry Lewis Labor Day Telethon. The work would last about two months but it was work and the type of work I enjoyed doing.

After this job ended, I took any call that came my way. I seemed to get a lot of show changes at many of the hotels but was hoping to find something a little more stable and permanent. I even took a job as a box boy at a nearby Skaggs Alpha Beta grocery store just to make a few extra dollars.

With our first child expected to arrive in April of 1984, I needed my financial situation to improve and the sooner the better. The universe heard my wish and was about to grant it.

Christmas time in 1983 was a great time for us. The struggles we went through with help from family were about to pay off. Andrew Zorne, the General Manager of the Mint Hotel and Casino called my father looking to find someone to manage and operate their newly remodeled lounge. My father asked if I had any interest to go there and look it over. I did. I went with him and Fred Josephs, the former owner of Design Concepts, to take a look at the operation. Sidro's Armada was playing on stage and I liked what I saw.

The job paid about three dollars an hour less than a comparable union job but I saw potential in this lounge. When you run a lounge, you do everything from lights, sound, spotlight, and stage maintenance. You are literally a one man show. Working out of Local 720 had not given me the opportunity to work in the audio field as much as I wanted to. This place could be my chance to do just that. When the job was offered to me I took it. Like I said, it paid less but there were good medical benefits working there.

I was hired in January 1984 and took to the job like a fish to water. Running the lights was fairly easy. The old system was still being utilized while we waited for the new console and dimmers to arrive. Running audio was nothing new to me. At first I had some frustration learning about the new high end gear and running it well. When a group came in and they had their own audio engineer, I picked their brain and learned everything I could from the. Some of them were quite good at the job while others were not so good. You learn something from both types.

I spent 1984 working on my audio and lighting skills. Lounge shows or sets were usually 45 minutes long. We (the band and Imyself) then had to strip the band gear from stage, set up new band gear, set microphones up, cable the microphones, line check the instruments, and get back to the control booth and dial everything up. We had 15 minutes to do all of this and then the next show began. I would mix everything as fast as possible while at the same time running the lights. A good technician can make it all happen and have the sound dialed in by the third song. My goal was having the sound set by the second song. It did not always work out that way.

This type of show turnover happened six times or more a night and six days a week. The better I got at my job, the more I enjoyed doing it. The year 1984 was one of the most memorable years of my career. I not only was able to sharply hone my audio skills, but I was privileged to work with some of the most incredible show bands and musicians in Las Vegas. In April 1984 our first child was born. We named him Michael. It was one of the greatest days of my life to have him in our family. It was nearly 22 years to the day that I was born while my Father worked at the Mint Hotel in the lounge. History seems to have repeated itself a little here.

If the universe gave me 1984 to polish and perfect my audio and lighting skills, then it was because of why I would need them in 1985. The Mint had signed a musical comedy revue called 'Bottoms Up '85' {BU85}, for a short engagement and if all went well, they would be back for a six month to a year residency. This is when I first met Breck Wall, Patrick Maes, and Michael Darrin. I was about to get an education from these men of how to present a fast paced vaudeville style revue. Let the lessons begin.

I am sure I went home during the four days of loading in the new show, lighting the numbers, and rehearing the show but it is all a blur to me nearly 40 years later. I do remember working the show bands at night from 8PM until 4AM and then catching a couple hours of shut eye before work began at 9AM with the BU85 cast and crew. At 5PM the BU85 gang would leave for the day and I would find somewhere to lie down for an hour or two then start the whole process over again. This experience was awesome and horrible all at the same time.

On opening night of BU85 I was as close to a walking zombie as anyone could imagine. On my first performance with these performers, I missed several lighting cues. For Michael Darrin, the show's choreographer and lighting designer this was sacrilege. The second presentation went much better but it wasn't up to the level of perfection expected. After the second BU85 show I was grateful to have a band for the remainder of the night to work with. I spent the night running the show and re-programming the BU85 show into the lighting console.

When the acts were over I went home and crashed for five or six hours. It was glorious. When I woke up, I had to go back in and finish the programming before the BU85 gang showed up. From that night forward the production maintained the quality they had expected from me. A month later the BU85 show closed but would return in a couple months with another one of their productions in tow.

When Bottoms Up returned in April of 85, I was ready for them. I had already re-gelled and focused the lights back to how they were three months earlier. Everything was restored on stage to their previous marks and presets. I had even reloaded the BU85 show back into the lighting console hoping we could use most if not all of those cues. We rehearsed the BU85 show for a couple of days and opened it with a near perfect technical aspect of our work.

The BU85 ran for two weeks as the only act in the lounge while we rehearsed and did the lighting programming for their other production. It was called Flamboyant Follies. It was an all male female impersonator or drag queen Presentation. Thirteen years after performing in drag as a witch in Hansel and Gretel, here I was working with a stage filled with Drag Queens. It was a blast. I am not sure if I ever enjoyed working performances as much as I did working those two shows. Every person in both productions were masters at their craft, so it was an honor to spend five nights a week with them. Flamboyant Follies would not be my only drag queen presentation to work in my career.

Both Bottoms Up and Flamboyant follies performed two times a night each Tuesday through Thursday and three times each on Friday and Saturday. They were off on Sunday and Monday but our room wasn't dark. On Sunday afternoon and evening, we hosted the Sandy Hackett Talent Showcase. Sandy is the son of legendary comedian Buddy Hackett and every once in a while I would work his act. I still bump into him once in a while. The other show we did on Monday nights was a big band music and dance presentation. I hired Talbot Snow to run these two nights so I could get a couple days off a week.

In March 85 we added another child to our clan. We named him David and he increased not only the size of our family, but the joy within our family. He had been born just before Bottoms Up returned to our stage along with Flamboyant Follies. Both shows would depart in December '85 and in January '86 I was ready for my next big adventure.

It had been nearly three years since we left Australia and Lillian had seen her mother. She wanted to go back for a visit with Michael and David or maybe go back and live there for a while. I was not opposed to the idea of returning to Australia and living there for a year or more. In February '86 we packed our bags and took the 22 hour flight back to Perth.

Within two weeks of our arriving back in Australia, I had found full time employment at one of the most luxurious hotels in Perth. The name of the hotel was the Merlin Perth Hotel. At the time the Merlin had the largest convention space of any other hotel in the city. My job was to set up the lights and sound for conventions, weddings, parties, anniversaries, car shows, and any other meeting a client desired. When compared to my work at the Mint, it was different but rather simple to do. The best part of working there was the hours. We were usually through by five o'clock at night and this gave me what I hadn't had in Las Vegas: a home and family life.

Nine months after arriving in Perth, I had the overwhelming feeling of wanting to be back into Showbiz in Las Vegas. I could feel the strings of entertainment pulling me towards them some 12,000 miles away. I told Lillian what I was thinking and she agreed with me. She had had her reunion with her family and now wanted to return to Las Vegas. In November of 86, we packed up our belongings, (all five suitcases of them) Michael, David, and another child yet to be born and returned to Las Vegas.

As soon as we arrived, I signed back in at Local 720 and started looking for work again. I went back to the Mint Hotel to say hello to some old friends and to see how they were doing. When I saw my former assistant, who was now the boss, Garry Sherman, he asked me if I wanted to work there again. He had had some employees leave and he was finding it difficult to replace them. Having no other immediate prospects, I took him up on the offer. The old team was back together but in different positions. Garry and I had worked together since the first run of Bottoms Up in '85. He worked for me for nearly two years after that. He took over for me when I left on my adventure Down Under.

I was back at the Mint but it wasn't where I wanted to be. The job I was doing had been done by me two years already and now it was just a source of income with little challenge to it. During this time I thought it might be interesting to be in law enforcement. I tried several times to join the force but failed the running part of the physical exam. I was always a terrible long distance runner. I knew I was ready to work on the big stages in the other hotels if only I could get the chance. Once again the universe heard me and was going to take me on a journey the long way into the big showrooms.

In May of 87 our third child was born. We named her Sharron-Marie. Thus far, all of my children had been born while I was an employee of the Mint Hotel. The job I was doing again at the Mint was easy maybe too easy but it gave me time away from the work to have somewhat of a family life. All the acts on stage liked me running their shows and the continually told Garry and his boss this fact. This made Garry nervous and I should have seen what was coming a mile away.

I was fired from the Mint in September 87 for moonlighting or working at union properties on my time off. It was a phony reason but it was within their rights to do so. I was more upset with myself for not seeing this coming even though the warning signs were there for a week or more. Oh well, another lesson learned. It was Friday and I signed back into Local 720 hoping for a show change or anything over the weekend. On Monday I needed to have some form of income and work. It didn't matter a great deal to me what it was.

The next chapter in my life was about to begin. It would be a short one but at this time in my life it was important for the universe to guide me through it.

CHAPTER FOUR: OUT OF SHOWBIZ, SORT OF.

The first week of September 1987 found me once again looking for work. I had been told by a friend that a company called Recreational Development which was a partner company to Chris Aquatech Pools was looking for a welder to build a water fountain at the Imperial Palace Hotel. When I arrived at the jobsite, my interview was to weld some of the pieces for the frame on the water fall. It was all 3/16" thick angle iron and flat bar that needed to be arc or stick welded together.

My first pass wasn't as good as my usual work. The second and third passes were more to my standards. It had been four or five years since I had stick welded and by the fourth pass my hand-eye coordination was back. Bill Whittle, the owner offered me the job and I took it. The job didn't pay very well but it was sufficient for our needs. We worked 6AM until 2:30PM, Monday through Friday. This gave me the weekends off in order to pick up work with Local 720.

Even in my youth, I was always building something. My time in the scenery shops gave me some marketable skills that were now going to provide me with some income. The waterfall and mini lake we were building was about 130 feet wide, 30 feet deep, and in places it was 20 feet tall. I don't think I stopped welding for almost two months straight. When the welding was complete, I thought they would let me go but when asked if I wanted to stay and finish the concrete work, I jumped at the chance.

I had never done concrete work before and when they put a trowel in my hands it felt like it belonged there. I was shown how to finish the concrete so it would look like natural rock. I guess I am a quick learner because within a few hours, the owner wanted to keep a trowel in my hands to finish all of the concrete. I didn't think it was all that difficult to work the mud. It was a little like stick welding. You just need good hand-eye coordination.

On really big pours, I was in charge of the concrete pumper. The mud had to be a certain thickness for the pump to work properly. I spent much of my time checking the concrete trucks out and having them adjust their thickness with water. When the pour was done, I would break down the pump and hoses and clean them out. Any concrete left in the hoses or pump would harden and damage the system. It wasn't as enjoyable to operate the pump as it was to trowel the concrete but it was a critical job and needed to be done right every pour.

The owner eventually put me in charge of troubleshooting problems on pools and waterfalls. If there was a leak or blockage on one of their pools or waterfalls, I was sent out to find and fix it. I had a pretty good success rate doing this work.

While I was working on waterfalls and pools I would still take work calls from Local 720 at night and on the weekends. For eight months I had worked for Rec-Dev and enjoyed the work immensely. Building gets my creative juices flowing and I consider it art. What some people do with paint and canvas, some of us do with concrete and steel. My time in construction came to an end in May 1988 with a single phone call from Local 720.

The next chapter in my life was about to start and oh what a chapter it would be.

CHAPTER FIVE: OK, THIS IS WHAT I AM GOING TO DO.

My day job building high dollar waterfalls and swimming pools for Rec-Dev was going well. I was spending time at night with the family, working with Talbot Snow on re-building KAZZ, and I was getting more and more calls for night and weekend work through Local 720. The universe had heard me several months earlier wanting the chance to again work shows (preferably in a main showroom setting). The ASAP call from Local 720 at 6:30PM one night changed my future for the better.

One of the stage crew working Jeff Kutash's 'Splash' show at the Riviera Hotel and Casino had injured himself and they needed a replacement there by 7PM for the half hour show call. I lived about a mile from the Riviera and was there with time to spare. My first stepmother Barbara Hayes, (there have been several stepmothers), was the Entertainment Director for the hotel and had concerns her bosses wouldn't like having a relative working there. So I was told I would only be working the one night for the two performances. This was fine by me. I was just glad to be working in a showroom doing real shows again.

During the first performance I was told what to do and did my best to memorize the cues. The second performance I did all my cues with limited help from others on the crew. It was fun being there and working on a show again. At the end of the night I was about to leave and stopped by Barbara's office to say goodbye and thank her for the opportunity. When I stepped into her office she had a concerned look on her face. I was about to leave when she informed me I would be back the next night and as far into the future as she could see. Was I supposed to smile or look worried at that moment? I asked her to explain the sudden change from 5 hours earlier and now wanting me to work there full time.

She told me she didn't want a crew rebellion so she had to keep me and figure out how to present this dilemma to her bosses upstairs. A what? A crew rebellion? I needed her to elaborate. She explained that by the second show, the Head Carpenter, Carl Sandahl, and several others informed her she was to keep me. It was rare that a stagehand came on an open call and knew all their cues after one show. I didn't think doing cues was very difficult and I rather enjoyed doing them. Barbara told me I was a keeper and if she didn't, her crew would be very unhappy with her. Now I was smiling because I was back in Showbiz!

To play it safe and earn a few extra dollars, I worked my waterfall and pool construction job during the days and worked Splash six nights a week. I figured I could keep this up for a few months or longer. I was wrong. I was wearing myself out fast working in the heat of spring all day and doing my cues at night. Something had to give. The medical bills from Sharron being born a year earlier were almost paid by the additional income. I knew what I wanted to do and I knew a career in Showbiz was my destiny.

The choice was really clear and easy to make. I could stay in construction doing something I enjoyed and making a livable wage, or I could work shows again with good pay and benefits. What to do, what to do? My final two weeks with Rec-Dev were busy ones. We had big pump and pours on a few of those days starting at 4AM and lasting until 4PM. Then it was home for a meal and a shower and off to work Splash. I left Rec-Dev under good terms with Bill Whittle. Even though he was not glad to see me go he was happy for me and my new career. Eventually a couple of his sons, one of whom I worked with for seven months at Rec-Dev, would become stagehands at other hotels.

In May of 1988, I became a full time employee of the Riviera Hotel and became a member of the International or IATSE Local 720. I would remain at the Riviera for the next six years until July 31, 1994. The next six years would be an E-Ticket ride, (if you don't know what this means you can Google it or ask an old person to explain it to you), in my career, personal, and business life.

I think I should give a better 'lay of the land' concerning the Riviera Hotel and all the shows under its roof. In the main showroom called the Versailles Room, Jeff Kutash's show named 'Splash' played two shows a night seven days a week, 50 weeks a year. It required 18 stage techs to operate it. This number does not include the several full time employees to cover days off and vacations. I was low man on the Totem Pole in May 1988. Normally, a stage tech at the bottom of the Totem Pole in seniority would spend their week covering several positions on stage and I did just that. The difference with me and other stage techs was my solid audio skills.

The Riviera had three mini showrooms called the Mardi Gras Rooms and a lounge in their casino. The shows in the Mardi Gras Rooms were as follows: Bud Friedman's 'The Improv,' (a comedy club), 'Crazy Girls,' (a nude dance and striptease show), and 'An Evening at La Cage,' (an all male-female impersonator or Drag Queen show). I worked all of these productions from time to time running their sound on other stage tech's days off and vacations. La Cage was my second of three Drag Queen shows I worked. There was only one left.

Needless to say, between Splash, the Mardi Gras Rooms, and the lounge, I had plenty of work to keep two stage techs busy. I was running sound almost every night somewhere in the hotel except for the one room I wanted. There was one thing on my career goals list yet to be checked off. I would not wait much longer for the universe to grant my wish.

I had worked the deck audio position or cues many times for the past several months. Helping the carpenters move scenery was secondary to maintaining and passing out the microphones to the performers. Henry 'Hank' Crossen, the relief Head Audio tech was going to the lounge and work there fulltime. Splash needed a new relief for the Head Audio tech Dale Dudley. All eyes slowly turned and looked at me. Everyone knew I was the perfect fit for the job; everyone except for the Head Audio tech.

Over the past several months, Dale had been watching me operate sound in the Mardi Gras Rooms and in the lounge. He also knew I took good care of his mics during Splash. He admitted I had good audio skills but he didn't want me running sound for Splash. His reason for not wanting me: I was too much of a cowboy or a shoot from the hip audio engineer. He wanted someone to be his clone or robot and do everything exactly like him. For a brief moment, I saw my goal of being a Head Audio tech in a major Las Vegas Showroom flying out the window.

I wasn't about to go down without a fight. I thought for a moment and came up with a plan. I would dazzle him with my audio engineering brilliance. Yeah, that would show him. No, wait a minute, another plan came to mind. I would be who he wanted and be the best relief engineer he ever had. Yes! That is the plan I went with. I chose wisely. Common sense: one. Ego: zero. Even after a couple conversations and me promising to tow the line as he wished, Dale still didn't want me as his relief.

I admit Dale was right. I was a cowboy. I shot from the hip on everything audio for several years. While at the Mint Hotel, running the sound meant shooting from the hip. There was no time for a proper line check, let alone a sound check. The first song of each set was the sound check. You had to plug and go and mix even faster. I loved those early days in my career and hoped they wouldn't be my undoing now.

Throughout my career, for one reason or another, there have been several instances when someone stood up for me and opened or kept a door open for me to pass through. This time it would be Barbara. Several months earlier the crew had insisted on me being one of the Splash Crew. She had acquiesced and it proved to be beneficial for the property and her department. Now her job was to overcome the objections of a resistant employee and Department Head.

Dale agreed with Barbara on one thing. I was the most qualified person in the hotel let alone the Splash show to run audio for the show. Now she had to give him something to sweeten the deal. She told Dale he had to train me and use me for two months. At the end of two months, if he still didn't want me in his department, she would find him another replacement and use me elsewhere. It was the best deal he was going to get. The next arrangement would have been an offer he couldn't refuse. He took the deal and conditions attached to it.

My time learning to run the sound for Splash just like Dale was the hardest mental work I had ever done. He had written out on a spread sheet everything he did and when he did it during the show. Sounds easy to read, follow directions, and do as written, right? It wasn't. I was working hard to convert my thinking over to Dale's thinking. This meant de-converting much of my shoot from the hip mentality. It took a couple weeks to really start locking in on the way Dale did audio, but after a month I was the clone or robot he wanted me to be.

When Barbara approached Dale at the end of their two month timetable, her question was simple. Did he want to keep me in his department or did she need to look for another audio tech to replace me? My time in his department would continue. He not only wanted me to be his relief at front of house, he wanted me to run sound for Splash five nights a week and he would run it the other two nights. Over the next five years we continued to have a good working relationship and became friends. There's much I learned from Dale and am grateful for all he did with and for me.

My goal of running sound in a major Las Vegas Hotel showroom was coming to fruition. I was even operating the audio console, (the Yamaha PM2000), I had wanted to run since first seeing one in 1980. As far as I was concerned, I was living the dream.

In all honesty, for the first five years working Splash and other rooms, I was never bored. I was a full time employee but I never had a position or set of cues assigned to me. Just for Splash I knew 12 of the 18 positions or tracks or sets of cues. I would do each of these cues from time to time just to keep them in my memory banks. When running sound, the cast, orchestra, dancers, and specialty acts rotated during the week for days off. This changed the show almost every night. The slogan of Splash was: 'To come see us again because we never do the same show twice.' So true, so very true.

I thought it would be appropriate here to list all of the positions I worked for Splash. Let's see, there were all four assistant carpenter positions, assistant deck electric, assistant deck audio, Head Deck Electric, Head Carpenter, Head Audio, Head Lasers, Head Cue Caller, Job Steward, and Stage Manager. I also worked the Head Lounge positions for the three Mardi Gras Rooms and the casino lounge. It's easy to see why I never got bored or didn't enjoy going to work every night. Could things get any better?

In 1990 the Riviera Hotel made a change in its entertainment policy. Splash was the hottest show in town to see even after five years of nightly shows. Ownership and management wanted to push the entertainment envelope even more by signing headline entertainers to perform in the Splash or Versailles Showroom. The idea was to have Splash perform 24 nights in a row followed by four nights of headliner entertainment. This schedule didn't affect the crew very much. We still had our scheduled one night off a week. The change really affected the dancers in Splash. They didn't get their usual one night off a week to rest and heal. It was brutal on them.

On the 24th night of Splash shows, I was promoted to acting Head Carpenter for the load out of Splash and the load in of whichever act was to perform the next night. My primary job besides clearing the stage of anything 'Splash' was to help the deck audio clear the orchestra pit of all band gear, chairs, microphones, cables, clear com, (the wired and wireless headset communication system for the stage) and trash. There was always lots of trash. Musicians can be real pigs. We would also have to clear some space for the visiting audio console and outboard gear. This was usually right next to the house audio booth.

While the audio work was being done, the stage was being transformed into the set or plot for the headliner. Lighting trusses needed to be hung, cabling needed to be run, band or orchestra risers were brought in and set up, audio monitors were put in place and cabled, monitor consoles were set in place, lighting dimmers were placed and powered, and visiting act lighting consoles were set up near the audio booth in the audience. Once this was all done, we would leave around 9AM and let the next crew finish the set up and make the stage look presentable. I usually returned to the showroom around 6PM for final checks and clean up prior to the doors opening. This sounds like a brutal schedule, and it is, but I enjoyed every day or night of those headliner shows.

For nearly 40 years, I have had the privilege and honor of working with some of the biggest names in live entertainment. One of the best things about the line of work I am in is to get paid very well for seeing the best shows in the world. This was true for my tenure at the Riviera Hotel. Our lineup included the 'Chairman of the Board,' Frank Sinatra, Liza Minelli, Paul Anka, Jerry Lewis, Tony Orlando, Mickey Rooney, Donald O'Connor, Perry Como, Jerry Van Dyke, Pia Zadora, Richie Havens, and one of my favorites; George Burns. (Once again if you don't know who these people are, Google, You Tube them, or ask an old person who they are.)

Here is where I really enjoyed my time as the front of house (FOH), audio engineer at the Riviera. About half of the headliners brought their own audio engineers and lighting designers. This meant Dale and I would get to mix the other half's shows. I was in hog heaven. I was doing what I had set out to do since 18. It only took me ten years to get here but it was worth it. I could now cross this off my 'To Do List.'

There was a third and final Drag Queen Show I worked during my career. I had been working late nights on Friday and Saturday at the Sahara Hotel in the Congo Showroom. I would run follow spot for the Red Foxx Show at 12:30AM after the second show of Splash. I would also pick up a gell-call (changing the colored filters in stage lights) every two weeks with Rick Keller the Head Electrician. He had a new show coming into the showroom and needed some help loading it in and lighting it. I was available, so…

The name of the show was Kenny Kerr's 'Boylesque.' It was the original Las Vegas Drag Queen Show. I worked during the days helping Rick in any way necessary to make his job a little easier. (This is what a good assistant is supposed to do). Once the load in was finished and rehearsals were concluded, I was to return only when needed to run a follow spot. There it is, the three Drag Queen shows worked by yours truly.

Okay, I have to admit I enjoyed working those productions. They are some of the most talented people in their craft and the shows are always hilarious.

It was during that time period that Talbot Snow and I decided to end the ten year run of KAZZ Mobile DJ Service. We had not come to a business partner impasse and breakup. No, we decided to take our skills to another level and open a 16 track recording studio. We partnered up with Quentin Stephenson who is the son of James Stephenson, the CEO of Big O Tires. James was a God-send for us. He not only put up the initial capital to start the studio, he educated us regarding how to operate a business successfully. He even came up with the name of our studio: Sound Masters Las Vegas Recording Studio. The studio has been open and operating for 30 years to this date.

It took some time for us to build a clientele base but when we did, the studio kept busy, well busy enough to pay for what Talbot and I were about to jump into. We had decided to write, produce, record, and sell our very own albums. It was during that time when Quentin decided he didn't want to own a studio and asked Talbot and I to buy him out. Talbot and I assumed all the debt on Sound Masters and bought Quentin's shares in the studio. Talbot and I were now in complete control of what we used the studio for. We were also in a good deal of debt. Oh well, that seems to be the American way.

Here is another question for you. What do you get if you work Splash six nights a week and work seven days a week at Caesar's Palace at the same time for over six months? The obvious answer is tired and you would be correct, but the correct answer is: Divorced, you get divorced. I guess this was inevitable or at the least very likely to occur. In 1980 as an apprentice at the MGM Scenery Studios I had been told by an older stagehand; "If you haven't been fired and divorced at least one time, then you're not a real stagehand." I had been fired from the Mint Hotel in September of 1987 and by November 1991, I would be divorced. I was now, according to Angelo Moreno's definition, a real stagehand. Hooray for me.

I can't really blame Lillian for having had enough of my lifestyle. In 1988 we bought our first home and in order to secure the down payment, I worked on the install of Siegfried and Roy's show at the Mirage. I worked from 6:30PM 'til 12AM six nights a week at Splash and then drove down the street to the Mirage Hotel and worked from 12:30AM 'til 1:30PM, went home, took a nap, and started this all over again. I lasted for one month doing this before calling it quits at the Mirage Hotel. I earned enough for the down payment on our house and took a break from all the work madness for a while.

Recuperating from the past month at the Mirage Hotel took about a week. I started working heavily on the album with Talbot during the day and working Splash at night. Then I was offered a job which was supposed to last one month at Caesar's Palace running sound for their pageant. The conditions of the job were starting at 9AM and ending at 3PM and you had to work seven days a week. I took the job thinking it was short term. I finally quit the job after six months. This extended job and my time at the studio were the last straws for Lillian.

We were divorced in November 1991 and she eventually left America and went back to Australia. Now I was a single Dad with three kids to raise and a living to earn. Nothing lasted forever, including being single.

After my divorce, I decided if marriage were to happen with me again, the woman would need to know every aspect of my life, especially my career. I had three kids at home with me and a career that drives many marriages off the tracks. She would need to accompany me to work a few times and see the job I did and the atmosphere in which the job took place.

In January of 1992, I started going to some social gatherings just to look around. It was at one of these gatherings that I met Linda Dennis. She was five years older than I and a Special Education Teacher. I saw potential in this relationship. After a few more social gatherings it was time for her to see my life and decide if she wanted to go any further. She came with me to Splash and sat with me as I ran the sound for the show a few times. She also accompanied me backstage to meet the crew and half naked dancers in the show. She seemed to be unfazed by everything.

We were married in August of 1992.

For our Honeymoon, we went to Los Angeles and saw Andrew Lloyd Webber's Phantom of the Opera and spent two days at Disneyland at the Disneyland Hotel. It was a really wonderful time. It was a short honeymoon due to her having to be back at work at her elementary school and I needed to be at Splash.

One of the most significant realizations in my life took place on our Honeymoon. As I watched Phantom of the Opera, I knew I wanted to work a show of its caliber. The drive back to Las Vegas and a conversation with Linda firmly rooted in my mind what my next move in Showbiz was to be. I knew my time at Splash was coming to an end, but I didn't know how or why. I just knew the universe was listening and would answer me soon. For now it was time to work, have family stability, and finish a project with Talbot.

In July 1993, Linda and I added another child to our family. We named him Wesley. He was my fourth child and Linda's first. That year was shaping up to be a very interesting one.

As 1992 turned into 1993, Talbot and I worked like madmen every chance we had to finish up the first of two planned albums. The first album was titled: Talbot Snow- 'Contrary to Popular Belief.' The album also featured Dani, Michael James, 1-800, and Saxx. The second album was titled: Talbot Snow- 'Prime Time Chameleons.' It would feature Craig L. Hayes and three other artists. Everything was recorded at Sound Masters, produced by the HSP Hit Factory, published through TTS Publishing and released by

KAZZ PHASE TWO 1989.

East of LA Records. Every one of these separate companies is owned by two people: Talbot Snow and Craig L. Hayes. We both decided when getting started on the albums we would hold all rights, publishing, and production under our names. We also decided we would only accept a distribution deal from any major label or no deal at all. This may or may not have been the right thing to do but neither Talbot or I wanted to be a puppet for any major record label.

SOUNDMASTERS LAS VEGAS RECORDING STUDIO 1990.

The album was completed and pressed into its compact disc form in September 1993. We had completed one of our goals. It had taken almost three years to do so, but we did it. The album received some air play in town but not enough to generate the interest needed to make it a success. A few record stores like Tower Records let us put the CD on their shelves and it sold some, but not enough units for our liking. After a few months, we came to the conclusion the product was very good but we just didn't know enough about the industry to make it a regional hit let alone a chart topping album. What we did learn was invaluable and we had accomplished one of our goals.

I still consider our first album a success in many ways. If nothing else, it was the best business card we could show potential clients at that time about Sound Masters. All we had to do is play the CD and show them on the insert it was recorded in the very studio they were standing in and they booked time. The studio was doing well and Talbot was making a living from it. In 1995, I turned my interest in the studio over to Talbot because of what happened to me in July of 1994, but first let me finish off my tenure at the Riviera Hotel.

By May 1994, I had been at the Riviera Hotel for six years. At the age of 32 years old, there was still a lot of ambition left inside of me. My career had advanced as far as it could at the Riviera Hotel. The past year was nothing more than making a paycheck. I wanted a challenge. I wanted to make my mark on a bigger stage. In September 1992, after seeing Phantom of the Opera, I had put it out in the universe what I wanted to do. The universe had heard me and was about to give me exactly what I asked for two years earlier. The next chapter of my career was about to unfold.

CHAPTER SIX: MY LIFE ON ELVIS' STAGE

July 31, 1994 is a very special date for me for two reasons. First, it is the 25th Anniversary of the opening night for the International Hotel and Casino / Las Vegas Hilton / LVH / Westgate Resort Las Vegas. The second reason I like this date is it was the day I was hired as Head Carpenter for the main showroom. My time on Elvis' stage had officially begun.

I had worked many times on Elvis' stage during the 1980's on show changes and even a few show runs. I had worked the deck for Wayne Newton, BB King, Gladys Night, and so on. I had even run a follow spot for some Barry Manilow shows. Going back further to my early teen years I had watched several shows from the box boom lighting positions. (This is an area in the audience on the far left and right of the showroom.) I saw Bill Cosby, Charlie Rich, Liberace, Sha Na Na, the Osmond Brothers, and many more in those years. Now I was standing on the stage as Head Carpenter and Crew Chief. Was this destiny or just great luck?

I owe a debt of gratitude to Carl Sandahl and Ed McDonnell for inviting me to leave the Riviera Hotel and join them at the Las Vegas Hilton. I had worked with them both at the Riviera for several years. Carl was the Head Carpenter on Splash and was one of the crew members who demanded Barbara keep me on the crew. Ed ran the Mardi Gras Rooms and I had worked for him many times there. Now, Carl was Stage Manager and Ed was Stage Director for Andrew Lloyd Webber's 'Starlight Express'

Ed and Carl had a problem in need of solving. The LV Hilton's showroom Head Carpenter, Mickey Geebler was retiring and they needed to find someone to fill his sizeable shoes. Three people were asked to interview for the job. The other two candidates were older and more experienced but somehow I got the job. Once again, the universe smiled on me. Call it luck or destiny or whatever else you wish to call it; I was the new Head Carpenter on Elvis' stage.

When I was offered the position, I was amazed at how lucrative the offer was. My starting weekly guarantee was twice that of what I earned at the Riviera. Then I was told there were other shows in the works that would raise my weekly earnings even more. Like I said before, Mama didn't raise any fools. I took the job. I gave my notice to Splash and finished off my last two weeks working at the Riviera Hotel. I was thankful for the wonderful experiences obtained there but they were soon in my rear view mirror. I went across Paradise Road to start my next big adventure.

Some things in life are surreal. For the first few weeks as the Head Carpenter on one of the most iconic stages in the world, there were days I would ask myself if this was a dream or a dream come true? I had been the relief Head Carpenter for Alan 'AD' Davis many times at the Riviera Hotel, but now I was in the full time hot seat. I had asked for just such a thing two years earlier while watching Andrew Lloyd Webber's 'Phantom of the Opera.' Now here I was working one of his shows at one of my favorite hotels to work in. Blessed, I am blessed.

THE STARLIGHT EXPRESS STAGE 1993-1997.

Perhaps I should take a moment and explain to those outside of our industry what it means to be the Head Carpenter in Showbiz on a major hotel showroom stage.

The Head Carpenter is the highest authority on a stage other than the Stage Manager, Technical Director, Entertainment Director, or Vice President of Entertainment. All other departments such as the Head Props, Electrician, Audio, Flyman, and Automation operate under his or her direction. The only other Department Head on equal ground is the Head Wardrobe person. Each of these Head of Department positions can have several, if not dozens of personnel under their individual supervision. On Starlight Express, there were 24 stage techs and 24 wardrobe dressers. Big shows equal big crews.

Every production show I have ever worked requires a certain number of stage technicians and wardrobe to function. This was true concerning Starlight Express. Every move of scenery, props, electrical fixtures audio, and pyro, are done on either music cues or on headset by the cue caller. Starlight Express was a little different. Every move backstage by every person was choreographed with the performers.

The skaters would skate around backstage very quickly in order to get to the other side of the stage for their entrance. If you happened to be in the wrong place at the wrong time then you would very likely be involved in a literal train wreck. (Did I mention Starlight Express was the story about trains racing to see who was the fasted, mixed in with a love story and much intrigue?) I was involved in one of those train wrecks one and only one time. When one of the skaters had a wheel break during the show he sped off stage to have it fixed. As we crossed paths and collided it was as if I had been tackled in a football game by a very hard hitting linebacker. Luckily, neither one of us was injured in the incident.

The best thing about working Starlight Express was the never ending maintenance and work calls. The differences between the two types of calls varied greatly. Maintenance calls were performed every day in order to keep the show looking fresh and new. This included the daily sweeping and mopping of the stage, cleaning the Plexiglas shields around the stage, vacuuming needed areas, dusting, wiping down all areas, emptying trash receptacles, filling water stations, and quality control or checking every piece of moving equipment. The electrical department would repair or replace all burn outs or broken fixtures. The audio department checked and re-checked every audio component and microphone to ensure peak performance. These are all daily maintenance calls.

Work calls were for the purpose of repairing a major problem. If a section of the stage broke or needed special attention, we would begin the work call immediately after the last performance of the night. On several occasions we would need to replace large sections of the stage overnight and have everything ready to go by the next show. The demolition, fabrication, painting, and sealing of the new section of stage would require an around the clock effort by everyone in order to be show ready. There was never a show cancelled due to the crew not having the stage ready after any repair work call. I must admit, it was close a couple times though.

Starlight Express ran from 1993-1997. Everyone on the crew made really good money during those years. There was never a lack of work in those years for everyone. In fact, the new entertainment policy that was about to be implemented would require even more hours to be spent on the stage. You weren't there, but I was smiling with gleeful anticipation.

The new entertainment policy would include headline entertainers on Friday nights when Starlight Express was dark. This was all very familiar to me. I had been at Splash when this type of policy was implemented and I loved every minute of it. We started off doing this Friday night concert series only once a month but within a few months we were having a Friday night concert almost every dark night of Starlight Express. For the next three years, I believe I only had 10-20 days off each year. My move from Splash to the Las Vegas Hilton had proven to be very challenging. I was now developing new skills and honing my leadership abilities

THE LAS VEGAS HILTON STAGE 1997-2005.

One quick note to point out here. Around 1995-1996 Paramount Studios and the Las Vegas Hilton teamed up and brought Star Trek: The Experience to the property. You could zip around the galaxy on the Starship Enterprise and it would drop you off on Deep Space Nine where you could shop at one of the many stores or grab a meal at Quark's. It was a fun adventure and I really liked having a meal at Quark's. Okay, I too am a Star Trek fan.

Back on Elvis' stage, Starlight Express closed in November 1997. We painted the stage a glossy black and loaded in the Oak Ridge Boys to film their Las Vegas spectacular. There were 60 different acts over the next couple of weeks along with every song made popular by the group. They were the last group to perform on the stage built for Starlight Express. A few days later the stage was removed and a new traditional stage was installed. In January 1998 we started the year off with a bang. The Consumer Electronics Show (CES) began with a ten day run of set up, keynote speakers, and load out. Three days later we loaded in Wheel of Fortune for a three week run. This began a two year cycle of Broadway Shows, concerts, television, and industrial shows on Elvis' stage.

I really enjoy doing television shows and industrials except for one aspect: The weight gain from them. Those shows have big budgets and are constantly feeding the crews. We would call Wheel of Fortune, Jeopardy and other industrial shows; "Ten pound shows" because that is how much weight everyone gained during those weeks. We would easily work off those extra pounds over the next few shows.

From 1998-2000 some of the Broadway Shows we did were Rent, Andrew Lloyd Webber's Joseph and the Amazing Technicolor Dream Coat, the Buddy Holly Story, and Grease. We even did an official Graceland Production called: Elvis Live. This show utilized three Sony Jumbotron video walls. The center wall had Elvis on it. The two side video walls showed clips of the band and backup singers 20 plus years earlier and currently on them. Elvis' actual band played along with the video images just as they had years earlier. To make everything fit and give the best sight lines for the audience, the band was positioned under the giant video walls. It was as real as you could get. In fact, there were parts of the show when Elvis would wave at people in the back of the showroom, and they would wave back to the video wall. They were true fans.

Even though we were busy doing Broadway Shows, television, industrials, and headline acts such as Styx, Kansas, Chicago, REO Speedwagon, Heart, Johnny Mathis, and the list goes on and on, there was one form of entertainment we hadn't put on stage yet; Boxing and MMA fights had not yet made it to center stage in our showroom. Once the commitment was made to do fights, we had to work out logistics for the stage and seating areas. We would set up the rings near the edge of the stage towards the audience and set up the ringside seats all over the stage. We also would have to hang a lighting truss over the ring and set up camera platforms for live television broadcast or recordings. When it was all over, we would spend the next day cleaning up the mess.

I almost forgot to discuss what happened in 1997. In that year Hilton Gaming Properties, Bally's gaming, and Caesar's Palace merged to form Park Place Entertainment (PPE). A major shakeup occurred at every property within the new corporation. Once a new President of the Las Vegas Hilton was in place things started to change. His first move was to give Starlight Express their 6 month notice of closure. His second move was brilliant. (I am being very, very sarcastic here). He wanted to tear out Elvis' stage and showroom and turn it into a food court. He believed showroom headline entertainment was dead in Las Vegas and even proclaimed that "Not even Tony Bennett could fill Elvis' showroom."

One man saved the room and stage Elvis built. When Barron Hilton heard about the brilliant (more sarcasm) plan proposed by Dean, (This is his first name), he put an end to it immediately. Thank Heaven for Barron Hilton. Dean was eventually made the President of Caesar's Palace and one of the first things he did was to demolish the Circus Maximus showroom and build a hotel tower in its place.

It was not long after Dean left the Las Vegas Hilton that we booked; wait for it, Tony Bennett in our showroom. Tony sold out every performance. We even took a picture of Tony on stage and the sold out audience and sent it to Dean. We never heard from him again.

When the Las Vegas Convention and Visitors Authority outbid other venues for the National Finals Rodeo, it was a stroke of brilliance. We reserved the first two weeks of December to offer top tier country music acts to the cowboys and cowgirls. We even had the very popular Nashville Network show called Prime Time Country (PTC) on our stage during the rodeo days. After PTC would change over to country music shows like Brooks and Dunn, Brad Paisley, Big and Rich, Wynona, Reba, and a slew of others for a late show. Then we would reset the stage for Prime Time Country and start the whole process over again. You had to be a Tetras Grand Master to make all this work backstage. Our venue was even named as the Country Music Venue of the Year by the Country Music Awards or CMA's. These were truly good times.

Over the next few years there was a slowdown in business at the property and in our showroom. It was if the lifeblood of the property was being drained and Park Place Entertainment was doing just enough to keep the doors open on the Las Vegas Hilton but nothing more. We soon found out what was happening and why.

By 2003 Park Place Entertainment had siphoned off all of the high rollers from the Las Vegas Hilton and taken them down to Caesar's Palace. There was only one thing left for those corporate gaming raiders to do. When word came down that the Las Vegas Hilton was put on the auction block by PPE, it was a gut punch to every employee on the property. The price tag on the property was around $300 million. I checked my bank account balance and found I was well over $299 million short of being able to buy it myself so we all waited to see what would happen.

Interest was shown by the Las Vegas Convention Center (LVCC), Marriott Hotels, and a few other gaming corporations. The worst of these would have been the LVCC buying it. They would have demolished the hotel and built a new addition to the LVCC and added more parking garages. In the end, none of the Las Vegas gaming companies acquired the Las Vegas Hilton.

The new owners of the property were from Atlantic City, New Jersey. Their company name was Colony Capital. They not only bought the hotel, they also wanted to keep the name on the building. We were now a franchise Hilton Hotel. Within a few months they were remodeling and upgrading the entire property. The company also bought several other Hilton, Bally's, and Caesar's gaming properties around the country. Remodeling the Las Vegas Hilton wasn't the only big plans they had for the property.

Colony Capital understood what the mob knew many years earlier. Entertainment, concerts, special events, and conventions are what bring people into your casino and hotel. Their first goal was to get Elvis' showroom back up to full speed. They started looking for a couple artists to put in the showroom as resident headliners. Our showroom has about 1,600 seats for customers. There is a certain price point for a headliner and all the other associated expenses that must make financial sense. The search for the perfect fit was on. Once found, the negotiations with the artist's manager and agent could begin.

As soon as the negotiations were complete, the press conference was scheduled for three weeks later. The biggest possible splash is what is desired at one of these events. I was brought in at the end of the negotiations and sworn to secrecy for our meetings. There was much to plan and prepare for even before any mention of the new headline residency could be announced. For the next three weeks I had to work covertly with my crew in order to make a work schedule and timetable for what would occur hours after the press conference.

Within hours of the agreement being signed with the artist and the hotel, rumors began to fly around the property. It was confirmed they had signed an artist to a residency but no other information would be given until the press conference. My crew asked me multiple times if the rumors were true and if I knew who the artist was. I was allowed to confirm the hotel had signed a residency agreement with an artist but was forbidden to disclose who it was. I never told a single person who the artist was. Everyone found out at the same time at the press conference.

I had told my crew to start making plans for a complete revamp when "Artist X" was announced at the press conference in three weeks. We had a great deal of prep work to do prior to the revamp and load in. We just had to wait three weeks. The press conference went perfectly and now everyone knew our headliner residency artist was Barry Manilow. His show would open in February 2005. The clock was now ticking.

The amount of work needing to be accomplished before we would start the load in of Barry's show was daunting. We still had a good deal of elements on stage from Starlight Express. The demolition of hard surfaced walls and skate tracks only took a few days to accomplish. While we were removing those items, the electricians were removing cables and light fixtures off the massive dead hung *'spider'* truss over the stage. The walls and skate tracks went into the trash or recycling dumpsters. Everything electrical went out to the parking garage to be checked, cleaned, repaired, recoiled, labeled, stacked, and prepared to be brought back into the showroom when needed.

There were far too many people working on the stage at the same time all needing the same space to do their work. I split the crews into two shifts of 12 hours each. Twelve electricians and four riggers worked the 7PM-7AM shift and fifteen carpenters and four riggers worked the 7AM-7PM shift seven days a week. The audio crew came and went as they needed. The push on removing everything Starlight Express was on.

It only took just over a week to finish removing the last remnants of Starlight Express. The dead hung steel truss was cut up into flat pieces by three people and placed in two recycling bins. Everything else ended up in the landfill at Apex. The work of loading in Barry's show didn't wait for us to complete the demolition and reactivation of all showroom systems. They had to be done at the same time or our timetable would fall apart.

As sections of the stage and truss were cleared, riggers worked to upgrade and repair the Flyrail and moving pipes system. While this was going on, the carpenters hung new curtains while the electricians installed new lights and cabled them. As every line-set or flying pipe was upgraded, repaired, and reactivated, the two flymen and eight riggers worked feverishly to keep up with hanging all the scenic elements that arrived daily. An additional crew of eight riggers was called in to rig Barry's flying bridge over the audience.

The final scenic elements and the band carts came in the first day of the last week for load in. Once everything was assembled, it was time for the audio and electric crews to cable them in preparation for band gear and light fixtures. Even with all the surprises and fixing broken systems, the work of loading in Barry's show was completed on time and without a day to spare. The next step in opening a major act was ready to begin.

It was time for technical rehearsals to begin. In less than a week, Barry, his band, and his backup singers would be on stage and show rehearsals would begin. The toughest part of technical rehearsals fell on the band cart drivers. They had to drive their carts from underneath the band in the dark and follow a taped line on stage to guide them. They had to hit their marks every time or they would crash into each other. Other moving pieces in the show could also crash into them if they were out of position. Band cart driving school lasted several hours a day for a few days until they were perfect every time they moved.

While driving school took place, the electricians were making sure every light they hung and cabled worked exactly like it should. If it didn't, then it was replaced or repaired. Lights were focused and gelled with the colors required by Barry's lighting designer, Seth Jackson. The creating of lighting looks took place while driving school continued. The goal was to have as many basic looks as possible preprogrammed in the lighting consoles prior to show rehearsals commencing. This would save time and time was a very valuable commodity and in short supply.

A small window of time was carved out of technical rehearsals in order to place all the band gear on the band carts and cable them. Line checks or verifying that each instrument was plugged into the proper channel on the audio consoles took place while driving school continued. Nothing in the show was being left to chance.

The automated winch system that flew Barry's bridge over the audience needed to be learned by a crew member and operated over and over again to work out any and all kinks in the operation of it. Being over the audience's heads meant this had to work perfectly every time or it could seriously injure people.

The flymen kept busy during this time by continuing to upgrade pipes and line sets every chance they had. They also fine tuned the counterweight system and finalized every in and out trim spike. One of Barry's flying scenic elements weighed in at 4,500 pounds. It had to run perfectly or someone on stage could get squashed like a bug when it came in.

The wardrobe department was now fully invested in work at this time fitting and repairing costumes and preparing dressing rooms for soon to be arriving guests. Their work is perhaps the most important of everyone's in the show. The audience can see every flaw in a suit or costume not properly checked and prepped. Attention to detail is their mantra.

And just like that, our technical rehearsal time was over. Barry would be on stage tomorrow and everything had to be ready for him. It was. Our days would now go from 10-12 hours of work each day to 12-16 hours of rehearsals a day for the next three weeks. If you weren't already exhausted by now, you would be by opening night.

I can describe the next three weeks of show rehearsals in six words: Rehearse, rehearse, and rehearse some more. When the show opened after all those rehearsals, it was a smash hit. It would run for the next five years and be seen by over half a million fans.

I know I have given a lot of details concerning the amount of work it takes to load in a show such as Barry Manilow's. I wanted people outside our industry to gain a little insight into the magic of Showbiz.

The key to being able to pull off a feat such as the load in, rehearsal, and nightly performances of a Barry Manilow show, is to surround yourself with the most talented and hardest working people you can find. This is exactly what I have always done. By doing so we accomplished the nearly impossible on one of the tightest timetables I have ever experienced. The nearly 50 people it took to make opening night happen have my deepest appreciation and respect for their hard work and professionalism.

The only other shows I have worked on that required so much time and work from load in to opening night are magic shows.

During the weeks when Barry was away, we usually did other traveling headline shows or concerts. We would also fill in the holes with conventions or boxing events. We stayed very busy. It seemed like the good times and hard earned paychecks would never end. Never say never.

In 2008 everything in our economy changed…for the worse. The housing bubble finally burst destroying trillions of dollars in wealth in our nation and the world. The owners of the Las Vegas Hilton walked away from most if not all of their gaming properties including our hotel. We were now a toxic asset on the books of Goldman Sachs. To their credit, the Wall Street banking giant hired a gaming company to operate the property and maintain its value while they looked for a buyer to remove it from their ledger.

The five year run of Barry Manilow's show ended in 2009. It had taken us about three weeks to load in his show five years earlier but now it only took a week to load it out. It's almost always sad when a show closes; this was no exception. I lost half of my full time crew due to a reduction in shows and needed labor.

Once Barry Manilow was gone, we spent another two weeks transforming the room back into a touring act roadhouse. We ordered and hung a lot of drapes to cover everything on the stage that Barry's fiber optic curtains had previously masked. We also changed the entire lighting plot to make it more user friendly for touring acts. Up to this point the Manilow lighting plot had stayed in place and untouched by our lighting crew and touring lighting designers.

The 2009 recession ushered in by the housing bubble collapse had a devastating impact on Las Vegas. While the rest of the nation was nearing the bottom of the housing bubble impact, here in our hometown we had bigger issues. We led the nation in housing foreclosures and bankruptcies. Every hotel was trying everything they could think of trying to draw people back to Las Vegas for a good time.

Even though the Las Vegas Hilton was in receivership by Goldman Sachs, nothing in hotel operation changed for the most part. We were still busy in the showroom due to our Vice President of Entertainment, Rick White, trying anything he could to keep business coming in our doors. I think Rick used the 'throwing spaghetti at a wall and see what sticks' method in order to find the next big hit for our room. I know I am but one of many grateful souls for all of his efforts.

If you had a show or convention in need of a fully equipped stage, Elvis' stage was available to you. From 2009-2012 we hosted shows such as the Daytime Emmy Awards, magicians, concerts, conventions, television, MMA and boxing events, along with any other production willing to rent the venue. We stayed gainfully employed and had a fairly decent variety of shows to work on. Then 2012 would change everything on the property for the worse.

The $350 million mortgage Goldman Sacs was holding on the property was dragging on their balance sheets. They had been paying the $6 million annual licensing fee to Hilton Hotels just to keep the name on the building. They had maintained operations in the hotel and casino in order to maintain the value on their asset. The proverbial straw that broke the camel's back was when Hilton Hotels ordered Goldman Sachs to spend over $24 million in upgrades and improvements on the property or they would terminate their franchise agreement. Goldman Sachs made the decision to not invest any more money in a property they were trying to sell. The Las Vegas Hilton signs were removed from every part of the property. We would now be called the Las Vegas Hotel or LVH.

As I watched them take the big red 'HILTON' name off the giant gold marquis in front of the hotel, I felt as if someone punched me in the gut. I had always been proud to tell everyone who asked where I worked; I work on Elvis' stage at the Las Vegas Hilton. Now only half of that statement would be true. The consequences of removing Hilton from the property impacted the hotel immediately. There was no international Hilton reservation and rewards system in place.

The LVH was now a lone swimmer in a sea of corporate gaming giants. Occupancy dropped off drastically and revenues plummeted. The value of the property took a massive blow to its asking price. Goldman Sachs would never see their full $350 million owed them on the place. The ripples of cause and effect went through the entire property including the showroom. Rick White was now only allowed to book four-wall shows or shows that pay all costs within the showroom. There aren't many of those type shows in the entertainment industry, and I think they all tried their luck on Elvis' stage.

During the Goldman Sachs years we had two magic shows. The first illusionists were Larry and Rafael or LaRaf. Their show was called 'Triumph.' It was a steam punk dance-magic show. It was an unusual concept and had several really good parts throughout the show. The problem was the several good parts didn't compensate for other parts that needed much more help in order to have a hit show. The show vanished in about a month, and we loaded it out never to re-appear again. See what I did there?

The other magic show appearing nightly was Steve Wyrick: Ultra Magician. All I can say about his show is this: It was heavy and huge. I have never worked on any show as hard as I worked for Mr. Wyrick. In fact, I lost 15 pounds in the two months we had him on stage. He would disappear from many of his tricks only to re-appear in other places in the showroom. He also made things, very large things, appear in mere seconds. He opened his show appearing in a full size helicopter and at the end of his show he made a full size, 49' long Lear Jet appear in six seconds. It is truly a spectacular illusion. It was sad to see the show leave after just two months due to low ticket sales.

Here's some advice concerning magicians and their tricks. Never ask them how their tricks are done, they won't tell you. Ask the stage crew how the tricks are done. They won't tell you either.

There are stark differences between stagehands working on a musical concert or comedian and working on a magic show. For a concert or comedian, the stage crew loads in the show, sets it up, helps with any requirements from the production crew and then waits for the end of the show to re-set it or load it out. The musicians or comic are in full control of their show and need little if anything from the stage crew.

With magicians it is a completely different story. The stage crew never stops working to set the tricks and operate the illusions. The magician walks around the stage 'selling' the trick or his ability to bend nature and physics to his will. Magicians may have their names on the Marquis but the real stars of the show, if you ask me, are the stage crews hiding behind curtains and working their magic.

The other major residency act taking their shot at fame and fortune on Elvis' stage during the LVH years was Raiding the Rock Vault. This was a concept/presentation created by John Payne, the lead singer and bass player of Asia. The show had several top musicians from big rock groups featured singing the rock and roll hits of the 60's, 70's, 80's, and later. It was a great act to work on. It eventually left the LVH and went down the street to the Tropicana Hotel.

We didn't know it when it occurred but the time period of having the LVH logo on the side of the building and on the marquis would only last two years. There were financial decisions and deals being set up for the next chapter in the life of "the old grey lady" as Barron Hilton called the Las Vegas Hilton. I want to tell you about one very special event on Elvis' stage in August of 2012.

One of the greatest showmen of the 20th Century was Liberace. He performed regularly on Elvis' stage through the early 1970's into the early 1980's. It was only fitting that HBO made a movie about his life and filmed it on the LVH stage. The movie starred Michael Douglas as Liberace and Matt Damon as Scott Thorson.

The movie required us to return the showroom back to its 70's and 80's appearance. This meant we had to remove the theater style seats from the audience and store them in shipping containers outside. We also had to create different seating levels with platforms and level them. Next was the installation of carpet, booths, tables and chairs. The audience seating area now looked as it did when the real Liberace performed. By raising and leveling the audience seating areas, it reproduced the look needed for the audience shots; it also created other problems on stage.

The elevated audience seating areas meant the stage was only 18 inches above the audience floor. The solution was to raise the entire stage from back to front and side to side 20 inches. It took a lot of four feet wide by eight feet long by 20 inch high risers to raise our stage which is about 75 feet wide by nearly 80 feet deep. If you ever get bored, you can do the math on this problem.

It took an incredible amount of work to transform the showroom and stage back 30-40 years and then restore it to its 2012 look. I remember telling my boss Tony Tauber it was all worth the effort when we would see the smiles on the little kid's faces. I was only joking with him. This film is rated 'R' and should only be viewed by mature audiences. Whew, that was a close one.

In 2014 Goldman Sachs had had enough of being a casino hotel owner. They had watched the value of their $350 million asset dwindle and wanted it off their books. They put out the word the LVH was going on the auction block and the highest bidder, no matter the price, would be the winner. Several bids were put in by a few familiar faces one of them being the LVCC who saw an opportunity to buy the property at a bargain price. The LVCC offered $130 million but were defeated by David Siegel and his time share company called Westgate Resorts. David's winning bid was $150 million. I know I can speak for all 2,500 people working at this hotel: Thank You David Siegel for saving this legendary property and saving all of our jobs.

Nothing changed in the hotel's entertainment operations for about a year. The new ownership was focusing all of their attention on upgrading hotel rooms, the gift shop, retail space, the convention area, sports book, and the restaurants. When they did venture into the entertainment areas, they started with the Westgate Cabaret. This is a 300 seat showroom just 75 feet from the main showroom. They upgraded the lighting and sound systems and added a video wall structure to the stage. They then signed Suzanne Summers to perform in the room. It was a very positive move concerning the future of entertainment by the new ownership.

The second year of Westgate Resorts owning the property meant changes to every department including the licensed operators of the hotel and casino. Navegante Group, who had operated the hotel through the Goldman Sachs years, was out and Paragon Asset Management Group was in. My bosses, Tony Tauber and Rick White saw the writing on the wall. Tony took a job running the stages at the Tropicana Hotel. After helping the new entertainment company hired to book and manage all shows was up to speed on upcoming events, Rick departed and retired.

The new company's name was Red Mercury Entertainment or RME. I was not impressed by them from day one and to this day have nothing positive to say about their business. In fact, as I understand it, the reason Suzanne Summers left the Cabaret showroom was due to RME wanting her time slot for one of their acts. Suzanne was four walling the room and was very happy to pay all the costs associated with her show. She was the perfect headliner for the hotel. She loved performing and had very deep pockets to compensate for any shortfalls in ticket sales. Nevertheless, she was out and her classy show that was self financed left the property. Sometimes you just have to shake your head and say, "WOW!"

You may be asking yourself how we ended up with Paragon and Red Mercury at our hotel. I blame the LVCC. Both Paragon and RME were operating the Riviera Hotel for Sheraton Hotels when the LVCC came calling. The LVCC had lost the bid on the LVH but needed to expand and build another convention space somewhere. They offered Sheraton Hotels $180 million for the Riviera. It was an offer too good to refuse. When the Riviera closed its doors, Paragon and RME were hired to replace Navegante.

The LVCC demolished the Riviera Hotel and built their new 328,000 square feet addition on the land where the Landmark Hotel and Riviera once stood. Now everybody was happy. Well, not everyone.

As is customary when one management team is hired, they bring their underlings to replace the existing managers. Rick White was replaced by RME and Tony Tauber was replaced by John Peer, formerly John Hanson. John had been the Business Representative for Local 720 for several years before being voted out of office by the membership. He then decided to try his hand in entertainment management and was hired by RME and Paragon as the Entertainment and Technical Director at the Riviera and had moved to the Westgate with the rest of the Paragon family.

One of the first residency acts brought to the main showroom by RME was Dirk Arthur-Big Cat Magic. Dirk is a very talented magician and showman. His tricks are very well done. He has paced his show to keep the audience wowed and wanting more. He also has one thing other magicians don't have: big cats. He has several tigers, a liger (a cross breed between a male lion and a female tiger), a bobcat, leopard, and a few very nervous birds.

I thoroughly enjoyed working Dirk's magic tricks and loved being around the big cats. The audiences were very receptive to his show but in the end it closed because of low ticket sales. We loaded Dirk's show out the fall of 2015.

The next show RME brought into the showroom was called 'Twisted Vegas.' The star of the show was a popular entertainer from France. His show poked fun at many of the other shows in Las Vegas. There were contortionists, a slack wire walker, a dwarf, drag queens, and a slew of other unusual acts in the show. I liked the concept but it didn't translate very well to the audience.

You have to give credit where credit is due. The investors and RME did everything possible to make the act a hit. The show ran out of money in a couple of months and we loaded it out.

In the last few weeks of Twisted Vegas, management added a second show to the showroom. Purple Reign-The Prince Tribute Show had been playing in the Cabaret for many months. It had been decided by all parties involved to move them to the big room after Twisted Vegas. By mid-March Twisted Vegas was gone and the main showroom's sole occupier was Purple Reign.

Moving Purple Reign from the Cabaret into the Main showroom caused me to do something I hadn't done in a very long time. Jason Tenner, the star of Purple Reign was four walling the show. This meant he needed to keep control of his costs in order to make a profit for himself. To this end, I announced I would run the front of house (FOH) sound for his show. This caused some confusion on behalf of my crew. None of them knew I was a FOH engineer in my pre-Hilton life.

There had only been a few million changes to audio consoles since the last time I ran one 22 years earlier. Analog consoles had given way to the digital age. Almost all audio consoles were nothing more than computers with touch screens to control sound. For a moment I thought I had bitten off way more than I could chew. I knew audio and how to mix a show very well, but doing these things while learning the latest technology would prove to be more difficult than expected.

The first couple of shows were rough. The learning curve on new technology was steep. By the end of the first week I had found my groove and was learning enough about the console to get around in the programs fairly well. I was spending nights running sound for a show again and working during the day to fix blown speakers and replace old amplifiers. I had made the full circle and become a Head Sound operator again. It felt good.

On April 21, 2016 the entertainment world lost a legend. Prince had passed away form an accidental drug overdose. The tragedy made Purple Reign the most popular show in Las Vegas to see. The audience numbers went from 200-300 per show up to 800 or more each show. Jason was making money on an extra 500 tickets being sold a night. It was good for him and everyone in the hotel. This boom in business was crushed within three weeks.

Contract talks between Local 720 and the Westgate had been going on for a while with no agreement in sight. The lead negotiator for Westgate's corporate office must have thought he could force a bad contract on us. Sighting a slowdown in business he decided to close the showroom in mid-May for the summer. It was an obvious ploy to punish Mark Broedling the Head Electrician and myself for rejecting their poor proposals. Being a vocal critic about some things will sometimes put a target on you by some short sighted people.

The only person this foolish action hurt was Jason Tenner. He had been making extra money and wanted to expand his show's production content. He now had to put that on hold as he returned to the Cabaret. All other stagehands on the property kept working with no disruption in business. There were only two full time stagehands affected by this decision.

I kept working in other parts of the hotel three days a week and picked up a lot of calls at other hotels. Mark did the same. At the end of summer two things happened; Phil (the first name of the Westgate negotiator) had been fired for violating some labor laws during negotiations. The second thing was Mark and I were back in the main showroom full time. Purple Reign was once again moved back into the big room with us.

I felt bad for Jason. The summer had passed by and the large crowds wanting to see Prince again had passed with it. This is what happens when people make emotional decisions instead of business ones. Vengeance is never a good negotiating tactic. Purple Reign would play on our stage until October 2017. They would take up residency at the Tropicana Hotel as one of RME's acts.

It would not take but a few months to find a really good show to replace Purple Reign.

In January 2018 a new act with a couple of Las Vegas entertainment veterans arrived on Elvis' stage. Clint Holmes and Earl Turner created a show called Sound Track. I really loved this production. It had everything a top rated performance should have. There was great music and songs mixed with stories from their lives. The band was phenomenal and the staging was superb. It has always been a mystery to me how some mediocre shows seem to survive, yet other quality shows don't survive the test of time. As much as I hated to do it, we loaded out Sound Track after two months of shows. We were clearing the stage for a new-former entertainer to return.

There are always rumors swirling around every hotel in Las Vegas. The rumor making its rounds here at the Westgate concerned a new headliner act. I had some suspicions and hopes of who it could be. A couple years earlier I had seen Barry Manilow's manager Garry Kief and Ken Ciancimino, the Executive Vice President during the Colony Capital years walking around the casino and in the showroom. I point blankly asked them when Barry was going to return. Their answer of: 'Anything is possible' told me everything I wanted to know. It was just a matter of time.

In January or February of 2018, (while Sound Track was still performing nightly), it was announced that hotel management and Barry Manilow were in negotiation to bring his show back to Elvis' stage. When Barry and his posse arrived for a sight survey to plan their show, it was like a family reunion on stage. It was great to see everyone again. Barry had told me many times during his 2004-2009 show run that he loved performing on our stage. Now here he was again almost ten years later.

My main job for this visit was to walk the stage with Barry and remind him of what we did ten years earlier. As he recalled the details and where the scenic elements were placed he looked at me and said,' I better figure out what kind of show we are going to do.' That is when I knew the deal was already done. I was thrilled we would be doing his act again.

With the deal signed and opening night scheduled for the end of April or early May 2018, (it actually opened in mid May), my question to my bosses was, when can we start load in? When I was told load in wouldn't be able to begin until late March or early April, I wondered how to pull this off. The scenery, rigging, video, and other companies would have to work around the clock to even meet the early April load in deadline. I looked into my crystal ball and saw a two to three week load in, one week tech rehearsal, and Barry's three week show rehearsal being crammed into four weeks. I thought, well, this should be interesting.

In the previous show, Barry had a lot of physical scenery all over the stage. This time we would replace all the physical scenery with massive video walls positioned everywhere. The largest of the video walls was positioned upstage or at the back of the stage. It measured 60 feet wide by 30 feet tall and weighed over 6,000 pounds. It had to run up and down smoothly at a variety of speeds to blend in with the music being played. He could now sing his songs and the video walls would transport him to any location on earth or space he wanted to go.

For Barry's Copacabana number, we would be flying a horseshoe shaped bridge over the audience so he could dance right over their heads. This scenic element would require 14 half ton winches to operate. Between the video wall and flying bridge, the automation operator had 20 winches to program, maintain, and operate. He would also control the piano cart as it drives on and off stage several times during the show. When the automation system works perfectly, it adds a whole new dimension to the presentation.

The two week deadline for load in and technical rehearsals meant I had to make daily creative schedules. Everyone needs time to run their equipment and fix all flaws. My job was to find everyone their needed time and still maintain the load in work schedule. If you could purchase time, it would have been the most valuable commodity during those two weeks of load in. Our load in and tech rehearsal time went by in the blink of an eye. We didn't even have hours to spare before the show rehearsals with Barry began.

Needless to say, Barry opened to sell out crowds and delighted fans. He would perform three shows a week, two weeks a month for the remainder of the year. When Barry was away, we stayed busy with other headliner shows, beauty pageants, corporate shows, and football on Sundays. The International Showroom never slept.

In 2020 the economy was roaring and Las Vegas was forecast to have one of its biggest and most profitable years in its history. Ticket sales for all of the venue's shows were strong. Barry's January performances were sell outs and his February presentations were also closing in on sell out status. Yes 2020 looked like it would be a stellar year until the bottom fell out.

On March 15, 2020 the Governor of Nevada, Steve Sisolak decided he had the authority to shut every casino, convention center, and any other business he deemed non-essential over a cold virus. Nevada went from an unemployment rate of 4% to 30% overnight. His unilateral decision to force over 200,000 people out of work and close businesses was to be for only two weeks to "flatten the curve." I write this story 14 months later and I am still unemployed along with most of my stagehand brothers and sisters. We have been told Barry will be back in September 2021. That will make our two week layoff a total of 18 months.

It is unfortunate that when some people have a little authority they begin to exercise unrighteous dominion over others. The truly sad part of all this is Governor Sisolak doesn't seem to be bothered by his destruction of so many fellow Nevadans and their lives. I hope this is a lesson learned.

Here we are in May 2021 and there is life slowly being breathed into Las Vegas and the entertainment industry. Fourteen months after the two week shut down we are witnessing some showrooms opening. Here at the Westgate Resort, the Cabaret has opened for three nights of shows a week. It is a good start. We have been informed that Barry will return in mid September to perform. Now it's a waiting game and looking for any work as our industry awakens. Like so many other fellow stagehands, we are all waiting for the next chapter in our lives to begin.

CHAPTER SEVEN: ALMOST DONE. WHAT'S NEXT?

Well, here I sit in May of 2021 along with most of my fellow stagehands waiting for the all clear to go back to work. For this chapter I was going to look into my crystal ball and give my predictions for what the Las Vegas Entertainment Industry would look like in the future. Even with smaller showrooms opening up to limits in seating with social distancing requirements, the main showrooms will lag behind them and open to full capacity in September. I have heard Caesars Entertainment is already closing some long running entertainment venues and canceling shows that have done good business for many years.

I had suspected some of these properties would take advantage of the year long shutdown and trim their bottom lines. It just never ceases to amaze me how some Las Vegas Gaming Corporations feel the need to take 'Entertainment' out of the "Entertainment Capitol of the World." In six months when revenues show a decline, these CEO's will look for more ways to cut costs. Perhaps the best way to do so is to find smarter CEO's. Just saying.

Here at my home away from home, the Westgate Resorts Las Vegas, we have opened the Cabaret and have shows playing Friday, Saturday, and Sunday. Barry Manilow will return mid-September. This means we will have been out of work for 18 months. We very well may have been able to go back and be stagehands in June, July, or August but it is hard to turn on and off a show like Barry's at the drop of a hat or on the whim of a Governor. Big shows have big expenses and it is better to wait a couple extra months in order not to anger your fans and the property's guests.

As for the entertainment in Las Vegas, I see a rocky time ahead for many of the showrooms and properties. It will take some time; I believe about a year to shake off the cobwebs and get this industry back up to full steam. The hotels that take chances and aggressively pursue a strong entertainment policy will prosper and those who are afraid to take a chance will always lag far behind the others. It's always interesting to see which hotels have leaders and visionaries and which ones just follow and mimic the successful properties.

What do I see for my future, you ask? Well here I am on the precipice of being able to retire in three years. I will be 62 then and every year after that will be taken one year at a time. I have already worked out of Local 720 for over 40 years to this point. If this last year has taught me anything, it is this: I really enjoy and miss working in Showbiz. I saw a bumper sticker that said, "You can take my gun when you pry it from my cold dead hand." It is very possible I will leave Showbiz when you pry my cold dead body off the International Showroom Stage.

There are a few projects I will be working on over the next couple years. There are still a few books on other topics I would like to write. There is also an unfinished album titled Talbot Snow: Prime Time Chameleons we started in 1993 and I think it is time to get it done. The album will star Talbot Snow just like Contrary To Popular Belief did and feature a different group of four artists. I will write and perform one or two of the songs on the album along with three other undetermined artists. It should be released in 2023. This may very well be our last album together. One album every 30 years is a grueling pace.

I am also mulling over producing my own podcast. I would like to do it with a variety of guests and on a plethora of topics. Entertainment will be featured heavily in it. The arts, science, science fiction, politics, religion, and any other hot topic of the day will be discussed at length and with civility. I want to do it right and if/when I decide to do it; I will make it the very best podcast possible. Who knows, I may even join forces with Talbot Snow on this project. Who knows?

Here are a few current photos of my longtime business partner and friend Talbot Snow and I. Photos from June 2021.

THE HSP HIT FACTORY 2021, FEATURING TALBOT SNOW AND CRAIG HAYES.

CHAPTER EIGHT: STORIES FROM FRIENDS

This book is not just about my family and me. I have worked with hundreds and maybe even thousands of performers and technicians over my career. To not give some of them a voice within these pages would be selfish and a huge oversight on my part. So, without further delay, I present to you my friends and their stories.

RON STONE

Hello everyone, my name is Ron Stone and it's a great honor to be included in Craig's latest book. Growing up in rural Washington, I was the little boy who sat on the fence at the end of the runway and said, "Someday, I'm going to be a pilot!" Ultimately I achieved my goal to fly. I became licensed to fly commercial aircraft and became a flight instructor on single and multi-engine aircraft. Flying is one love, entertainment is another. I have been very blessed in my life to have had two amazing careers that I thoroughly enjoyed. I had a combined 32 years in the U.S. Army and U.S. Army National Guard, and the U.S. Air Force Reserves where I served as flight engineer on a C-130 Hercules. I had

50 amazing years in entertainment, with my dual careers overlapping for many years. I retired from the U.S. Army in 2009 as a Chief Warrant Officer.

I was always blessed to be in the right place at the right time. I feel very fortunate that I was part of Las Vegas in its heyday. It was an exciting time in the history of the Las Vegas Strip. People got dressed up in elegant clothes to attend shows in those days, as it was still the era of the Rat Pack. It was what people now call the **'old** Las Vegas'. I met and worked with many famous stars that some kids today probably have never heard of, such as Ann-Margret, Jim Nabors (who once came to dinner at my Reno home!), Wayne Newton, Liberace, and Frank Sinatra, just to name a few.

I retired from show business in December 2019 having worked mostly in Las Vegas. I was also privileged to travel and work on shows in New York City, Atlantic City, and Branson. I came to Las Vegas from Seattle, in 1970. I was 23-years-old and had recently returned after serving in Vietnam, where I was a Huey helicopter crew chief/gunner, for the U.S. Army. When I arrived in Las Vegas I had a 'Spanish red metallic' '57 Chevy and twenty-five dollars in my pocket and I took the first job I found, as a cook at the Silver Slipper.

As a teenager, I knew I wanted more than anything to work in entertainment after I saw 'Kiss Me Kate' at the Seattle Metropolitan Opera House. I wanted to be one of the crew who made the magic happen. After two years at the Silver Slipper I got my first stagehand job as spotlight operator in the lounge at the International, later known as the Las Vegas

Hilton, now known as the Westgate. Soon I worked spotlight in the main showroom where Johnny Cash was performing at the time.

In the middle of my first decade in Las Vegas I met and married the beautiful and talented Sheila Sparr, who was then lead singer at the Stardust in the Lido. We were married 30 years when, quite suddenly in October 2006, God called on Sheila to join Heaven's choir. Sheila and I had recently returned to Las Vegas after 12 years in Reno at MGM, where she sang in Hello Hollywood Hello, and I was the Technical Director at Sahara Reno. Several years later I was a stagehand at MGM with Hello Hollywood Hello, and I was still flying with the Guard. After HHH ran its course in Reno, we returned to Las Vegas and Sheila retired from entertainment.

I took a position as Technical Director at Bally's, and after seven years I was invited by my boss and dear friend Joel Fischman to work at the Luxor as Technical Director. I was later promoted to Director of Property Operations at the Luxor. In 2005 while still serving in the Guard I was called back for full-time active duty in the U.S. Army. Leaving my position with the Luxor I spent the next five years flying many Counter Drug Task Force missions with some of the finest soldiers in this country. During my final years of military service I met the lovely lady who would later become my wife.

After Sheila passed away I didn't think I'd marry again, but God had other plans. My sweetheart Becki is my very best friend, and she has stood by my side through everything life has thrown at me since we met. She's my treasure and has brought much joy to my life.

I met the talented and amazing Craig Hayes while working at the former Hilton, now the Westgate. He has been a long time friend, and is one of the best stage managers you'll ever encounter. He is truly a leader in the entertainment industry. Craig always had a knack for making the crew feel important, and valued as individuals. We worked together for many years and with Craig the atmosphere was always easy going, with no chaos. One of the nicest compliments I ever received from Craig was during my time as lead spotlight operator in the showroom, with four other spotlights working Barry Manilow's, 'The Hit's Come Home'. One evening right before the show began, Craig told me as long as I was up in the light booth, he wasn't worried. I was glad to do my job so well that I had Craig's total confidence.

He may have limited eyesight but believe me, he sees everything, and he mysteriously always knows where everyone is, and everything going on! I didn't know Craig was a published author until he shared three of his books with me. If you haven't read it yet, please read his last book, 'After Our Fall'! It's eye opening! Craig is a man of many talents, and endless energy, patience, and kindness!

Wow, I have so many memorable experiences. One that I like to tell friends is about the time I was working with Wayne Newton. One evening I was running spotlight on Wayne's show and we had a full house. At one point I had to reach back with my left hand to adjust the carbons, with the 'nero knob'. (As a fun fact, the carbons inside the spotlight are locked in jaws that are positive and negative powered, and while running would give the appearance much like welding, creating very bright light. The carbons are made of carbon and lime, hence the theatrical/stage term, 'in the limelight'!)

During the show I was sitting at the spotlight in an ordinary office chair, the type with wheels. As I was leaning far back to make the carbon adjustment, right in the middle of Wayne singing 'Rhinestone Cowboy', the entire back of my chair broke clean off, leaving me flailing around like a bronco buster. The spotlight tipped up, and the beam flew up to the ceiling, well away from its subject. Wayne stopped singing, wondering like the entire audience, what had happened. He looked up and saw my feet and arms in the air, grabbing for a hold. After learning from the stage crew on headset what had happened, he could not stop laughing. I was so embarrassed! Forever after, every time Wayne sang 'Rhinestone Cowboy,' he'd look up towards my spotlight and enunciate, 'like a Ron Stone cowboy'!

Another time, I was working on a show with Bobbie Gentry. Part of the scenery for her show included a river scene with a full moon that was to rise slowly over the river at a particular point in her song. I was running the light console that evening, so I had free time to go get a cup of coffee from the pot in our light booth. As I was walking back to the light console I looked at the stage and saw the river drop slowly flying out, and the moon still standing in front of the orchestra. Bobbie was singing a fairly long song, and as the music for it was a taped recording, the musicians were able to get up and move around for a quick break.

Being in constant communication with the backstage by headset, I informed the flyman that he was pulling the wrong line. For anyone who may not know, these are the ropes that move the scenery up and down, and he had grabbed the wrong rope! When he realized what he had done, the river scene came quickly back onto the stage floor in a split second! Then the moon went full up in half that time. As all this was going on there was poor Bobbie Gentry still singing her heart out, the only person in the showroom who couldn't figure out why the entire audience was laughing uncontrollably.

So many good times, and great memories! I know every stagehand has thousands of stories, and it has been an honor to share mine with all of you, and an even greater honor to have my memories featured in Craig's wonderful book, 'Showtime'! Thank you Craig, for being a friend! As Bob Hope always said, "Thanks for the Memories!" God bless you Craig.

TONY TAUBER

My career in Entertainment began on the bright end of the follow spot. I had just graduated high school and finished two boring years of business school when the Ice Capades came to Hershey PA. They were desperate for chorus boys and with my limited ability as a rink rat at a local ice arena I was hired and skated for four years. They must have noticed that my creative interest and ability in lighting far exceeded my skating talent. I apprenticed and later I became Ice Capades Lighting Director for the national touring show for 11 years. With the dawn of gaming and entertainment in Atlantic City the opportunity arose as Lighting Director at the Playboy Hotel and Casino. After 8 years I moved up the boardwalk to Caesars Hotel and Casino serving fifteen years as Head of Lighting in the Circus Maximus Theater. Like the game of Monopoly I moved around the board to Resorts International Casino for two years before moving to Las Vegas.

I accepted a position with the Las Vegas Hilton as the Entertainment Technical Director. After ten years and prior to retiring in 2017 I was Director of Entertainment Technical Operations at the Tropicana Casino.

Craig Hayes, Head Carpenter in the Las Vegas Hilton Theater was my 'Go To' person for ten years. When I met Craig no one had to tell me how experienced and competent he was in his position. This position is not only a job it is his passion. Show operations, installations and turnarounds are all huge tasks that he makes look easy. His professional handling of last minute, sometimes bizarre requests from headline entertainers, producers and corporate clients was a natural skill for him. During our ten year run in the showroom it was my pleasure to have him on my team and I consider him a close friend. After formulating a schedule or working on a budget we would jokingly say; "We've got this, what's the worst that could happen?" Sometimes we found out.

Odd Senior Moments in the Casino Entertainment World

In Caesar's Palace Circus Maximus Theater in Atlantic City, Myron Cohen, a famous comedian during the 1970's and 80's, now in his 80's, was booked for a three day engagement.

On his opening night he walked confidently on the stage like he had done for half a century. The stage was brightly lit with dozens of wash lights and two hard-edge spotlights. The audience who was anticipating an evening of his famous one liners began applauding. After delivering fast-pace jokes one after an other, for approximately 15 minutes, he stopped. He then proceeded to walk off stage. The bewildered spot operators followed him off stage and then went out.

The stage was now lit and empty. Chatter started over the headset. The audience was surprised and started murmuring among themselves. "Is he sick?" "Is this it?" "Is he coming back out?" was the conversation that drifted up to the lighting booth. A stunned stage tech followed Mr. Cohen back to his dressing room to find out what happened. Cohen was sitting on the couch with his jacket draped over the back of a chair and a beverage in his hand. He took a drink from the glass and asked the tech who was standing in the doorway "How did I do?" The tech replied, "You were great. But, you only were on stage for 15 minutes." Without so much as a second look or word to the tech, he stood up, slipped his jacket on and started back to the stage. "He's coming back on stage." The tech shouted over the headset. "Everybody stand by." As he hit the stage the spot operators picked him up, and followed him to center stage. He finished another 45 minutes of jokes and one-liners that the audience loved and they never realized that this was a senior moment.

Wait For the GO

When the band, Chicago came to Caesars Circus Maximus Theater in Atlantic City, Ian Peacock, their lighting director had a design request for six follow spots from the front of house position. His cue structure introduced each member of the band and highlighted musical changes and solos, which created a complex cue track for follow spots. He was confident playing our house, since we requested the same six experienced spotlight operators for each of their engagements. All six spotlights were required to be set with a soft edge focus. During this engagement only five of the six requested operators were available. The sixth operator who was dispatched was not known to me or anyone on the crew.

My assistant and I loaded the color frames in the spots and set all the spot edges to a soft focus. As we were leaving the booth, we met the new spot operator. For this story we will call him, Larry. "You're on spot one," I said. "This is a good time to familiarize yourself with the light before the house opens." When we returned from break, Larry said, "Don't worry, I got all the spotlights fixed." I perceived this as Larry's sense of humor. Ian arrives at the booth with his Scottish humor, and a bag of jelly beans that he always consumed during the show. He gave the operators their assignments. Spot 1, which was Larry, was to pick up the first band member, the founding member of Chicago, James Pankow. Spot 2 was to pick up Lee Loughnane as he entered the stage. This sequence continued until all six band members were on stage.

The house lights go out. The stage is dark. The announcer's voice booms over the speakers, "Ladies and Gentlemen, Please welcome, Chicago!" The sold-out house goes crazy. The announcer begins the band introduction, "James Pankow!" The fans jump to their feet. Ian says, "Spot 1, GO."

James Pankow carrying his trombone enters a black stage. Ian again says, "Spot 1, GO!" The spot is still out. Spot 2, since he knows the show, picks up Pankow to cover for Spot 1. The announcer continues to introduce each member as they enter the stage. "Lee Loughnane!" Ian realizing the cueing is out of sequence, he asks Spot 3 to pick up Lee for Spot 2. "Walter Parazaider" was announced. Ian says, "Spot 4 pick up Walter." "Keith Howland!" "Spot 5 pick up Keith" came over the head set. "Lou Pardini!" "Spot 6 pick up Lou." "Tris Imboden!" Ian asks, "Spot 1, can you pick up the drummer?" No response from Larry on Spot 1. The drummer has no spotlight.

I ran over to Larry, who tells me the spot is not working. Pointing the light on the booth floor I demonstrated that light would never come out because he was opening the douser and closing the chopper at the same time. When that failed, he would close the douser and open the chopper. I showed him how to only open the douser and to use the iris to adjust the size. Ian's instructions for the third song were that all spots would be on their home positions in no color. Larry is now on James. "All spots, stand by to go to color frame #3," Ian cued. Larry in his panic immediately snaps in frame #3. "I didn't say GO. Wait for the GO!!!" Larry yanks out the color and is in open white. Ian, now standing and visibly upset shouts "you already had the color in why did you take it out?" Larry slams the color back in. Ian has lost his Scottish sense of humor and has not consumed one jelly bean.

The song ends, and all spots black out. The next cue is for Spot 1 to pick up James in full body no color. Ian gives the

GO cue and again nothing happens. Spot 2 covers again. Larry opened his light with a tiny pin spot on the side wall of the theater because he lost his position. I watched the pin spot sliding down the wall and across the front of the stage. When it reached James feet, Larry popped open the iris to full body. Now, totally frustrated with Larry, Ian gave a slow and deliberate warning cue "All…spots…STANDBY… for a black out." Without waiting for a GO, Larry blacked out. Ian yelled, "wait for the GO CUE!" Larry snapped the light back on. "Don't go back on you were already out." Larry blacked out again! That was Larry's final cue of the show. I asked for Larry's headset, took over his light and told him to punch out.

When song four of the set began, Ian asked "Tony, why are all the lights Hard Edge?" It wasn't Larry's sense of humor when he said "I fixed all the lights" he actually changed all six lights to a hard edge!

When Chicago returned, Ian couldn't wait to tell me that whenever a spot operator messes up, he'd say "Nice Job Larry!"

BRADLEY SNOW

Hello. My name is Bradley Snow. I am a Native of New Zealand When I was around 12 years old I moved to Las Vegas in 1980 with my family. My brother Talbot had been a DJ in New Zealand before we came to America and he wanted to continue doing so here. I helped him move his audio gear from function to function during those early years. These were my earliest experiences being in Showbiz.

In my teen years I took classes in technical theater at Valley High School. This helped prepare me for what was coming in just a few short years. By 1985 I was out of high school and looking for work. This is when Craig Hayes stepped up and hired me as a relief stage tech to run lights and sound at the Mint Hotel. This was my true start working as a stagehand. Eventually I worked out of Local 720 as a carpenter, electrician, audio tech, rigger, and camera operator. I worked out of Local 720 until 2009 when I returned to New Zealand. I now live a life working various jobs and living at the beach or going fishing.

I first met Craig Hayes shortly after arriving in Las Vegas. My brother Talbot and Craig bumped into each other a few times before learning about each other's interest in everything audio. They soon became friends and business partners and I was always around and included in their exploits. As stated before, in 1985 Craig hired me fresh out of high school as one of his relief techs at the Mint Hotel. It was an awesome job.

When Craig was hired as the Head Carpenter at the Las Vegas Hilton, he brought me onto his show crew during the Starlight Express years. I would eventually work in several positions from 1995 until 2009. My years at the Las Vegas Hilton were some of the best years in my career and life. I still stay in close contact with Craig and have always enjoyed working with him.

One of my most memorable stories was while working the Tim Conway and Harvey Korman Show. They were doing their 'Boring' skit that was all about Harvey speaking at a corn grower's convention. During the skit Tim gets bored and starts looking for something to keep him awake. Tim pulls out a cigar and is supposed to light it and blow smoke on everyone at the table. On this night, Tim's Zippo didn't work so he couldn't light the cigar. I was watching from the side of the stage and saw what was happening. I showed Tim my Zippo and he motioned for me to throw it to him. I did as requested and hence the meaning of the term; "The show must go on."

The second story I have is one out of Ripley's Believe It Or Not. Magicians Penn and Teller filmed their Las Vegas Show Sin City Spectacular for the FX Network on the Las Vegas Hilton's stage. For one of their illusions they needed over twenty blow-up sex dolls. So here I was backstage by the large roll up door, which was open, with Walter Winn blowing the dolls up and placing black tape over their private parts. Soon we had a large stack of blow-up dolls and every hotel employee who walked by just laughed and shook their heads. I am sure they were thinking there was some seriously kinky stuff going on in the showroom.

These are my stories and I just wanted to thank Craig for making me a part of this book.

CHUCK ROUNDS

My name is Chuck Rounds. I've been involved, in many different capacities, in the entertainment world for over 40 years...starting out performing as a street mime in my late teens. I worked as an actor, as a stuntman, and as a crew member. I decided to go back to school and get my graduate degrees and became a professor of Theatre. I did that for nine years before deciding to go back into the professional world. I became the editor of the entertainment trade paper in Las Vegas, *Callback News*...also known as *Dirt Alert,* and I also reviewed all of the shows in Vegas (http://www.igoshows.com). I now produce and direct productions across the country, and I've been doing that for the past 16 years.

I like staying busy, so whenever I had some free time in my schedule, I would pick up a little extra work through the stagehands union. It was on one of these calls that I met Craig Hayes. It was in the late 1990's, and he was in need of an extra spotlight operator. It was apparent that he liked my work because he kept calling me back, and for the next 5 years, I became a regular fixture at that property. Then I got busy producing productions and events for the next 15 years, and it was after that when I happened to be reviewing a show at the Westgate, and I once again ran into Craig. "Are you still interested in running a spotlight?" He asked me. I was interested, and once again, quickly became a steady regular at the property.

There are many tidbits and stories about Las Vegas entertainment that are fun to share:

As caustic as Don Rickles was on stage, he was kind, respectful, and gentle off stage. Don Rickles' wife would sit in the dressing room during his show and make friends with all of the dancers and showgirls.

Before going on stage, Vic Damone would be on a backstage phone with his then wife, Diane Carroll, and they would sing love songs to each other.

The managers of the Four Tops and the Temptations made it a point to go around and meet every stagehand, thank them for their work, and give them an envelope with a generous tip.

Johnny Carson had the best comic timing of anyone in history.

Magicians have both the biggest and most fragile egos of any performer; primarily because most stage magicians don't actually have any talent. The illusions are performed by the stagehands and assistants, and the magician takes all the credit as the front man…and magicians usually have no idea what to do if something goes wrong because they aren't the ones operating the illusion.

Showgirls will not help or assist other performers, if you fall down, they will step over you. As opposed to a dancer who will pick up a fallen comrade. Showgirls and dancers were subjected to weekly weigh-ins (if they gained weight, they would be put on notice…three weight notices in a row, and you would be fired.) They also had to pass the "pencil" test. A pencil would be placed under their boobs, and if it stayed there, their breasts were considered too saggy.

As the editor of the local entertainment trade paper, my staff and I would get to know most every performer in town. As a show critique, I would generally see a couple of shows a week and was always treated like a VIP. It was wonderful…for the most part. Yes, I got to see all of the greatest shows that the city had to offer, but…I also suffered through all of the miserable shows that rotated in and out of the smaller theatres.

On one occasion, my date and I were going to go see Tom Jones. We were given the front row, center table next to the stage. We were sent cocktails, and we sat back to enjoy a true master of the stage. Now I had heard about the tradition of women throwing their panties onto the stage at Tom Jones performances, but had never experienced it. Well, it was true. As soon as the lights went down, panties were being flung toward the stage…sadly, though, so many of the women throwing these objects just didn't have the arm to support their objective. Those panties that fell short of the stage fell directly on me and my date. The first one landed directly into her cocktail…and then on her head. I did my best to quickly and inconspicuously remove these items…I hoped that they were clean. Women saved their panties for their favorite song, creating a steady stream of incoming underwear throughout the night. There was no fighting it…it became a joke. We started to judge the quality of each piece, we tossed some back to have the thrower try again, but we both got headaches by the end of the night because so many of the panties had been doused with a variety of heavy perfumes. Of course in between the barrage of the panty brigade, Tom Jones was wonderful.

Another memorable evening came when my (same) date and I went to see "Jubilee"…one of the largest showgirl extravaganzas. Again, we were treated well, and again, we were given seats next to the stage, this time on the house left side. Now to understand this story, you have to understand that performers get very excited to see someone they know in the audience, and I was friends with most of these performers. They noticed me at the end of the first big number when the line of showgirls was exiting stage right. "Chuck," the first one proclaimed. "Hi, Chuck! Hey," as she looked down the line of women, "Chuck's here!" One after another greeted me, blew kisses, shook their breasts, and waved. I was truly enjoying the spectacle...until I looked at my date. She was not sharing the same joy and exuberance. To be fair, it had to be daunting to have thirty of the most beautiful women in the world, wearing only a g-string and a smile, flirting with your date from the stage. She wasn't looking at the women...only at me with a dark and deepening disdain. I really tried to not enjoy it so much, but that was a lost cause.

Life in and around the stages of Las Vegas has been exceedingly fulfilling. I often have to pause and reflect upon how lucky I've been. It's been a great way to earn a living, and it sure beats sitting at a desk in an office for forty hours a week.

KELLEY WASHAM

Hi there. My name is Kelley Washam and this is my contribution to Craig's book. Just to set the table correctly, let me tell you I am a theater geek. I am originally from Denver, Colorado where I lived until the age of 14. My next stop on where I would live was in Missouri. While in high school and college, I stage managed every play I could to gain experience on stage. I attended Missouri State University graduating Cum Lade with a Bachelors of Fine Arts degree in theater with an emphasis in stage management. While going to college, I worked full time in a country music club and built sets for the university's theater program. I also helped open the new performing arts center on campus.

After graduation I traveled to Branson, Missouri and took a job as Head of Wardrobe at the Shoji Tabuchi Theater. I would spend the next two years in that position. Shoji Tabuchi is an exquisite violin player and his shows are filled with singers, dancers, a large orchestra, and beautiful costumes. He would often travel to Las Vegas and watch many of the shows playing at the hotels and incorporate some of their production ideas into his show.

It was while working in Branson that I met my husband Johnny. We would move to Las Vegas in 1996 and I was offered a position in wardrobe at the MGM Grand Hotel working on the FX show. It is fair to say I was making a living working in wardrobe but it wasn't what I wanted to do for the rest of my career. I desired a job in theater management and worked to find a career in my new hometown.

When the Orleans Hotel opened I took a job as Stage Supervisor/Manager on the Rex Allen Jr's show titled 'Gone Country.' The show lasted for six months and then we went to having headliner entertainers from that point forward. A couple of my favorite stars were the Smothers Brothers, Lou Rawls, and the Righteous Brothers.

In 2000 I went to the Rio Hotel in their audio visual department as an Administrator and Coordinator for PRG Show Pay. In 2001 Magicians Penn and Teller opened their show in the theater. They would share the room with shows such as Louie Anderson, Jeff Foxworthy, David Spade, Peter

Frampton, and David Cassidy. We also had a late night topless revue called 'Showgirls' performing nightly. During the day time Bob Barker took over the stage with 'The Price is Right'. It was a very busy showroom. Not to be left out by 'Showgirls', 'Chippendale's' male revue was brought in for the ladies. For horse lovers, we even had the 'Cavali Horse Show' for a time.

The Rio never stopped looking for ways to bring customers through their doors. They had a Mardi Gras Carnival every day in the hotel. The difference with the Rio's and other cities was our carnival floated above everyone's heads in the hotel. It was amazing. My final show to open was Prince. He brought his show to our nightclub for an extended residency.

In 2006 Johnny and I moved back to Missouri. I returned to working as a real estate agent and Johnny went on the road from time to time as an electrician on corporate conventions and shows. Ten years later we returned to Las Vegas and I joined the Westgate Resorts Team as an entertainment manager. Johnny worked out of the Stagehand's local and did his corporate shows until March 2020. We were both deemed non-essential as the Governor shut down the State due to COVID 19. I have once again turned to my real estate license to help us make ends meet.

I first met the notorious Craig in 2018 after I was hired by Westgate as an Entertainment Manager. My original read on Craig was that he was skeptical of me and thought I wouldn't last long. If you take COVID 19 as it is, then he was right.

On one occasion Craig took my husband and son on a tour all over the showroom. They went into places very few people outside our industry even know exist. To this day, my son still talks about his amazing tour backstage.

Craig is a rock. You know that everything is going to be ok when Craig is there. He is the dad you always wanted combined with that voice of reason that is so crucial when things go sideways. On the several occasions I have walked in the back door to the showroom with Barry he has said 'when he comes in the room and sees Craig on stage he knows everything will work well for the show.' This is high praise and deservedly so.

I was asked to tell as few stories about Showbiz. My stories are short but give a little insight into theater life.

When we were filming 'The Price is Right' (TPIR) at the Rio Hotel there was a 20 feet by 20 feet elevator in the middle of the stage. It was used to bring up set pieces for our various shows. For TPIR they decided to use it for their car reveals. Rehearsals went perfectly but once the audience was loaded in and showtime started the elevator broke down. It took a Herculean effort on everyone's part including the hotel engineers to make it work again. We never used the elevator again.

I was stage managing a show that had a female magician as the star. Her assistants were all little people. (In the past they were known as midgets or dwarfs.) On one fateful day the gaggle of geese in the show got loose and were running and flying around the stage and showroom. The little people and stage crew were running around trying to catch them and put them back in their cages. To say the least it was one of the most bizarre sights ever seen. Luckily it was just a rehearsal.

Lou Rawls is one of the nicest and most talented singers of our time. One night while I was stage managing his show I was talking on our Clear Com intercom system telling everyone how much I loved Lou's show and him as a person. The next thing I heard was Lou talking back to me on the Clear Com teasing me. The base station at my desk had malfunctioned and sent our conversations to the dressing rooms by mistake. Thank Heaven I didn't say anything improper at that time. My lesson was to be leery of where the Clear Com is going and who is listening.

I can't imagine doing anything other than Showbiz. I love the entertainment industry, the people in it, and the comradery with those people. Making a show happen, even in the worst of circumstances, gets your juices going. Our payoff is seeing the smiles on everyone as they leave our showroom. There truly is no business like show business.

BEAU DOYLE

Hello everybody. My name is Beau Doyle and entertainment has been in my blood for quite a long time. I am a third generation drummer/percussionist/entertainer. I have also been a professional mascot, dancer, cheerleader/MC, stagehand/stage tech, and personal body/security guard. I've been very blessed to have had the opportunity to perform all over the world in one or more of these roles.

These experiences are some of the greatest days of my life.

As a kid, I helped set up stages for my dad; Jerry Doyle, who is also a drummer and a stagehand. I learned about back line or band gear and how to set it up and stage it. At nine years old I was baptized as a stage drummer. Concerning this experience, let's just say I was hooked. Throughout my career as a musician, I've had the incredible opportunity of playing with garage bands to Grammy award winning and platinum album holding musicians. Some of those bands and musicians are Barry Manilow's band, Tom Jones, Celine Dion, Buddy Rich Big Band, Living Colour, Quiet Riot, Ratt, Julio Iglesias, Gloria Estefan, and the list goes on and on. I have played in small clubs and large main stages all over the country and world. Las Vegas has always been my main stay of my greatest gigs. I've had a great career. When I wasn't on stage or doing security, I was backstage as a stage tech.

It was while working as a stage tech I met Craig Hayes. I'm not sure how long ago that was; but it was most likely in the late 90's or the early 2000's. It's all kind of a blur. What I do remember is Craig and my father working together since the late 90's. Then I started coming into the old Las Vegas Hilton Theater as a rigger where Craig was; and still is; the Head Carpenter. Again, it's all a bit of a blur, but we've had some great times together in that legendary theater. We worked on many shows together from Starlight Express, Jeopardy, Wheel of Fortune, Mrs. America Pageants, Barry Manilow, The Righteous Brothers, and many more.

I have worked on a large number of shows and have so many stories in entertainment, that it's a bit difficult to narrow them down to just one or two for my part in this book. It's especially difficult having been involved in diverse facets of entertainment. With that being said, I'll try to quickly run through a few stories.

In college, I gave up a full-ride scholarship to be a mascot and Cheerleader. This all started at UNLV where I was the first and only mascot ever based on a coach. The mascot was based on Jerry Tarkanian, the UNLV National Championship winning coach. I was "Tark the Shark." After college I went on to mascot for the Las Vegas Dust Devils, an arena soccer team, the Las Vegas Sting, an arena football team, and the Las Vegas Thunder, an IHL hockey team. I've been several teams' mascot all over the US, Canada, and Japan. I earned a living jumping and dancing around in a mascot suit while performing in front of a few hundred people to over 60,000 people. It's a rush to say the least. I've been in three Sports Illustrated Magazines in 1990-1991, been featured on newspaper covers all over the US 1990-1991, and was on the "Top 10 plays of The Day, Month, and of The Year" in 1991.

During 1990-1991 and for a few years after, I did security & bodyguard work. Many of my stories from those years may not be suitable for this book. These are a few of the people I've been able to work for: Pauly Shore, The Oakridge Boys, U2, Metallica, The Grateful Dead, Jo Koy, and many more. It would be improper to talk about many of these experiences because they tend to get a bit R-rated to X-rated. So I'll just leave that there.

As a musician opening for bands like The Bangles, Berlin, Seven Nations, Dreams Come True, (one of the biggest Japanese pop acts of all time), I had the pleasure of being able to live a rock star type of life for a short time. Party like there's no tomorrow…and so forth. You've seen the lifestyle on TV and movies, and let's just say it's all true! Playing intimate shows to just a handful of people to 10,000 plus spectator arena shows is a natural high that has no comparison. When you are behind the drums laying down a groove and looking at the audience groove along with you, it is one of the coolest feelings I've ever had. When I was part of a duo that opened for Dreams Come True; the curtain opened and everybody there was like, "who the hell is this?" After a few seconds of awkward silence, we started throwing down musically. Within a few minutes of playing music, we received some cheers and applause. That's when I started remembering some Japanese phrases; from when I lived and performed there previously. The place started going crazy! So we just rocked their socks off for 45 minutes. After the curtain closed the main producer asked if we could finish their tour as the opening act. Unfortunately we weren't able to make the dates. None the less, the experience was life changing at the time.

Now for a story about one of the coolest things I've ever done. This one takes place one day when I was doing some high rigging. There was a George Strait concert playing at the Las Vegas Speedway, and I was invited to play on the rigging team for the show. It was an early March week when the weather was finally getting warm and there was a nice 10 mph breeze keeping us cool. We were in our rigging harnesses hanging about 65 feet up in the air on a scaffolding rig hanging the rigging points for the sound system. All of a sudden eight stock cars started racing around the track. If you know anything about stock cars, they are extremely loud and rumble everything around them. At this same time, fighter jets and air tankers from Nellis Air Force Base started flying over us. It was the annual Red Flag Air Games. Their runway was just a few miles south of the speedway and every plane took off and landed right over our heads. So there I was hanging from scaffolding, swinging in the breeze, stock cars racing around me, and fighter jets and tankers flying a few hundred feet above me. WOW! What a rush of a day! Let's just say that was one of, if not the coolest days I've ever had in my 28+ years of rigging for shows.

I'll say it again; 'Entertainment has been a great life!'

MIKE CRISWELL

"Life IS a journey. I've enjoyed the ride."

Please allow me to introduce myself, I'm a man… Sorry about that. I had a Rolling Stones flashback. Hello, my name is Mike Criswell and this is my contribution to Craig's next book. I started my career in Showbiz in 1967 working at the Sahara Tahoe Hotel and Casino. I joined the IATSE in the Reno Local number 363 in 1968. I worked for one year on the stage, three years in the electrical/follow spot department, and two years in the sound department. Working in Lake Tahoe was one of the most beautiful environments on earth. After five years, I was ready for a new adventure.

I hopped in my red and white VW camper van, (I still own it), and headed south. I arrived in Las Vegas June 15, 1973 and learned immediately what hot weather means. It was 115 degrees on that day and I had no air conditioning in my van. John Stephens, who I had worked with in Lake Tahoe, helped me find employment very quickly. I started my Las Vegas Showbiz career at the Desert Inn Hotel and Casino. I worked with Craig's Uncle Gilbert who was a fellow stagehand and Craig's cousin Bonnie, who was the resort's Entertainment Director, for several years.

When an opening as Head Soundman came open, Randy Wood had two candidates in mind for the position. Gilbert Hayes was very qualified for the job but bowed out of consideration so I could take on the job. It was 1974 and Gilbert was looking at the end of a very full career and felt I was younger and would enjoy the challenges more than he would. I would stay at the Desert Inn for only four years.

In 1977 I left one of the most incredible showrooms in Las Vegas and took a position as the Head Soundman in the showroom at the Frontier Hotel and Casino. Todd Dougall had hired me as the Head of Audio in 1977 and now asked me to make a change in my job location. In 1982 until 1984 he asked me to work in the lounges within the hotel and help him take back jurisdiction in the convention areas from the Operating Engineers. It was a successful change for me and we did take over the jurisdiction for all things Showbiz in the convention areas. Truth be told, the Operating Engineers didn't want to keep the work in the convention areas and gladly turned it over to Local 720.

In 1984, Ed McDonnell, another Lake Tahoe stagehand paid me a visit and offered me a job at the Riviera Hotel working as a deck electrician in the Versailles Showroom. The show was called Solid Gold. It was a live stage version of the hit TV show hosted by Dionne Warwick. This is where I met Barbara Hayes, Craig's stepmother and the Stage

Manager for the showroom. To this point in time, I had still not met Craig. That would change in about four years. I worked for one year on Solid Gold when we were informed a new show called 'Splash' was coming to the Riviera showroom. I would get my Pyro Technician's License and became the Head Pyro Tech on Splash from 1985 until 1996.

I met Craig around April 1988 and worked closely with him for six years until he left Splash. When Craig left Splash in 1994 he had been the Job Steward for about a year. I was voted in as Job Steward after his departure. For the next two years I created an appeals committee for our showroom to handle any small incidents arising on stage. This was done to lighten the load of unnecessary grievances by Local 720. I also secured all extra work in the convention area on a rotating basis. My final accomplishment during my tenure as Job Steward was aided by Phil Carter, the Head Carpenter. We insisted that everyone wear black clothes whether on stage or front of house. This made us a well defined and unified crew in appearance.

In 1996 I received a phone call from Craig Hayes the Head Carpenter at the Las Vegas Hilton. He wanted to know if I had any interest in working on the Starlight Express show with him as the Head Pyro Tech. I started two weeks later working in another legendary showroom. When Starlight Express closed in 1997 I went to work for John Stephens in the Las Vegas Hilton convention area. This is where I learned my audio-visual skills.

In 1999 I went to work at Bally's-Paris convention areas for Encore Productions. This was enjoyable work and it gave me the opportunity to go into business as a labor coordinator. My partners in the business were Tom Gerard and Dan Morrison. The name of our company was Desert Crew Call. I was only a partner in the business from 2008-2010.

In 2014 I was promoted by Keith Purser to the position of Technical Director for Encore Productions at Bally's-Paris Convention areas. My promotion didn't exclude me from fulfilling my other duties as an audio-visual tech. This was my final highlight in a long and rewarding career.

I first met Craig in 1988 when he was called in to fill a position for an injured stagehand. We hit it off from the start. We had a really good working relationship through the years at Splash and at the Las Vegas Hilton. I also became a customer at his and his partner Talbot Snow's recording studio. I even brought my bicycle pump to be recorded one session.

I have thoroughly enjoyed my many years of being friends with Craig. I am honored to have been asked by him to participate in this, his latest book.

T-BONED IN TULSA

Over my many years being the Head Audio Tech in several hotels, I have had the opportunity to mix audio for many top entertainers. Roy Clark was one of my favorites entertainers to mix, but not until we had a serious discussion about his guitar's stage volume. Roy liked his guitar amplifier loud, too loud. I recorded his show one night and played it back for him. He hadn't realized how loud and out of balance his guitar amp was. He turned down his amp and we re-balanced the sound for that night's show. Roy appreciated and respected me for being willing to tell him the truth and bring up an issue about his show to him.

When Roy went on tour he asked Todd Dougall if he could take me with him as his FOH engineer. Todd gave his blessing and it was off to Tulsa, Oklahoma where Roy lives for rehearsals. On one of those trips Roy and his wife Barbara picked me up at the airport and we headed to his home for the night. As Roy drove us home through town we were t-boned in an intersection by a driver in a pickup who had run a red light. The other driver became very belligerent with us until he realized he had just crashed into 'Mr. Tulsa'. He quickly changed his attitude and thought he was going to jail for slamming into the city's favorite son.

Roy is one of the kindest people on earth. He put the other driver at ease and fixed the situation with the police. He even helped with the repairs to the other man's truck.

Roy was also one of the most talented and gifted musicians on the planet. He would play music on his guitar or steam powered organ I have never heard from anyone else. He was not just a country music artist. He could play any style or genre of music you could think of. My time with Roy is one of my most valued memories of my time in Showbiz.

THE FALL OF ANNE MARGARET

In the early 70's it was a common practice for headliner entertainers to bring their new show to Lake Tahoe casinos and work out all of the bugs before taking their shows to Las Vegas. While working at the Sahara Tahoe Hotel in my early career, Anne Margaret brought her show to our room for two weeks. In her show she had a flying platform in the form of an open hand with the thumb pointing up in the air. She would stand in the middle of this platform and be lifted into the air about 22 feet and then float in for her opening number.

Her opening number was 'After Midnight' by Eric Clapton. Her dancers wore costumes of all creatures nocturnal. She wore an evening dress with a large heavy cape with a metal ring in the top to keep its shape. On that evening, the opening act, comics Mitzi and Charlie Brill were wrapping up their number and it was time for Anne to get loaded on her flying hand. Everyone on stage got into position behind the Main Curtain and Anne rose to her position over everyone on stage.

Suddenly, her flying platform started rocking out of control and Anne fell off it 'head first' towards the stage floor. Without a miracle or two, Anne would be dead in a couple seconds. She received her miracles in the form of her heavy cape catching on the flying hand and turning her on her side instead of her head. The other miracle was a stagehand by the name of Charlie Manchester was underneath her and broke her fall.

As bedlam broke out on stage, I ran over to Anne and found her to still be alive but seriously injured. Charlie though injured himself by her fall had literally saved Anne's life. That part of her opening number was not used again.

MY SOUTH AFRICAN ROMANCE

In 1976 Juliet Prowse took her show to South Africa on a tour. I went along with her as the FOH Engineer. When I arrived at the venue, I walked the room with one of the stage techs named Ian. As I looked the room over something caught my eye. She was one of the most beautiful women I have ever laid eyes on. I asked Ian who she was and told me her name was Rene. He also told me not to waste my time because every man in the place had tried to get dates with her. I told him to introduce me to her.

I was mesmerized. She had won a look-a-like contest and was known to everyone as the South African Olivia Newton-John. We started dating two weeks later.

Juliette could see I was very interested in Rene and wanted to give me some advice on my situation. She told me South African women are heartbreakers and I should take it slow. I appreciated her sisterly advice but decided to continue dating Rene. After the tour we all went our separate ways and I returned to Las Vegas without Rene…for now.

In 1990, some 14 years later my romance with Rene was re-kindled and she moved to Las Vegas and became my wife. We are still married to this day, some 30 years later. Some things take a while to get right.

A FINAL THOUGHT

I concluded my career in Showbiz in 2017. I have had a great career. My favorite quote is by Sir Isaac Newton. He said: "If I have seen further than others it is because I have stood on the shoulders of giants." I have mentioned some of those giants here. I want to thank every person I have ever worked with for their friendship and professional interactions. Of all the different places you can find Showbiz, my absolute favorite venues are showrooms and theaters. There is a special magic in them.

For those who are new to the business and some of you seasoned veterans; whatever job or position you have on a stage, it is the greatest work on earth. When you retire and leave this business, your stories and memories will be your greatest treasures.

DALLAS HALL

Howdy folks. My name is Dallas Hall. When Craig asked me to write a few words or stories about my time in entertainment, I was curious why he would ask me. You see, I have never been a stagehand even though I worked side by side with them at the Golden Nugget Hotel in Las Vegas. I am an electrician by trade in the International Brotherhood of Electrical Workers or IBEW. I will get to my stories and observations about Showbiz in a moment but first let me give you some background of who I am.

I was born in Ogden, Utah and lived there for about eight years. I lived on a farm and knew the meaning of hard work from an early age. Some time in my eighth or ninth year we moved to Hayward, California. It was outside of San Francisco and it too was a rural farming community. I lived there for ten years. After serving a proselytizing mission for my church, I came home to a new town. While I was away for two years, my parents had moved to a small town 40 miles north-northwest of St. George, Utah called Enterprise. I was only home for a short time before heading off to work as a driller and blaster at the Pan Am mine.

After a year working in the mines I decided to find a trade to work in. At age 22 I began my four year apprenticeship as an electrician in St. George. I actually finished my apprenticeship in three and a half years. After taking the electrician's test and passing it, I now had a trade to support my family with. I moved to Las Vegas and signed up with the local IBEW union and waited for some work. I didn't have to wait long. I was offered employment at the Nevada Test Site (NTS) as an electrician and took the job.

After two years at the NTS I returned to Las Vegas. The next stop in my career was working for Steve Wynn at the Golden Nugget as a non-union electrician. This is where I was introduced into the world of Showbiz. After four years at the Golden Nugget, I left to work once again at the NTS for a year. I finished my time in Las Vegas working construction as an electrician for three more years. My total time spent in Las Vegas was ten years.

In 1990 I returned to Enterprise, Utah and worked for the most part in Southern Utah as an electrician. During that time period I traveled to every western State and worked on construction sites as an electrician. Today, I am retired but still work on some construction jobs in my trade.

In 2010 I moved to Alaska and worked in construction and as an electrician with other members of my family. I even worked as an electrician in a gold mine that was so remote the only way to get there and back was by airplane. I only worked there for a short time. During this time I worked on the North Slope oil fields. Alaska is a truly amazing State but after five years of Alaskan winters I returned to Southern Utah to finish my career as an electrician.

I first met Craig in 2008 after he, his wife Linda, and son Wesley moved to Enterprise. My late wife Melanie and Linda quickly became friends and through them I was introduced to Craig. We learned we had some commonality in our lives from working in Showbiz. I feel we are kindred spirits and have enjoyed reading and discussing the several books written by him. I am honored to have been asked to be a small part of his next book.

I was asked by Craig to tell a few stories about my time working around stagehands and entertainers at the Golden Nugget. He thought my perspective of not being a stagehand but working side by side with them on shows would be interesting. With my disclaimer in place, I will tell you a couple short stories and some observations about Showbiz.

I found some entertainers to be all business and others that loved performing and loved the people they performed for. Merle Haggard was one of those entertainers who loved to perform and I believe he really loved his audience. When he would start his midnight show he would come out on stage and start singing for about an hour. He would then take a short break and return wearing sneakers. Wearing his cowboy boots for what was about to come would have been too uncomfortable. In his sneakers and cowboy hat he would continue his show and sing his songs for the next two to three hours. He always gave his fans what they came to see.

John Denver was not only one of the most talented musicians and songwriters I have ever known, he was another one of those entertainers that loved to perform and loved his fans. He had a vocal range that was incredible. He could sing anything from rock and roll, soul, jazz, and even opera. His 8PM show would last about an hour and a half, but his midnight show would last for several hours. He at times would play his songs and sing for his fans until 6AM.

John was very athletic. Even if he played all night and into the early hours of the morning, he would get up at 7AM and go to the Union Plaza Hotel and play tennis until 10AM. He then came back to the Golden Nugget and played songs on whatever instrument he wanted until 4PM. If you wanted, you could join him on stage and play with him on any available instrument or sing along with him. He also had a buffet set up for anyone who came into the auditorium. They could eat and listen for free or they could join in on the fun. He was truly amazing.

I have one more, brief story about John Denver. I had gotten to know him quite well over the years and we both loved hiking in the mountains. He did most of his hiking in Colorado and New Mexico. I did my hiking in Utah. Any ways, he told me when he goes hiking songs just pop into his head. He would pull out his notebook and write those songs down and continue with his hike. These hikes are where his biggest hits came to him.

I had mentioned earlier there are some entertainers who are very good at their craft but treat their shows more like a business. Kenny Rogers is one of those performers. When you went to a Kenny Rogers show, you got exactly what you went there for. His show was highly polished and perfected. He sounded in concert just like he does on his albums. When he was done with his show, he was done. He would play for 59 minutes and walk off the stage and go to his room. No amount of cheering could bring him back for an encore. Paul Anka was a lot like Kenny. The difference was Paul would go back out and sing a few more songs for his audience if they cheered loud and long enough.

I am grateful for the opportunity to have worked with some of the most talented and amazing entertainers in the world. Even though I was an electrician for the showroom at the Golden Nugget and not an official stagehand, I appreciated the work and talent of those who make shows come alive every night. Theirs is a craft to take great pride in. I cherish the memories of working for just a few years in and around Showbiz.

JOHN PEER

Hello everyone. My name is John Peer formerly known as John Hanson. I feel it is a privilege to be included in Craig's latest book. Before I tell a couple stories from my time in Showbiz, I would like to tell you just a little about myself.

I am a true native of Las Vegas having been born in our fair city at Women's Hospital on Sahara and Spencer Avenues. The hospital is no longer there having given way to a car dealership. I lived most of my youth in the neighborhood behind the now non-existent Showboat Hotel and Casino. The closest main roads to my house would be St. Louis and Boulder Highway. As far as schooling is concerned, I attended John F.Miller Elementary, K.O. Knudsen Jr. High, and Valley High Schools.

I grew up in a very pro-union home. My adopted father, Don Hanson had been an assembly line worker for the United Auto Workers Union or UAW in a few car plants back east. In Las Vegas, he was a member of the Teamsters Union and did various jobs under their jurisdiction including driving a Taxi Cab. My dad always believed in unions and instilled in me a desire to be part of one someday. He was an admirer of UAW President Walter Ruther in the 50's and 60's for all the work he had done on behalf of his members.

In junior high school at K.O. Knudsen I became involved with the school's Audio Visual department. Our school had a closed circuit TV station in it and I became a news director for our monthly 15 minute news broadcast. I never appeared on camera but liked editing and producing shows on our one inch Beta Tape machines. I also enjoyed setting up projectors and screens in classes around the campus. I didn't know it then but I would be doing this type of work in convention rooms all over town one day.

My high school years at Valley High were filled with several activities. I played J.V. basketball, ran track, and ran cross country events. In my junior and senior years I gave up basketball except for LDS church basketball with my friends Glenn Horlacher, Tony Christianson, and Wayne Horlacher. I did run track and cross country in my junior and senior years though. I had no involvement in the Valley High AV department during my high school years.

To make a few dollars in high school, I worked at USS Fish and Chips, at Sears as a watch and jewelry repairman, and a few other un-remember-able jobs. One year after graduating from high school, I became a paid campaign staff member on one of Harry Reid's runs for the U.S. Congress. After the election, I found a job as a runner for a large law firm in Las Vegas and was sent as a courier to the U.S. Embassy or Consulate in Monterey, Mexico several times with legal document for the families of some people killed in the MGM Grand Hotel fire.

While working as a runner for the law firm, I applied to become a firefighter. I didn't do well on the test and I never tried out again. I was looking for something else to make a career and didn't know what to do or where I should start looking. One of the law firm's secretaries referred me to an Audio Visual Company that was looking for help.

The name of the company was Nevada Audio Visual and the owner's name was Larry Little. I got the job as a field representative, (a delivery man and trouble shooter) and started doing what I had done in junior high school. I worked there for two years and left to work at Caesar's Palace as an Operating Engineer out of Local 501 in their convention areas. I worked at Caesar's for ten years from 1985-1995. In 1994 IATSE Local 720 was signing up people to work out of their hall. I signed up thinking it would be a good second job and a fall back employment office if I ever quit working at Caesar's.

A year later I left Caesar's and was offered a job working for Larry Hamm, the owner of Las Vegas Video Sound Rental. It was familiar work having been employed at Nevada Audio Visual many years earlier. I was once called out to be the company representative on a movie called 'Fools Rush In'. All it meant was standing around during the shoot in case one of our pieces of equipment had any issues and solving the problem. It was easy money.

In 1996 I ran into Julius Lightfoot and BJ Thomas (not the singer) and they suggested coming down to Local 720 and volunteering some time on a few endorsed political campaigns. It was by doing this simple thing that I made some contacts and started working steadily at the Tropicana Hotel, Las Vegas Hilton Hotel, and Riviera Hotel convention areas. This was the year my career with Local 720 truly began and took off. I spent the next ten years working as an AV Lead and Job Steward in most of the town's convention facilities.

During this time, I decided to get more involved in the

internal workings and politics of Local 720 by running for Craft Two Representative and being on the exam board. This was just a prelude for what was to come.

While working on one of the larger conventions in town, Dan'l Cook, Ron Poveromo, and I all decided to run for leadership positions in Local 720. Dan'l would run for President, Ron would run for Secretary/Treasurer, and I would run for Business Representative. We all won on the first ballot. Prior to our running for office, I had been hired by Jeff Coleman our Business Representative to be one of his Business Agents over the Film and Television jurisdiction within our local. This was invaluable knowledge and a priceless experience.

In 2008, once we were elected to our various offices, my first contract to negotiate was at the Las Vegas Hilton. This is where I first got to know Craig and witnessed his involvement in securing the most lucrative contract for Local 720 in Las Vegas. It set the wages and benefits package bar very high for all other hotel contracts to live up to.

When I ran for my second term as Business Representative I once again won on the first ballot. During my second term in office, I implemented a new dispatch system for our local and negotiated a new contract with the operators of the Electric Daisy Carnival or EDC. With a good number of successes under my belt you would think my election for a third term was a shoe-in. It wasn't. The membership decided to go another direction and with a different Business Representative.

In 2014 I would leave the leadership of Local 720 and find a few job offers from Freeman Audio Visual as a labor coordinator and PRG AV as one of their Representatives. The offer that intrigued me the most and the one I went with was from Red Mercury Entertainment or RME. They were in charge of all entertainment at the Riviera Hotel and wanted me to be in charge of all technical and labor issues for them and their shows. This was my first true venture into the showroom aspect of our industry. I had a big learning curve to overcome.

Just over a year after taking the job with RME at the Riviera it was announced the hotel had been sold to the Las Vegas Convention Center and would be demolished in order to build another convention hall. I thought I would be out looking for work again until I was told I would be going with the Riviera management team over to the Westgate Resorts as the Director of Entertainment and Technical Operations. I have been in this position for six years and am looking forward to being here for many years to come.

I probably crossed paths with Craig several hundred times at Valley High School. The interesting part of this is we never really knew each other back then. He was in the Class of 1980 and I was in the Class of 1981. The only way we knew of each other was from LDS church basketball. We were both friends of the Horlachers but Craig went to a different chapel than Glenn and Wayne. Prior to the official basketball season, Craig and Glenn would bring their opposing teams to some pre-season games for a tune up. I played on Glenn's team and all I remember is the battle royal of street ball. It was a good tune up.

Like I said earlier, my first real business interaction with Craig was during contract negotiations in 2008-2009. Now I am his direct supervisor. I have found him to be well spoken and a good leader of his crew. He has a vast knowledge acquired over his 40 years working in entertainment of everything relating to stage operations and management. Every client that comes to our showroom leaves giving high praise to the crew under Craig's direction.

I was asked by Craig to tell a couple stories about my time working in Showbiz. Even though most of my time working out of Local 720 has been in the convention audio/visual departments and representing the membership as the union's business representative, I was able to come up with some stories or observations concerning stage craft.

Story 1: While working at Caesar's Palace from 1985-1995 under the jurisdiction of the Operating Engineers Local 501, in the sound department, it was not uncommon for the leadership and membership of Local 720 to vocally give their displeasure about what they believed to be our union doing stage work. There were many heated arguments about jurisdiction between Job Stewards and Business Representatives over this work. This is not a bad thing. Unions all over town are constantly fighting over jurisdiction in order to expand employment opportunities for their membership. These conflicts usually get resolved in the grievance and arbitration process or management steps in and assigns the work to one of the disputing unions. The conflict between Locals 720 and 501 was settled by management in contract negotiations.

When Caesar's Palace expanded their convention space, management decided to assign all convention sound, lighting, video, carpentry, and rigging to Local 720. The members of 501 were signed up in Local 720 and were made full time employees in the convention area. I believe it was a huge victory for Local 720 not just because of them being assigned the convention area jurisdiction, but some of the Local 501's sound department employees, absorbed by Local 720, were the strongest fighters for 501 jurisdiction. Some of these men went on to be elected as leaders in Local 720.

Story 2: I was elected as Business Representative in 2007 and took office in January 2008. There is a massive learning curve for the position and I spent many days in classes, on job sites, and collapsing from exhaustion at night. In 2011 I had one of the best wins for one of the members in Local 720. A spotlight operator at Bally's Hotel on the Hollywood Jubilee show brought in some gun parts to work on between shows. Once again, I said, 'gun parts,' not a gun. It was a barrel and the grips to one of his pistols and he wanted to polish it on his down time. This was probably not the smartest thing to do as we live in an era of fear concerning firearms. Anyway, one of the crew members notified security. They arrived and promptly confiscated his parts and escorted him off property. As he left, security returned his parts to him. He was terminated for bringing a firearm on the property.

I filed a grievance for him being wrongfully terminated and we began our ten month journey through the grievance process. When the arbitrator was presented with the facts that the employee never brought a firearm to work, only a couple parts of a firearm, and he had not threatened anyone with his parts, and security had even given him his parts back as he left the property, the arbitrator ruled he was to receive his job back with back pay for the past ten months. If I recall correctly, it was a back pay of around 40 thousand dollars. It felt great to have such a big win for one of 720's members.

One thing is for sure as the Business Representative of a union: you can't win them all. When a member does something so blatantly indefensible such as bringing his motorcycle on stage to work on it between shows and starts welding on it with a full tank of gasoline, the outcome is certain and swift. This very thing happened at the Tropicana Hotel and of course, the employee was terminated for putting the property in danger. Remember, Las Vegas has some of the toughest fire codes in the nation because of the MGM Grand and Las Vegas Hilton fires.

When the member asks you to fight for his job, you file the grievance paperwork and prepare your case for the employee. But, after seeing the evidence, you know in your heart there is little if any chance to win the case. Nevertheless, you are obligated to fight your hardest for the member. In the end, you have to accept the termination as being valid and hope you don't have many more losses like this one.

Story 3: When I ran for re-election as Business Representative for a third term, I really thought I would win and probably win a fourth or fifth term before retiring. This was not the case. The membership decided to elect another person to office and I was forced to seek employment in the workforce I once represented. Working as a job Steward or in an audio/visual department would have been logical but not rewarding. I decided to take a job with RME at the Riviera hotel as Entertainment Technical Director. I was about to have a new learning curve forced upon me.

I had worked in audio/visual positions for many years prior to this and new my way around quite well. Other than having worked as the Business Representative for stage hands, I had not worked on a proper stage during my career. The Riviera was the ideal location for me to jump in with both feet into stage craft. They had three small showrooms and a lounge for me to oversee. During this time, I learned what I would here a couple years later from Craig as the difference between 'convention techs' and 'Stagehands.' There is something unique about lounges and showroom stages that is hard to describe, other than them having a 'magic' in them.

The several shows we changed out and brought in helped give me a better insight for what would happen next.

Story 4: When the Riviera hotel was sold, I was fortunate enough to be taken with the management team from the Riviera to the Westgate Resort right across the street. The Westgate has a Cabaret Showroom seating 300 people just like some of the showrooms at the Riviera. Unlike the Riviera's Versailles Showroom which had been dark for several years, the Westgate has Elvis' showroom or the International Showroom on property and actually operating. This was something new for me to get my head wrapped around. With some help from the crew, I soon had a good feel for the room and how it operates.

We would spend the next few years doing concerts, fights, beauty pageants, industrial presentations, and production shows. When it was announced that Barry Manilow was returning to the property for another residency, I had to rely on Craig and his crew to make a very short load in and rehearsal schedule work in order to open the show on schedule. I am proud to say everything worked out and fell into place on time and on budget, for the most part.

When it was opening night for Barry, Craig told me to be in the audience and see how the room goes wild when Barry walks out on stage. He also told me to watch the people when they leave and see how they react after his show. The magic and electricity in the air and seeing his fans react is why so many people love working in Showbiz. I did what Craig asked and now understand a little better the magic of Showbiz.

Final thoughts: The career path I started on in the early 80's has led me to finally being involved in Showbiz for the last eight years. I would love nothing more than to finish my career working in the industry and for the company (Westgate Resorts) that has taken such good care of me. Showbiz, particularly in Las Vegas, is an amazing industry to work in. I sometimes wish I had pursued working on a stage sooner in my career. It truly is magical.

NICOLE BRYANT-STEPHENS

Hello and greetings to everyone.

My name is Nicole Anne Bryant Stephens, and I am proud Craig asked me to contribute to his book. Putting 'pen to paper' about myself is a little outside my comfort zone, so, please bear with me.

Originally from North Tarrytown, New York, the site of Washington Irving's 1820 short story, "The Legend of Sleepy Hollow." And no, I have never seen the *Headless Horseman* riding around my hometown. I did not stay in New York for exceptionally long. Though my birth town is one of the most haunted places in the world, it was not the reason for my family's move to Fishkill NY, then heading west to Fremont CA, and making my forever home in Carmel, CA.

Born to artistically gifted parents, (my father was an architect and my mother was an incredible artist) it was no surprise I began my love of theatre arts in the fifth grade with an original puppet show based on '*The Elves and the Shoemaker*'. Mesmerized, the response from kindergarten audience fueled my passion for the arts at this early age.

Throughout middle and high school, The Frohman Academy, School of Dramatic Arts, in Carmel, CA, was instrumental in every aspect of my theatrical training for the stage. I was a performer, stagehand, spotlight operator, assistant stage manager, scenic assistant, artist, and any other position needed to produce a show. The time at Frohman Academy gave me a good basis for what I would learn in my college years.

University opportunities led me to the Midwest where I earned a Bachelor of Fine Arts degree in Scenic Design/Art, at The Theatre School, (formerly The Goodman School of Drama) at DePaul University in Chicago, Illinois. While in my university studies, I designed the musical "*Working*," by author, actor, historian, and broadcaster Studs Terkel. He even attended the opening night gala.

Developing my career in California theatres deeply blessed my life. I will always cherish the memories of collaborating and working relationships with my parents and brother on show productions. Their life skills and artistries ran from architecture, set and fashion design, and stage crew expertise. My fondest memories of working with my family were: '*Nutcracker, A Monterey Peninsula Tradition*', a full-length ballet produced by Dance Kids of Monterey County. It was a 27-year, three generation tradition for our family's holiday working season.

In 1996, Scenic Technologies in Las Vegas, NV, developed a new attraction at the world-renowned Caesar's Palace. "*Caesar's Magical Empire*" took its audience on a fine dining experience through ancient Rome while being entertained by magicians. I was tasked to turn wood, concrete, and other building materials into marble and granite throughout the attraction. This rare opportunity brought my talent and creativity in scenic art to a higher level.

While living in Las Vegas, Scenic Technologies created a Christmas display masterpiece for Opportunity Village. This is a nonprofit organization dedicated to providing people with disabilities employment opportunities through vocational training and community outreach programs and services. My imaginative design for the extravaganza (a fund-raising event) showcased the magic and glory of this special season and it was a tremendous financial benefit for a worthy organization.

With the 1997 opening of the Orleans Casino in Las Vegas, I was asked to design country music star and show creator, Rex Allen Jr.'s production called, '*Gone Country*'. I am grateful for his trust and aid in my career during these heady times.

During my time with Tri-Star Theme Builders I became a paint foreman of faux finishes, (my time and experience at Caesar's Magical Empire was seriously paying off now) working on the exterior of Sunset Station Hotel and Casino. I was a mere 26 years old at this time. This job provided me with the opportunity to run crews and drive and operate heavy equipment such as 40', 60' and 120' boom lifts and scissor lifts. These invaluable skills were a boon and benefit to future jobs and my resume'.

For one part of the project, Tri Star Theme Builders subcontracted my family business; 'Bottega Designs' to paint faux wall tiles on one side of Sunset Station. This helped grow my family business by opening the doors for more design work in construction and entertainment.

It was while working on the Sunset Station Hotel project that I met other scenic artists in the stagehand's union or IATSE (International Alliance of Theatre & Stage Employees) Local 720. A fortuitous meeting with Tom Walker, the union's Business Representative, gained my entrance into this coveted union. I would now work in a protected and secure working environment in the Las Vegas entertainment industry.

One of my first scenic artist assignments was for Rufino (Ruffy) Mugica, the Production Manager for the show '*Splash*' at the Riviera Hotel. I was to re-paint the 4,000 gallon water tank (used by the divers and swimmers) that sat on stage. I thought this was a prank. It was not. I showed up at the Riviera Hotel's Versailles Theater and there the tank was, waiting for me to re-paint it. I have had many firsts in my life and painting a diving tank, complete with mermaids, on a stage in Las Vegas rated a space on that list.

My initial trip into the Las Vegas Hilton was for Penn and Teller's '*Las Vegas Sin City Spectacular*' for the FX Network. This was when and where I first met Craig, the author of this book. He seemed to like my skills, work ethic, and attitude during the filming. He later hired me to work on the show run of '*Joseph and the Amazing Technicolor Dream Coat*'. Because of Craig's influence, weekly calls became incredible experiences. I worked on Wheel of Fortune, Jeopardy, boxing matches and an endless variety of Las Vegas concerts and shows. We developed a friendship and working relationship lasting throughout my career.

Nicknames abounded on stage. When you work 16-20 hours a day for weeks at a time, you get one of two things: You either get real grouchy, or you get real punchy and laugh at the slightest mistake or misspoken word. The co-author of this book, Kelli Wolf and I earned the moniker '*The Giggle*

Twins' from Craig as we often worked too many hours with too little sleep and found life situations quite entertaining.

While living and working in Las Vegas, I maintained many of my contacts in California and in Hollywood. In 1999 Tri Star Theme Builders hired me as the Field Art Director on the re-model of the Swiss Family Tree House in Disneyland. We were to transform it into Tarzan's Tree House at the Anaheim theme park. Once the tree house transformation was complete, I became one of the Art Directors for Disney's California Adventure. When my work at the California Adventure ended, I was offered a position as Field Art Director at Hong Kong Disneyland's PhilharMagic in Fantasyland. Soon after my work in Hong Kong concluded, the Shanghai Disneyland Field Art Director position was offered to me. I had to turn it down because I needed to stay close to home due my parents ailing health.

In collaboration with Kent McFan and Bruce Ryan, (television entertainment designers), I have plied my scenic art skills on many TV shows. My credits include The Billboard Awards, Teen Choice Awards, Kid's Choice, and the Source Awards. I did the set design for "Ask Rita" starring Rita Rudner. One late evening, while I was painting the floor of that set with my mother, I was horrified to realize my Old English Sheepdog Sashza left paw prints on the edge of the set in the wet paint. Arriving before I was able to erase the paw tracks, Ms. Rudner insisted they stay. It turns out she was an ardent dog lover. I guess you can call this a fortunate misfortune.

Back at the Magic Kingdom working for Mural Makers, better known as Disneyland, I became one of the assistant field art directors for Star Wars Galaxy's Edge. When we completed the work in a galaxy far, far away we walked over to the California Adventure and began painting Marvel's Avenger's Campus until it was shut down because of COVID-19. We have since finished the work in the Marvel Comic Universe and it is now open to the public. There is something very fulfilling about painting areas in theme parks and knowing millions of people will see and some will appreciate your work.

Craig asked me for a story or two about our business we call: *'SHOW'*.

I have had a life filled with unique experiences all while living my dreams working in the entertainment industry. This is not the case for many other people. My mom was born in 1942 and could have or should have been an artist. In her younger days, it was expected of women to pursue more traditional roles such as teachers, nurses, secretaries or homemakers. She did what was expected of her and put her art skills and dreams on the shelf and became a nurse. I would help her realize and fulfill her dreams one day.

Once retired, she joined me on many scenic art jobs such as *The Billboard Awards* and the *Nutcracker*. I was blessed to have my mom working side by side with me and give her the chance of being what she actually wanted to be so many years prior. She worked with me for over ten years doing the work we both love. It was not always smooth sailing when we worked together. In fact, she threatened to resign daily. If you think about it, the natural order of life declares children should take directions from parents and not the other way around. In the thick of things, there were times mom didn't enjoy taking direction from her daughter. I knew she wasn't serious.

Stagehands loved her presence and soon became 'Mom' to all. Introducing her as my business partner, Pauline Bryant, never seemed to fit her style. 'Mom' became her artistic identity, and she fulfilled many roles during the years we worked on stage together. While working with recording artist Pink, mom was tasked to find cases of Cool Whip as a cake icing for the singer's 'popping out of a cake' entrance. Mom was completely at ease no matter who the VIP on set was. She was at home with a paint brush in her hand or making her way through a cadre of bodyguards surrounding entertainers such as Britney Spears. The time we spent together on stage was priceless, but far too short.

Over the years, I have found some recording artists and film stars to be very warm and others to be reclusive. While working on the '*Billboard Music Awards*' show for the late producer Mo Morrison, I met one of my favorite country music stars: Garth Brooks. He was truly kind and generous with his time. I learned it was customary for him to take photos with fans and give autographs to every person asking for one. I was included in the group of fans who got a photo with him and his autograph. Thanks you Garth, for a significant memory.

Another job for Mo Morrison took me to the Caribbean for the '*One Love Bob Marley Tribute*' in Jamaica. The stage and set was produced on James Bond Beach. The night before the concert, I was finishing painting when Ziggy Marley, the family, Queen Latifah and numerous other celebrities arrived for sound checks and rehearsals. It was necessary for me to stop painting for the time being until they were done. I found a comfortable place to stay out of the way and enjoyed a private concert and preview of the following night's show.

While watching TV monitors backstage at an awards show, I stood next to Whitney Houston and Jerry Springer. As they watched the show, Whitney told Jerry how much she enjoyed his show. He thanked her for the compliment and continued watching the show. This confirmed to me that mega-stars aren't really different from any other person. Some of them like crazy things like a Jerry Springer Three-Ring Circus Freak Show.

Passing on your knowledge, education, insights, and skills to the next generation is some of the most rewarding time I have ever spent. Working with the local elementary school and putting on three plays a year gives me the opportunity to watch the growth of the kids in theatre arts. The kids work on every aspect of the play. They are performers, help build the sets, make costumes, run lights and sound, work as stage crew, and any other requirement needed to put on the play. Some of the kids participate in every play for their five years in elementary school. They go on to middle and high school having worked on fifteen shows to their credit. This gives them a tremendous advantage if they pursue classes in theatre. I love watching their growth and confidence develop over the years. It's so rewarding.

Show Business is one of the most amazing industries. Whether you are on stage or work behind the scenes, you share happiness, allow an escape from reality, and facilitate fantasy, if only for a few hours.

What job could be better?

TALBOT T. SNOW

Kia ora or in English: Hello there. My name is Talbot Snow and this is my second contribution to Craig's latest book. If you read the FOREWORD, I covered a lot of time and events from my 40 plus year friendship and business partnership with Craig. Even though I am honored to have been asked to contribute to this book, I must admit I was filled with some trepidation at the thought of writing something others would read. I have performed in front of large crowds in my past but writing this and the FOREWORD has taken me out of my comfort zone.

So without any further delays, let me tell you a little bit about me and share some stories from my time working in Showbiz.

In my business and line of work, I wear a few different hats such as: Musician, Producer, Director, Sound-Engineer, Photographer, Videographer, DJ, Dishwasher, and the list goes on and on. These different roles have evolved from a lifetime of being involved with Music and the Arts.

My love of music and art started when I was a boy, growing up first in New Zealand for sixteen years. From the age of sixteen, I worked at developing my artistic / creative abilities in Las Vegas. During my teenage years, I transitioned from the piano to electronic music and discovered my affinity for electronics and sound equipment. In the early 80's, I started DJ-ing around Las Vegas which is something that I had actually started doing in New Zealand. This of course reinforced my love of music and high end audio equipment.

Later, in the mid-80's, after serving a mission for the Church of Jesus Christ of Latter-day-Saints, my partners (Craig Hayes and Quentin Stephenson) and I took out a small business-loan, and we started our first recording studio. Sound Masters of Las Vegas (SMLV) was born, and some of my lifelong ambitions began to materialize.

For over thirty years, Sound Masters has been a studio serving thousands of different clients for their music and visual projects. Sound Masters has gone through many changes and studio upgrades over the years. At the current primary location, the studio has enough space to house a collection of state-of-the-art, and vintage sound equipment. The studio can also accommodate varying musical acts ranging in size from a single vocalist to an entire band.

Recently, I've expanded SMLV to include visual production. This includes professional photography, video filming and editing, graphic design, and website layout and design. To further improve the quality of my product, I've researched extensively, and acquired some of the best camera and lighting equipment available. Now having filmed and edited many music-videos, TV commercials, and company promos, I've become a confident competent Videographer / Photographer.

We all have dreams of what we would do if we won the lottery. If I won 100 million dollars, this is what I might do. I would design and create an entire media complex filled with multiple media studios, sound stages, a radio-station, and even a nightclub. It would be a multimedia Mecca under one roof, where clients / artists could work and even live.

How I met Craig...

As mentioned in the FOREWORD. Craig and I literally bumped into each other 40 years ago, quite by accident, in an LDS chapel gymnasium. I was walking through the room carrying my Sharp boom box and Craig was carrying his basketball. He noticed that I was walking though the gym with my extra-large boom box, and started asking questions. From there, we quickly ascertained that we had many things in common including a love of music, and a strong affinity toward stage and sound equipment. It wasn't long before we were hanging out, designing, and building our first mobile sound system called KAZZ. DJ-ing at every function we could get hired for was only the beginning. We would spend years increasing the size and abilities of our DJ service with a variety of bigger and more powerful eclectic sound systems. We still look back at the first KAZZ with fondness, remembering how it was cobbled together from a variety of different sources.

Over the last four plus decades, Craig and I have joined forces in creating and producing a variety of Music Artists, song projects, photo shoots, video shoots, stage productions, and events / gigs. What a blessing it has been to have such a creative, trusted, generous confidant, and co-producer as my good friend.

Craig asked all of us in CHAPTER EIGHT to tell a few stories about our time in Showbiz. Here are mine.

SHOWBIZ SHENANIGANS

Being involved with media content creation, music production, stage production, sound reinforcement, lighting design, and events or gigs of every size, has taken me to many interesting locations. My career has put me into some very interesting moments and smack-bang-in-the-middle of some very quirky situations. I'll give a quick description of what I am talking about.

I had been hired to DJ and perform with my band: Zodiac Dragon at a very popular Las Vegas nightclub on the 4th of July. While sitting backstage waiting for my segment to DJ and for my band's turn to go on stage, we found ourselves

Waiting in the changing room area (the green room) with dozens of stressed out, flirty, half-naked Drag-Queens. Here I am, along with my fellow performers and technicians trying NOT to look awkward or out of place as we awaited our turn to hit the stage.

Everyone loosened up after a short time and we all enjoyed the kinship of being fellow entertainers. The show went very well and those Masters of Hair and Makeup put on one of the most incredible shows I have ever seen. It will always be remembered by me as an evening of unusual experiences.

Has your heart ever stopped while getting ready to perform on stage? Mine has. When you are in a band and one of your instruments has issues, you do the best you can and push your way through the performance. But when your entire musical score is pre-recorded…well that's another story. My band, Zodiac Dragon and I were hired to perform at an outdoor concert event. There were thousands of concert-goers enjoying the day's entertainment lineup. When it was our turn, we were introduced by the MC. I pushed the "play" button on my Serato / Mac Laptop DJ Core Rig, only to hear the wonderful sound of silence. Looking at the screen made my heart stop. I was looking at the spinning beach-ball of death on my computer screen!

You could hear a pin-drop as the crowd held their breath waiting to see what would happen next. Everyone was watching me during that smothering, agonizing 10 plus seconds of silence. Holy crap! What to do? It was quickly discovered that there was some funky electrical fluctuations happening. The source of these problems was the portable power-generators powering my rig! These fluctuations had somehow messed with my laptop / DJ rig controller, and it (the controller) was, apparently re-setting or re-starting itself at the exact moment I was supposed to start DJ-ing and performing with Zodiac-Dragon. It took several seconds (which seemed like an eternity) to reset itself, but, the rig came back on and I was able to start the music / program. Whew!

DJ-ING

DJSnowManLV.com / Zodiac-Dragon.com

Over the years, I have DJ-ed in front of some fairly large crowds. I'm talking about audiences numbering thousands of people. At one particular New Year's Eve gig there were a couple thousand attendees. Another spring day time gig had some 12,000 people, in attendance. I point this out to show how big crowds transfer big energy to the performer.

To play great music and to hear that quality sound coming through a premium sound system; (a system that I purchased, put together, and set up) is a great feeling. To play music the crowd is responding positively to and watching them dancing, laughing, socializing, and having a good time, is a greater feeling still! Playing some popular line-dances and seeing groups of people clapping, stomping their feet, dancing in unison, is almost spiritual, for me.

I have DJ-ed at many functions like these! To call it almost spiritual might seem a little unusual, perhaps, but that's how it felt at the time.

Music is such a unifying, incentivizing, and universal language that EVERYONE understands! It brings people from all walks of life together in such a wonderful way. To play some small part in bringing good music and people together has been a wonderful part of my life.

CAMERA GIGS

TalbotSnow.com / SoundMastersLV.com/video

As a camera operator (photography / video), I'm always looking to capture amazing shots. On one occasion when I was shooting from a rooftop overhang at an Art Gallery in Downtown Las Vegas, I was trying to get a birds-eye-view for the event I was shooting / covering. While leaning over the edge of the roof that I was standing on with my somewhat heavy camera, I could see several people (attendees) below were looking up at me. They looked very worried that I was going to come falling or crashing down on them. Someone yelled out, "Watch out! Don't fall down!" Thinking back, I failed to thank them for their advice and help. I was trying to capture golden moments of the outdoor fashion-show parade that was going on down below. Thankfully, I didn't fall, and I DID get some nice shots!

Another time, I was shooting a local rock-group in an outdoor alleyway setting. As we went from one area to another, we noticed that there was a wash adjacent to the pathway next to us. I asked the guys if they felt like climbing down into the wash to get a more unique background in their promo-photos. We all agreed to do it. So, we jumped a fence, and climbed down into this 20 foot deep concrete aqueduct. I started taking more photos, and soon we were getting some great moments with body language and attitude from the guys. The tall concrete walls covered in graffiti behind them added an extra raw dimension to the shots.

While we were shooting, we started getting an audience. A group of homeless men, who apparently lived nearby, saw us jump the fence and climb down into the gorge and were now looking down at us from the top of the wash. I think we were on their turf. Some of them started yelling at us. Others started asking questions. Some of the guys in the band were getting a little nervous with the situation. So, we climbed out, planning to leave the area and their 'turf' behind us.. While we were coming out, one of the onlookers asked us what we were doing.

I told him we were shooting some promo-photos for a local rock-group and this seemed to satisfy his curiosity. Then an idea popped into my head. I asked them if they would like to be in some of our shots. After a minute or two of thought and not having any pressing obligations at that time, some of them agreed to be in the shots. The next thing you know, we had shot some very interesting photos combining the band members, the homeless men, and the graffiti covered walls. The shots were edgy, raw, and real.

I've done things like that many times, in order to get a better shot or angle; As a photographer, I will do almost anything humanly possible to get the perfect shot.

RECORDING MUSIC

www.SoundMastersLV.com

I have two stories about recording other's music.

One day, I was with a group of Rap Artists in the studio working on their Rap Song adding sound effects to their production. I was searching through a sound effects library, looking for sounds like gun-shots and police car sirens. I didn't realize that the fader on the console controlling the sound volume in the room was up at a very high level. Somehow, it had been turned up to almost full (ear bleeding) volume.

As I hit the play button, the gun shot sound effect went off. It was so loud it shook the whole room. What had been a crowded room was seemingly and suddenly empty. I looked around the room where the Rap Artists had been standing a few seconds earlier and couldn't see him. In fact, there was not one person to be seen. They had ALL instinctively ducked, or dived quickly behind the mixer-desk. They were all severely shocked by the volume of the gun shot sound.

I couldn't help but laugh as they gradually came back up from behind the mixer and other hiding places. Everyone who was there started busting up; laughing, and poking fun at each other and with me.

On one Saturday morning, an older gentleman called me up. He told me he was coming in from Arizona with a very special project. I said, "OK. What kind of project, and how much time will you need?"

He said, "I'll need your entire Saturday, and I'm bringing some assistants with me!" This sounded like a real important project.

When he came in, he was joined with three other senior-citizens. He was true to his word. One of them was on crutches, one was in a wheelchair, and one was on oxygen. They all looked like they were about to keel over at any moment. They were his "assistants" or maybe his fan club. I'm not sure which. He had brought these three friends along to help him with his project. Wait, it gets better.

He pulls out a cassette tape and tells me he has about an hour's worth of audio on the tape. It was a recording of himself and his son playing on the piano.

It turns out his son was mentally challenged. The father's idea or version of his son "playing the piano" was simply him banging random keys along with his father.

Now of course, I can appreciate the sentimentality behind an effort like this. The bond between a father, and his son, is precious. But the recording sounded like one person playing various actual songs while a second person was randomly banging away on piano keys for an hour straight.

My client wanted me to listen to this tape recording and put it into my Pro-Tools rig. He believed my very expensive computer recording system could analyze the recording and in his words: "Correct any bad notes." There was also some background noise in the recording. As I recall, there was a TV show and some other household sounds that could be heard in the background. Also, his son, who was obviously having a good time during the recording, could be heard laughing and hollering throughout the recording.

I tried to explain to my client how this process would probably not work out very well. But he wasn't hearing it. I told him that for anyone to sit there and "analyze" then "correct" the recording could take several days. Besides that, I wasn't sure what he meant when he said, "Correct it." He wasn't interested in excuses. He told me to identify any bad notes and pitch-correct them. So we proceeded.

Visualize this: Four elderly gentlemen and one very bewildered owner/operator of a recording studio all sitting there listening to this recording. He gave each of his "assistants" a note pad to take notes on as the cassette was playing and being internalized into my Pro-Tools System. I had had turned on time-counter display, showing the exact minutes and seconds passing. He wanted all of us to make notes of the exact time to the minute and second we heard a "bad note." Within about 15 minutes of playing this chaotic recording, all four of the older folks, including my client, had fallen asleep and were passed out in my studio. Soon, it was difficult to hear the recording over the snoring.

I have recorded / produced thousands of songs at Sound Masters of Las Vegas. It has been a privilege and an adventure to be involved with so many song projects. Craig and I have specifically recorded many of those song-projects together. Having his ear and his touch adds to any recording and always made it a better over-all MIX!

CONCLUSION

I have been blessed beyond all measure by being allowed to do the things spoken of previously. Creating multi-media products / services, exploring new places, meeting new people, (especially some very talented

Creative contemporaries and occasional VIPs) has been a blessing. Being able to write / produce music scratches one side of my creative itches. Developing a video script, directing those in the shoot, and editing the video into a finished product helps relieve the itch on another creative nerve. When I'm given the opportunity to capture moments, people, and places in photography sessions gives me a great deal of satisfaction. The icing on the cake is to perform / DJ in front of crowds and being rewarded for a job well done with applause and cheers. I have recently dived into website design for fascinating people and projects.

It has been an amazing journey over the past 40 years. And to think I get to do all of these creative projects while getting paid and making a good living along the way, has been a

DREAM-COME-TRUE.

No man is an island unto himself. I have found great success by associating with other talented people and working hard to achieve my goals. Processes that looked almost like "magical mysteries" to me a few decades ago have since turned into interesting chapters in my career of discovery, learning and proficiency.

I thank God, our Heavenly Father, Hs Son Jesus Christ, and the Holy Ghost for granting me a small part of their talent and insight. You are an extremely wealthy if you have just one good friend. I have one such friend in Craig Hayes. I don't know if I would have gone as far as I have without a supportive family like my

mum and dad: Matina and Brian Snow. Other family members and friends that believed in me are: Victoria Hart, Dani Carter, Colleen Dunn, Blake Snow, Raven Snow, and many others. Thank you again for your guidance, inspiration, and companionship throughout different parts of my journey.

KELLI DRAPER WOLF

Strangely I never thought of what I do as Showbiz …

When I got the email from Craig explaining what he had in mind for his latest book I reminded him, "*Book #4* was my last proofreading, editing, and ghostwriting labor of love." But Craig Hayes is a very persistent and patient taskmaster. He planted the seed and left me to germinate. He assured me this project was going to be entirely different from his other books. It would not be a 244 year chronologically accurate history of these United States like *'After Our Fall.'* Nor would it be a *compilation* of generations of children's Bible stories retold with *'modern day perspectives'* on *'Jesus'* and *'The Prophets.'*

God is a tough act to follow, but his third book: *'Just Thinking'* was the prequel of sorts that started everything. We had worked together for years before I discovered Craig was a writer. Having worked in journalism, since junior high with a plan to study broadcasting, life and an unforeseen diagnosis got in the way. So here I am again, living vicariously through his literary adventures, working on another book *with him* and this time having to talk about myself. Probably one of my least favorite things to do, but there is no other way to tell it. We will need to go back to when I was young, very young. Sorry. But mine is not a typical story.

My father made his living in construction. He was a Roofer by trade and an actual framing and finish Carpenter who also fabricated his own 60's custom psychedelic acrylic tile bathtub surrounds. Dad was a Marine who served as an aircraft mechanic in Korea 1956-1959. [This fact plays in later, when I speak about my predecessor.] My dad loved working with his hands. My mother was a telephone operator who became Head of Telecommunications for Clark County in Las Vegas in the 1970's. I was the youngest of their two daughters, with a brother between us. I did not come from a Showbiz family. I wasn't related to anyone who worked out of Local 720. My only exposure to Showbiz was one of my neighborhood friends was the child of a stagehand but I didn't learn that until years later when their very unique name came up at work.

I was the daughter of a Carpenter. I cut my teeth wrangling tools in my dad's shadow. I wanted to be at his side no matter what he was doing. I followed him up on ladders while he fixed the flashing on the chimney, to perch at the ready to grab or fetch him this tool or that.

It was Las Vegas, circa 1970. Our population was *125,787* a mere fraction of the more than two million people packed in our valley today. It seemed as if I could see the entire valley back then from that little flat roof top of our 2-bedroom brick house. It was nestled beneath the long-faded peace sign that once designated Sunrise Mountain on the east side of our valley...just another one of Las Vegas' landmarks that have disappeared through the hands of time.

I soon became dad's last apprentice. I was barely five years old and just learning to read at the little Baptist church pre-school that flanked the original Las Vegas High School, (now the '*Academy of the Arts*') when my dad was injured in a near fatal industrial accident involving the inhalation of toxic chemicals which left his heart permanently damaged. We didn't know it at the time, but he knew that his life was over. He was a dead man walking and still, he kept building. He was barely thirty-one and the doctors had all but signed his death certificate. It was only a matter of when. With no time to waste he invested in a 7-11 convenience store franchise. My dad spent those nine or ten months before I started kindergarten at Mountain View Elementary putting into place his plan for the future of his young family he would never see. My apprenticeship with my dad was too short.

ME WITH MY DAD, RALPH B. DRAPER AT MT CHARLESTON.

Within a few years, the half of his heart that had miraculously sustained him gave out. He died a few weeks after I turned nine years old, yet he had set in motion a lifeline that would employ and provide for us for generations. What does this have to do with Showbiz? Days off were rare and holidays were spent giving employees time with their families. The reality of physically demanding work coupled with the nonstop nature of living and working in a 24-hour store in a 24-hour town would serve me well when I found my way into Showbiz.

My mother's second husband was a Milkman at my dad's 7-11. My second father figure was 28 years old when he married my mom. She was eleven years his senior. His name is Buddy Hunter. Bud was a Teamster *in every sense of the word*, except he had retained most of his natural teeth! Never had there been a more influential character in my world than this Army Corps of Engineers, *four-tour* Vietnam Vet, turned *Teamster Milkman* everyone called *'Buddy.'*

Because of the nature of his industry, being a union driver through Local 995, 14 and 631, Bud had several popup gigs he would let my brother and I tag along on. My father's little grocery convenience store where I stocked shelves and ran the register was my day job from 5-16 years old. My favorite work story was my first summer job. I was a seasonal member of a four-man crew, except I was a twelve-year-old girl.

Initially, I tagged along out of boredom one sweltering summer day when I was invited to ride in the cab of a long-haul Kenworth semi-tractor-trailer with air conditioning and a bird's eye view of the world. We drove around town as the men in my family delivered sides of beef to local Vegas Village Shopping Centers. I would climb down and help the *driver's shotgun* unhitch the back doors of the trailers and secure them to the side of the rig. After a few trips, Bud had me muscle up with the boys. Brandishing my own meat hooks, my white butcher's coat having been smeared with the blood of the carcasses from my work, I was no *debutante*.

I soon learned I absolutely loved keeping up with the boys. A job well done meant a young girl who had unloaded her fair share between my brother Brad, my brother-in-law Ralph and my mother's new husband while being affectionately tortured in the long-standing tradition of being one of the boys. Trial by fire in a man's world just meant I had carried my own weight. There was no greater feeling than surviving the gauntlet / delivery of a remaining box of gizzards and livers thru the chicken room to the cold box. This required you to walk through a room temperature alcove space known as the chicken room. It was a stench no nose forgets!

Having seen an unspoken wink and nod between the guys, I knew something was up when I caught wind of the joke being played on me. But I emerged from the chicken room grinning ear to ear as if my nose hadn't been defiled. I was sincerely treated as one of the *guys*.

I found myself in a showroom setting forty years ago. It was 1981. That was the first time I walked into the Las Vegas Hilton Showroom. I was 16 years old. My best friend had dragged me to see Hank Williams Jr. perform. We had seats in the front row, house right directly in front of a double stack of speakers. I had a migraine for three days afterward. After that experience, I ended up leaving my job as a Teller at I.B.E.W. Plus Credit Union for my first union position as a front desk information clerk. My future husband, the nephew of a sign electrician here in Las Vegas, found me at the credit union. Or should I say, that is where destiny found me crossing paths with my future husband, my sixth-grade dodge ball partner, Jeff Wolf when he showed up at my teller window in 1984. Now married since 1987, these past 34 years have blessed us with two children and four grandchildren.

Soon, I worked my way up as a check-in clerk, guest service agent, (GSA) and night auditor running daily reports at the Flamingo Hilton. A long career working at the front desk was never really in the cards for me. In 1991, I woke up one morning after traveling to California with my mom and one year old son to help care for my grandmother who had suffered a heart attack.

I felt off. My hands were weak, and my face had gone slack as if I'd suffered a stroke. By the end of the day, I was hospitalized and within two weeks at a little Visalia hospital, having lost my ability to walk, I was given a diagnosis most people wouldn't have received after ten years of symptoms.

I had Multiple Sclerosis or MS. My prognosis was explained to me as a wheelchair and a life expectancy of 25 years from date of onset which translated as an early death by the age of 50. MS causes multiple areas of scarring throughout the brain and spinal column or central nervous system, (CNS). It swiftly and most unapologetically takes away pieces of you and sometimes gives them back. I could no longer ambulate or often hold my own head upright. Suddenly I found myself trapped in a never-ending cycle of wonder. I was barely 26 years old. One minute, I was a young mother and a wife attending college. By all accounts, I was a valid, vibrant young woman. Then in an instant - it was all gone. But Jeff wouldn't let me give up my dreams and at his insistence we took a leap of faith, and I left my vested union position.

More often than not, because I couldn't get up, I literally crawled on the ground with my infant and toddler and made it a game that lasted nearly five years. Little by little I was improving. The double vision eased. I would eventually drive again, and shop for my family. This might sound insignificant, but it eased the burden on my young husband. I could even travel across town on my own accord and visit with my mom again. These visits, one in particular, would change my life.

How I found my way to the stage was anything but typical.

I never knew I wanted to be a Stagehand. I didn't even know what one was before my first gig. It was a callout from my then union, Teamsters Local 995, looking for help to assist Local 720. They needed bodies to staff a load-out that night of an Ice Capades event that was built over the fountains at Caesar's Palace. They were looking for my stepdad, but he was out of town on a hunting trip. Mom slipped the receiver to her shoulder cupping the audio and asked if I wanted to go to work. I jumped at the opportunity. I spent the rest of the day scrambling around town to get the required tools and my credentials in order. I am here working out of Local 720 because of a phone call and a visit with my mom.

I finished the work the following day, in the wee hours of the morning, and eventually completed my paperwork to sign up with Local 720. The downside of working all night after having not worked for nearly five years, was once I sat down, I couldn't walk for three days. But as I lay there, unable to stand or gain my balance, I was actually dreaming of a future again. I was so tired of being a cripple with only a wheelchair in my mental future. Becoming a stagehand not only saved my life, it also gave me back my body. Doing something you love changes everything.

Like living so many, *'mini lives'* through each show start to finish was immediate gratification. It catapulted me and the more contacts I made my career took off. I never wanted to miss a moment. I grew stronger gig by gig. After that first exposure to the work that changed my life, I started taking Stagecraft 101 and every other Training Trust class or college course I could find. Before long I had eleven cards in Local 720's dispatch system. I was a stage and convention assistant electrician, an assistant stage and convention carpenter, and most excitedly received my Ground Rigger Certification and eventually head carpenter, props, assistant audio tech, and earned the title of A/V Tech. I found audio visual, AV Tech work to be less rewarding and challenging for my temperament. I have several other cards in wireless microphones and building flats, but these initial seven credentials served me well in building my future and letters of request, (*LOR*) kept me remarkably busy.

HOW I KNOW CRAIG

I was first introduced to Craig L. Hayes the day *'Starlight Express'* received notification that their show would be closing. I was taking an assistant audio class through local 720. We were touring the LV Hilton Showroom and had gathered at the Front of House audio booth when our instructor, Ralph Hamilton made the introductions. Craig stepped out of the shadows seemingly from out of nowhere. He politely made his greetings. Welcomed us to the adventure and quietly slipped into the background. Walking into the iconic room in1981 as a member of the audience was a remarkable experience. Touring backstage in 1997 was surreal.

It would be more than a year before our paths would cross again but I never forgot how it felt standing in that room. Ultimately, it was where I eventually discovered I wanted to be. But I had work to do first. I worked every call offered to me. At times more than one in a day. I was bouncing all over town starting at the Convention Center on another open a.s.a.p. call when my tools and gloves were stolen. *::insert eyeroll here::*, Some people! I learned fast, made connections, and always seemed to get callbacks. There were industrials, road shows, concerts, conventions, themed gatherings, and holiday parties. I did them all, whenever the phone rang which wasn't often the first three years. Somehow, my paperwork to join Local 720 kept disappearing. Not to be waylaid, I just kept submitting new packets.

Like Cinderella, I knew the clock would eventually strike midnight. The odds were I'd wake up one morning unable to get out of bed and it would all be over. One day, thanks to my husband's encouragement I just decided I could get hit by a bus as easily as ending up in a wheelchair, so I kept on building shows, a career, and kept learning everything I could about my trade.

What we do is unique. It seems like anyone who has been part of or performed in a kindergarten play or high school production can do our work. Just ask them and their faces will light up with fond remembrances. But like I said, I never had a clue about Showbiz. I just liked to build things. I love being a part of the process and the stronger I got, the more my body kept letting me.

That was until it came to running crews and all the behind the scenes work you don't get paid for. So much sitting, talking, planning, and never-ending changes because someone up the chain didn't do what Craig does, and think through the process, that eats up hours akin to babysitting when I could have been with my family. It just wasn't my cup of tea after a few years. Even though I loved the opportunity and the experience, I moved on after I was asked to join the Carrot Top's Atrium Theater at the Luxor and be a part of their Convention A/V Department. It was amazing being able to contribute to the completion of the work and being invited back over and over and over again.

Although I knew all too well the limitations of my physical body, when the phone rang, I was there. Because it seemed I now had an expiration date invisibly stamped on the bottom of my foot, being able to amplify my life thru the work and see start to finish from build out, show run and ultimate load out, was cathartic. It gave me purpose again.

Performers can't create their magic without ours. The Crew: ground riggers, basket riggers, flymen, high riggers, electricians, robotic light operators / programmers, audio engineers, carpenters, props masters, assistants, video engineers, teleprompter technicians, and the list goes on based on the scope of work and size of the ever-shrinking scale of the budget. This is only a part of what makes the magic happen it's not about pats on the back, the work does that for us!

Often, a shoestring budget can be stretched by the skills of stage craftsmen who make each and every show 'look and sound' like a high dollar production because together we can. The client is the beneficiary of technicians who have literally seen and done it all. This is what makes Craig an incredible asset because in his 55 years in Showbiz, he actually has. There always has to be someone in charge of everything on a stage. That person is Craig. He makes the work so much easier. He has planned it all. Made sure we had what we needed and a tight schedule to make it happen.

No matter the size or scale of the production he is always about the show and making it happen. He built a better mouse trap and cultivated an atmosphere of teamwork like I have never seen. The stage crew in the *"big room,"* is a family, in every sense of the word. At the risk of inflating his nonexistent ego, I will firmly add one final compliment with the hope his cranium will still fit through the large roll up door into the showroom. Craig astonishes me by the amount of energy, motivation, and never ending generosity he possesses. I learned years ago that every show or event landing on his desk is viewed in its entirety. He sees the end from the beginning and ensures everything operates like a well-oiled machine. This is skill, talent, and experience fully utilized and for someone who is visually impaired, he sees everything. Always.

He applies this same process to his writings. I'm sure he knew I would come along with this book long before he even asked me. It is highly annoying, and one of these days I am going to just have to tell him 'no.' But when I do, he just squares his shoulders and shoots back, 'I'll see you tomorrow,' and we leave it at that.

There are so many people I have treasured who gave me encouragement, opportunity, guidance and always answered when I called to staff a gig. Their names are too multiple to list in their entirety and in no particular order I have to name a few who lifted me up and gave me a chance. In Gratitude: Mike Gilligan, Dee Prince, Allen 'AD' Davis, Jerry Schmitz, Richard Kelly, Bill Murphy, Nicole Bryant Stephens, John Stephens, Bonnie Diamond and Thom Ferman.

There are story tellers and there is support staff. I ride strictly in the rumble seat of the latter. Jack of all trades hardly applies to me, but it does give you the snapshot of my job description as Head Props in the wake of my predecessor, Edwin Schauer. Ed was not a tough act to follow, he was impossible.

Ask anyone who ever worked with Ed. No one could fill his shoes or do what Ed did. He was / is a master fabricator and from the moment I met him he reminded me of my dad in so many ways also a master fabricator. When he shared with me that he had lost his father in Korea, that fact never left me. He could wield a welder like no other. I was barely fit to empty his trashcans when I found myself on an a.s.a.p. call from Local 720 late one night in 1997. Much of how I do my work today was learned from him. He was always kind and encouraging to me, as only Ed could be, reminiscent of my days hauling beef.

I will never forget the day he left the stage, as he knelt to assist a guest in the audience handing her a souvenir, I had no idea it wasn't just another vacation fishing trip. To me, from where I stand, respectfully there isn't a day that I don't recall his unmatched skill and talents, fondly.

Working behind the scenes isn't easy and never anything I talk about, let alone write about. Like Doctors and Lawyers, I am of the opinion that what we encounter behind the scenes is sacred ground and is ours to protect. Every day is my last day and I don't talk shop frivolously. With this being said, I was asked to share a story or two about my time in and around Showbiz.

1985: MY FIRST EXPERIENCE BEHIND THE SCENES

One of my first early memories of Showbiz was when I was nineteen in the cold of winter on one of those blustery frigid desert nights. I was working as a teller at IBEW Plus Credit Union when Bud invited me to come hang out with him on a production he was working transportation on. I did not know at the time, but it was an Alfred Hitchcock remake of *'Man from the South.'*

They were filming at Wilbur Clark's Desert Inn Hotel. I spent three evenings, after working all day, until the wee hours of the morning, traveling all over town, from one set to another. We were huddled together under the Marquee at the Sands, then Caesar's Palace, and back to the D.I. The hurry up and wait of Film making was excruciating but simply reminiscent of going to school all day and having to pull an all-nighter because the graveyard shift had not shown up at dad's store. It's just life in a 24-hour town. We did the work that had to be done. Sleep and holidays are not realities everyone gets to enjoy.

It was more than cold that first night under the Marquee when I showed up on Set out in front at the Sands Hotel Casino. I was dressed in an ankle length wool skirt, boots and layers of warmth, but the cold was still piercing unhindered by the large space heaters placed throughout the set. I knew how to hang in there, but I must have been shivering as disembodied voices had a broken, shorthand conversation over the radio with the two occupants of the crew van idling a few feet from me as Bud translated the information.

The next thing I knew Bud pulled open the sliding door and told me to hop in and take the very back bench seat. I did as directed without a word as my eyes met his he nodded to the man sitting in front of me and slid the door closed. He was grinning ear to ear when he threw me a glance with a tilt of his head as if to tell me to look at who I was sitting behind. It was Al Pacino's co-star of *'Scarface'* fame, Steven Bauer! John Huston, Director of *'The African Queen,'* starring Humphrey Bogart and Katherine Hepburn, was sitting in the front seat. I had seriously just died and gone to cinematic heaven. I never said a single word. I kept my mouth shut and my head down as I reveled in the presence of motion picture royalty. When the time came for me to climb out of the crew van, I paused and briefly extended a word of appreciation to both gentlemen for giving me a place to warm up between scenes. I was both humbled and mortified when they invited me to pose for pictures and autographs.

I spent the next three evenings watching John Huston, Melanie Griffith, {her husband at the time, Steven Bauer, who I had a mad teenaged crush on} and Kim Novak. Like a fly on the window, I had a front row seat to the life behind the scenes I wanted to be a part of. Those three unforgettable days also ultimately changed the course of my life.

ME WITH STEVEN BAUER.

ME WITH JOHN HUSTON.

MY DAD, RALPH B. DRAPER'S INDUSTRIAL ACCIDENT

In October 2020 I began doing background for this story by reaching out to a cousin back east. She filled in some blanks concerning my dad's accident. What I didn't know was that the accident took place at the International Hotel-Las Vegas Hilton-LVH-Westgate Resort during the final phases of construction for Elvis Presley's residency in 1969. I was stunned that the property I have called home for the majority of my 25-year career in Showbiz has such a connection to my family history.

MY TIME IN PARIS (THE HOTEL)

Have you ever abandoned your child in a hospital? I have!

In November 1999 I left my daughter in the recovery room of Valley Hospital after her tonsillectomy when I got the call to join the running crew of the off Broadway production of *'Notre Dame des Paris.'* My daughter of course couldn't speak having just had her tonsils out. But gave me a fragile little smile and an excited thumbs up when her dad and I explained the news. So, I went.

If you don't have a family behind you 150% in this business, you will never make it.

I quickly learned the magnitude of the little things that we do as Stagehands. Show business may, and often will, dish out a beating that is massive to the human body. Rehearsals and long hours magnify the frailty and often the strength of the soul. It does not discriminate between cast or crew. The extended hours can also be brutal. Safety Checks, procedures and protocols are carried out to prevent incidents and protect all concerned. Still accidents happen. People die doing what we do, and life can turn on a dime.

In 2000, one night deep into our show, it happened to one of our own. I was seated next to automation, in an elevated position backstage. This put me in direct line of sight of the acrobats performing in the bells. It was like any other night. Bells and acrobats began swinging from the automation center stage. The trim on these flying, scenic pieces was 26 feet above the deck to the top of the bell. It was 22 feet to the bottom of the bell where the crossbar was welded with a wrist anchor for the performer. These iconic renditions of the bells of *'Notre Dame des Paris'* provided a perch from which the acrobats would swing in the bells.

One young acrobat named Rodney lost his grip on the safety wrist harness and fell 22 feet to the deck, crumpled in a heap to the collective gasp of audience, cast, and crew. Because of his superior athletic physique, training, and natural ability and the custom specialized fabricated buoyancy in the flooring, he walked away from this accident with only a broken wrist. His career and life did not end that night. His schoolboy grin certainly lit up the room when he emerged the following night, smiling ear to ear as he held up his little white cast with a shrug. His sheepish, humble grin, (obviously he was just glad to be alive), comforted all who adored him.

MR. *WARMTH* AND *PERSONALITY*

I have worked with so many amazing artists and have fond memories of my years as a stagehand, but one memory stands out from the rest: Don Rickles. During his time performing at the Paris while I was Head Carpenter in the showroom and convention area there was especially remarkable for me. My mother had told me a story, a comment really that was more to one of her contemporaries, that my young ears never forgot after she and my father attended a show on the strip dressed to *'the nines'*. It was more of a *look* and a *gasp* in her remarks insisting that he was rather *'uncouth.'* Mom's story was from the early 70's when Don Rickles was *the opening act for many headliners.* The fact that I had the opportunity to stand on stage (*some*

30 years later) with this legendary performer I found to be *enlightening* and want to share a little about this man. First, he appeared to be *legally blind*, and you would never know it. His senses were keen. In the tones of light and dark his heightened awareness of his surroundings only increased his enthusiasm for his craft. It was remarkable to watch!

My responsibility during that show was to stand stage left at an exact point tucked into the wings against the curtain holding a white stage towel at a precise position. This was a part of his show because this 73 year old man, a consummate professional, would work so hard dancing and performing his skits and shoe bopping the length of the stage back and forth beneath the heat of the stage lighting he would sweat profusely. He gave this his all. If I wasn't exactly where I needed to be, he couldn't damp mop his face fast enough to maintain his timing and finish his performance. He was an exceptional gentleman who made his crass stage persona believable. I will never forget the honor of working with him and all he taught me about presentation. Definitely a class act.

A FINAL THOUGHT

I am constantly motivated by people who have disabilities that never let it stop them. Especially those in Showbiz who are transformed into their most miraculous selves, against all odds each and every time the music starts, and the curtain goes up. There are so many moving parts and pieces in entertainment that work together from load in, to audience and acrobat, there is nothing like Showbiz! I have always said they can pry my cold dead hands off the deck before I leave, and by the grace of God, I hope that it is true!

EPILOGUE

It has been said, 'If you find a career you love, you will never work another day in your life.' I am fortunate enough to have found such a career. I'm not saying some days on a stage are not long and filled with a great deal of stress, they are. I admit there are days filled with a lot of physical labor, sweat, and exhaustion. All I am saying is I would be hard pressed to find one day I would call 'work.' I can't imagine a life not filled with the experiences I have had.

The business I am in is called Showbiz. My family, friends, and co-workers take our craft very seriously. We also know making other people happy begins with us. If we can't find joy in our industry then how can anyone else who pays for our product find joy in it? This is the greatest industry in the world in the Entertainment Capitol of the World. Think about this for a moment. It's amazing to be a part of it.

The generational legacy of Leander Hayes will most likely end with me. Only three of Lea and Emma Hayes' sons made a career working full time in Showbiz. Of those three only my Father John had children working in 'The Business.'

My brothers John and Scott and sister Trina have all spent varying amounts of time working under the jurisdiction of Local 720. I was the first grandchild to pursue a career on the stages in Las Vegas and will probably be the last to exit. My first son Michael and nephew Jason both worked for a short time in the business but opted to find other employment and spend his time with their children. I am so proud of them for doing what I never could.

The day is coming when I will walk across Elvis' stage one last time and exit out the back door. When the door closes behind me it will probably be the end of 80 years of the Hayes family working in Las Vegas showrooms. This will be the conclusion of a long and incredible legacy for our family. I can only hope that whoever takes my place will continue or begin their own family legacy in Showbiz.

I truly hope you enjoyed this adventure through the history in Las Vegas on the stages where something magical happens almost every night of the week. I endeavored to be accurate concerning the characters and timelines they were involved with. If there are any errors, it is because many of the characters are no longer with us to give their personal autobiographical story. Those that did participate are in their advanced years when memories are not always accurate.

I feel it necessary to explain one more item to you. You may have noticed I spent some extra time describing my interactions with Breck Wall of Bottom's Up and Barry Manilow. I have worked with hundreds of performers and entertainers over my career. So why did I single these two out? The answer is quite simple. These two men have completely different shows to present to their fans. Breck's show is a music-comedy production and Barry sings his mega hits. Yet, each of them is a perfectionist at their craft.

In all the years I worked with each of these men, I never heard them say 'let's put on a show that's just good enough.' It was not uncommon for Breck to give me notes on his show so we could tighten up his delivery of music and comedy. You might get offended by this correcting because you think you had a really good show. Remember, it's not about what you think. It's all about what the entertainer thinks. It's his show.

Barry makes an audio and video recording of every show and watches it after his performance so he can make notes on what he sees as imperfection. We usually wait to hear from his production crew on his verdict. If the previous show went well, we can expect to have a quick sound check the following evening and prepare for the night's show. If he sees something in need of attention, we can expect to spend minutes or hours working out the issue to make it perfect.

I consider myself to be a perfectionist just like Breck and Barry. I strive to surround myself with other stage technicians who have that same drive for elevated job performance. I admire entertainers and others who are always in pursuit of the 'perfect show.

If you work with perfectionists, then you better be one too.

Once again, I hope you found this book interesting and learned about the greatest city on earth, Las Vegas and the shows we present every night.

What was that? Did you say: ENCORE, ENCORE!? Well, all right then. Let's keep this show going.

ENCORE, ENCORE!

In this 'BONUS CHAPTER' you will have the opportunity to obtain a little more insight into the history of Las Vegas. I have included an interview that was conducted by Mark Kevin Ryhlick with the University of Nevada Las Vegas Special Collections and Archives Oral History Research Center as part of the Ralph Roske Oral History Project on Early Las Vegas.

We owe a huge thank you to those involved in this interview for giving us another chance to hear the history of early Las Vegas entertainment from the man we called Grandpa.

The second part of this BONUS CHAPTER is the autobiography of Leander Fields Hayes. I have left it as he wrote it. There is some grammar, word usage, and language we might not use today within his story. It was difficult for me not to go into editor mode and correct them, but it needs to be kept intact, honest, and real. It's history.

I hope you enjoy this added material as much as I do.

UNLV University Libraries Leander Fields Hayes

An Interview with Leander Fields Hayes

An Oral History Conducted by Mark Kevin Ryhlick

Ralph Roske Oral History Project on Early Las Vegas Special Collections and Archives Oral History Research Center University Libraries University of Nevada, Las Vegas

UNLV University Libraries Leander Fields Hayes

Ralph Roske Oral History Project on Early Las Vegas University of Nevada, Las Vegas, 2019

UNLV University Libraries

Leander Fields Hayes The Oral History Research Center (OHRC) was formally established by the Board of Regents of the University of Nevada System in September 2003 as an entity of the UNLV University Libraries' Special Collections Division. The OHRC conducts oral interviews with individuals who are selected for their ability to provide first-hand observations on a variety of historical topics in Las Vegas and Southern Nevada. The OHRC is also home to legacy oral history interviews conducted prior to its establishment including many conducted by UNLV History Professor Ralph Roske and his students. This legacy interview transcript received minimal editing, such as the elimination of fragments, false starts, and repetitions in order to enhance the reader's understanding of the material. All measures have been taken to preserve the style and language of the narrator. The interviewee/narrator was not involved in the editing process.

UNLV University Libraries

Leander Fields Hayes

Abstract

On March 13, 1981, collector Mark Kevin Ryhlick interviewed local technician, Leander Fields Hayes (born on May 23rd, 1907 in Salt Lake City, Utah) in his home in Las Vegas, Nevada. This interview covers the history of entertainment in Las Vegas from the mid-forties to 1958. Brother Hayes, as he requests the collector to call him, specifically covers the local live music and comedy scenes. He also touches on the topic of segregation and how Black entertainers, such as Lena Horne, were treated when they came to perform in Las Vegas, Nevada.

UNLV University Libraries

Leander Fields Hayes

This interview is taking place on March 13th, 1981, at 4:30 P.M. The location is 88 Beasley Drive. The narrator's name is Leander Fields Hayes, and the interviewer's name is Mark Kevin Ryhlick. I will be referring to Leander Fields Hayes this afternoon as Brother Hayes, at his request.

MKR: Brother Hayes, I would—believe the first thing I would like to ask you is, what are you—the first experiences in which you remember? And what was the date in which you first came to Las Vegas?

LFH: I arrived here at about 10:30 P.M. December the 21st, 1941. And for those people that are young, that was two weeks after Pearl Harbor. And a lot of things were happening in Las Vegas that maybe the first time you heard that date it didn't mean anything to you. Submarines had been spotted off the Pacific Coast and the big power dam at Boulder City; they knew would be a prime target. So we had the military, marines, soldiers, sailors, everything, in here setting up guns, around Boulder Dam. To this day you can still see if you know where to look—machine gun mesh, up around the rim of the dam, to protect it from anyone trying to drop a bomb, you know, carry a bomb, in on the dam, or drop one down from the face of it. They were even loading a hundred and five millimeter canons that they were 'gonna use on aircraft, if that, those things starting coming over. Now I realize that this is not perhaps, show business. But it's show business in the fact that this is how it affects people. Here was a town that was supposed to have been all lights, and here was a town with their windows, with their casinos painted black. No lights outside at nights, blacker than pitch. Now that would be a hard thing to imagine today. In fact, it would be something that'd be darn hard to accomplish today, to get a blackout. Unless the power company just shut her down. Anyway, I had come down here at the request of the motion picture operator's local in this town, to give them some relief. They had not had a day off a week off or anything, vacation for nearly two years. So, my local in Logan, Utah gave me permission to come down here from works some vacations for these fellas, which they were just tickled to death to have me coming. And the date, if you recall the twenty-first of December brought me in close to New Years. So I saw first-hand, the first time Las Vegas had put on a New Year's Party, and little show. Now the little show consisted of four girls in the line. They called it the chorus line. And they did a little dance on these little platforms that they had. And no spotlight or anything like that, just a few lights outside, where a busboy would go turn on a switch or two like you use in your own home. That was at the El Rancho Vegas and I think this is maybe of some interest to people. The El Rancho Vegas was built to operate as a motel before gambling was legalized in the state of Nevada. When the gambling was legalized, the El Rancho Vegas opened up a casino. Put in the crap table and roulette wheels just like machines and the 21 tables. And made it pretty fancy for El Rancho Vegas. And it was a nice place but they had no facilities for show business and this was where my work started.

MKR: Brother Hayes, being an audio sound technician and working with the entertainment industry as it was just getting started, what are some of the advances and some of the stage techniques in which many of the new hotels that were opening up at that time innovated?

LFH: From the El Rancho we come to the big new—it was called a big new Last Frontier Hotel and I'd like to remember the name of the man who built it. 'Cause he was quite a—well, he loved good food, he loved beautiful women and he loved good shows. And I'm sorry that I can't remember the name, man's name, but I'll probably get it before we get through with this recording session. However, the Last Frontier was the first place to put on a real up-to-date show. Their show or stage facilities were very inadequate. They had built a little platform and that's about all you could say for it—for the band and for some of the entertainers to use. There was a little, like a twelve by sixteen foot hardwood floor for dancing. And the tables for dining were arranged all around that. And I have to say that with the very inadequate equipment, the young man who was operating the wires, what they call a stage electrician, was doing a beautiful job. And here's another name that I've got to wait another further to catch up with. He is now, or was up until two or three years ago, the golf pro of the Tropicana Golf Course, no, the Desert Inn Golf Course. That was right. He was the pro of the Desert Inn Golf Course. But he was the young man who was running the lights at the Last Frontier when I came into town.

MKR: What capacity did that showroom have for seating?

LFH: I think it would seat about two hundred.

MKR: About two hundred? LFH: Yes. And that's packing it.

MKR: How were the—was the business back then? Was the—did the theatre stay fairly busy?

LFH: Oh yes. But you must understand in those days, they never expected the dining facilities to pay for the show. No way. The casino paid for the show. The food charges—the price of the meals were such just to take care of the cost to the hotel, and the cost to the hotel of the food that was served and those people who served it. The show was paid for by the casino, which is entirely not that way today. And as I go along, I'll show you where the changeover was made and where people kind of got upset because of the price of seeing a show.

MKR: I see.

Oh, I'll say right in here now, when you went to a show, you didn't have to buy anything. Not a penny. They couldn't charge you a thing. If the maître D would send a captain to seat you, you got to see that show. You didn't have to order a drink or anything to eat. See the show, enjoy, and dance afterward, if you want. 'Cause they always had some good orchestras.

MKR: I see, so nothing was mandatory then, they could just go in and see the show if they wanted to and there was, had no—?

LFH: That's right. But you could understand, they had the maître D's controlling the people, which you would have to do.

MKR: But you mean only certain people would be allowed to do that, on the shows, back then, or was that—?

LFH: Well, now what I'm trying to say is—they just don't turn a flock of people loose in there to go ahead and get a table where they want to and ride corrals around. The captain or the maître D would instruct the captain to take this party, certain, certain table. But you never got to sit down and handed a ticket before you practically got your glass in your hand, like you do today. They were very accommodating. Very courteous.

MKR: A little more personal than they are today.

LFH: Yes. Yes. But yes. They were out to build up a business, and this is the way to do it. If there's one of these hotels that don't believe that just give 'em time and they'll go broke. (Laughs)

MKR: That's right.

LFH: Well, let's see, after the El Rancho—no, after the Last Frontier Hotel opened up, the two men who owned the Old Palace Theatre got the Golden Nugget Casino uptown going. And they, at that time, I've talked to 'em, of course, working for them, I knew them well, we knew them at first name association. They wanted that entire block in which today, I believe they own that entire block. But that took some maneuvering and patience to be able to acquire all that property and get that big fine casino and hotel up. And it is a beautiful place, today. But they understood because they were running a motion picture, they had association with our union and understood when I told them that their best bet was to pay a few dollars for a man to take care of their entertainers everyday there, than to just let it run wild. And the entertainers—unhappy when they were there. Unhappy when they left. Pay somebody to be a little personal service to them and watch how quick you get a topnotch show, which they did. And this is where they really made money, at the Golden Nugget.

MKR: Brother Hayes, who were some of the entertainers that the Golden Nugget was featuring? And what were the different forms of entertainment that the other hotels were offering at this time in Las Vegas?

LFH: Slim Whitman. He was one of the entertainers, which of course, if I could recall all of the wonderful western country music entertainers that come into the Golden Nugget, oh why they had it and drew the crown, believe me.

MKR: Was that one of the—kind of the top places for entertainment here in Las Vegas at that time?

LFH: Only for western and cowboy music.

MKR: I see.

LFH: What do they call it? Western?

MKR: Country music.

LFH: Country music, country and western music.

MKR: Yes.

LFH: That's the kind of entertainment they had there. And of course it fit right along with the, you know, as the Frontier and now when you go down to the Last Frontier Hotel, there you see the lavish, beautiful girls and beautiful dresses and fine music and wonderful food.

MKR: Was that more of a higher class establishment?

LFH: Yes. Yes. That was playing to the elite of the entire western part of the country, that's what that was.

MKR: I see.

LFH: And then, they started construction of the Flamingo Hotel. Now the Flamingo was built with materials that the war production board said were not available to anybody. But they got them. Steel, copper, concrete, hardwood. And they'd build a beautiful place, that Flamingo Hotel. And this man, Benny Siegel, it was quite open in all the papers and everything around, that he was one of the key men in Murder Incorporated of Chicago. Well, I got to know him personally in first name, the way we greet each other. And you would never, at least I would never know that he was a murderer or anything else. He was just a good employer. That's all I could say for him. And one who would tell you, you ask a question, he'd give you a straight out answer. Because after the Flamingo opened, which was—and this was quite a day, the 26th of December, the day after Christmas, 1946, and that's the day to remember. The first two days were invitational only. But it was free to you. You had of course, to play at your gambling, however the management would put the money in your hand, if they thought you wanted to gamble and didn't want to risk any of your own, I know of that because I'd seen it many times. But the show and the dinner or the second show, whenever it happened to be, was free to those people who got an invitation. And the unusual thing about this invitation was that it was delivered by courier in a big limousine. I know because I received one at my home on Fifteenth Street. Here this great long black Cadillac pulled up and a uniformed courier comes and brings this big beautiful invitation to my front door. So as I say, the first two nights were invitation. And then, they get them ready for the big New Year blowout. And a lot of people get it, a misconception of when the Flamingo opened and there have been a lot of people who have made positive statements, that it opened on Christmas, that is didn't open until the first of the year, you know, and some said it was in the 1940s, first of the year, 1948, practically. But it was New Year's or Christmas, before New Years of 1946, '47 that it opened up. It was the largest, most prestigious show that had ever been produced, out in the west. In the show were such names as Jimmy Durante, Rosemary, Xavier Cugat, and what was that girl's name? She's still around. Anyway, that was the show and this brought down a lot of criticism from the other hotels. The first show of the Flamingo Hotel was December the 26th, 1946. Now these are coming from papers that were written a long time ago. Jimmy Durante costarring Rosemary, Xavier Cugat Orchestra, and the June Taylor dancers. Now that in itself was a—normally a show. And this—oh yes. This entire show was a cost of five thousand dollars a week. Nobody had ever spent that kind of money on a show in Las Vegas or any place else around this country. This brought condemnation of Ben Siegel, by the Last Frontier and the El Rancho Vegas, because they've been putting on shows for maybe twelve hundred, fifteen hundred dollars. MKR: Now that was per week, again, right?

LFH: Yes. Mm-hmm.

MKR: I see.

LFH: Now all of a sudden the figures up to five thousand, would you believe?

MKR: Did that—were those figures kind of out of the reach of those other establishments at the other hotels?

LFH: Oh no. But they just didn't like to pay that kind of money for entertainment.

MKR: I see.

LFH: But from that day on, that's when this old man got his foot in the door. And I just kept pushing it open, pushing it open. Finally we came up with a show like at the Stardust hotel, no one had ever seen the likes of it in the United States. I had friends of mine who worked in the Radio City Musical, in New York City, come out here to see that. They didn't believe it could be done— what we had done, but we'll come back to more about that Last Front—or the Stardust Hotel, (Unintelligible) show, a little later here.

MKR: I had one question, that—as far as the entertainers when the entertainment was just getting started—how were the entertainers to work with as far as the, maybe some of the entertainers that were just breaking into the business versus some of the established oldtime entertainers? Well, you have to remember this—that no entertainer ever breaks in on any of these hotels even today, for the first time.

LFH: Well, they're all trained, they're all brought up to

understand what the rules are on the stage before they ever get there. But once in a while, one little smart aleck will get through but they'll cut him down now. That don't mean my people, supporting the entertainers. I mean to manager to the hotel would put that guy in his place real quick.

MKR: How were the entertainers to work with as far as, on a person-to-person level?

LFH: Always the—what we call the pros were beautiful to work with. They seem to understand your problems and would always try to work with you to alleviate the problem, to put them in the best show, atmosphere that's possible. But not demanding things that they couldn't get, beautiful. But again, like I say, the new beginners, some of the demands they make is ridiculous. But the thing that'll always amaze you would be how they come in and start demanding things. Not by their own experience but somebody who is managing them, their show manager, he will try to get somebody like—security at one of the lounges here, with no follow spot at all. And maybe a little keyboard that somebody has to push with their foot in the band a little change of lights. This fellow is trying to get a spotlight effect on him. Now there's where you have trouble. It's not really the entertainer, it's the person who is their manager that generally causes you the trouble. As soon as you could spread those to the part, and let each one of those understand what facilities you've got, and you'll give 'em the best they can. It cools down and maybe for a couple of weeks or a month, however long they stay, everything is happy.

MKR: How did the entertainers feel about Las Vegas then? How did they feel about appearing here?

LFH: Well, now here's quite a story. We're not 'gonna go off tape here are we? This is—oh, we should (unintelligible) alright. This is concerning—and since you asked that question, I must remind you, at that time when I came here—no black people were allowed in these resort hotels. So when you get entertainers like Lena Horne and I don't know whether you know of her but she was one of the top entertainers in the 1940s. She's still a pretty big star, she was on one of these big shows, Dean Martin Show not too long ago, I'd say within three or four weeks. Anyway, they had to stay at a woman's home, over on the Westside. And this is a terrible thing to say, I even hate to mention it. Because it's degrading to everybody. I don't even like to think that the people in Las Vegas would even sit still to see such a thing happen. If this person can come in and entertain all those people out in that beautiful dining room, they should be entitled to the best room in that hotel, if they want it. But this is the thing I'm bringing up. Anyone, who came here was supposed to follow those rules, Black or White. Such a people, as I said, Lena Horne, Pearl Bailey.

MKR: Brother Hayes. After these circumstances changed and there wasn't any segregation, where did many of the entertainers stay, that performed at the Flamingo Hotel?

LFH: So, then, Lena Horne, like, she gets to the big top suite in the Last Frontier Hotel, or Flamingo Hotel. Do you remember what the original building in the Flamingo Hotel looked like?

MKR: I remember what it looked like before, they recently changed it into the Flamingo Hilton.

LFH: Oh. Yes. That—

MKR: Probably in 1968, '69, '70.

LFH: Yes, well, that had been changed a lot before then. But that was the suite of rooms that Ben Siegel had. The only way you could get up there was the elevator. And he could stop the elevator any time he wanted to.

MKR: What did they call that?

LFH: The Penthouse. Yes. I got—(unintelligible) well, anyway, when—when the Flamingo got to operating for about the year, Wilbur Clark started building his Desert Inn Hotel. And this was then, we would call it, the fourth resort hotel in Las Vegas. And there of course, I got my foot in the door again, and then we began to build up show business right there. After they could see what we could do.

MKR: What are some of the changes in which you innovated into the industry at that time?

LFH: Oh yes. Now this, I'm glad you reminded me of that. Because this is quite important as far as I'm concerned, in that you have to remember—or you should be informed that the man that controls the lighting board was always on the stage. Either right stage or left stage and I'll always remember right stage or left stage is to the performer, not to the audience.

So you don't get mixed up. And down the stage was down towards the footlights and upstage is up towards the backdrop. Now there was no way for the man who was running the lighting control board to see what he was—if you would use, let me use the expression, the picture he's painting with lights. And if you go in there, you'll see where this is not my idea, this is some editorial wise guy who tells you that I did—I was the, was one of the great painters. I'll get to it. I said, the lighting controls have got to be out in the front where the man who is controlling them sees what the effect is.

MKR: In other words, sees what the audience sees.

LFH: That's right. He must see what his lights are doing. And if he has any artistic ability at all, he will paint a beautiful picture with the beautiful lights. And there again is where we come right out to the front. Las Vegas began right there, to be the showplace of the world. Because nobody else could do that, see. I wouldn't allow another place built in this town, but what—they let the lighting control be out in the front. Then I had to start fighting for the sound control. Always before they put the sound booths like at the Flamingo off on stage left, up above. Inside a little room. Now how in the sand hill does the man controlling the sound know what the poor audience out there is 'gonna hear. No way. I spent the next twenty-five years of my life fighting maître D's and owners of those places to get the sound, control man, the man controlling the sound out right in the middle of the audience. So he could hear what they were hearing. And by this everybody was happy.

MKR: Brother Hayes, what was the quality of the audio sound equipment that you had to work with at this time?

LFH: Well, this is a question that any student in electronics should be interested in following through to verify what I'm telling them. When the sound system was installed at the Flamingo Hotel it had a lot of small speakers in the ceiling. Now to the best of our knowledge in those days it was referred to as a seventy vault line to the speakers and then tap off transformers allowing a certain amount of power to go to that speaker column. And then many speakers on that single line. This is called a seventy vault line. The big problem there that we didn't recognize for quite a while and maybe engineers knew about it before I did. But I know for one man who began to ask questions why do we have all this distortion in the sound? Each one of those speakers reproduces a certain percentage of sound. And each speaker in those days had a different amount of clear sound reproduction or distortion. Each one of the little transformers added distortion. The microphones added distortion. The amplifier itself in those days, the specifications for sound systems were eight percent distortion. Now if you ask somebody just coming up in the audio sound business today, how would you like to have an amplifier with the best possible response, eight percent distortion? That man would tell you immediately, you can't run it. You got distortion before you got any output sound. That was it.

MKR: Brother Hayes, who were some of the great entertainers that you remember that were playing back at the Flamingo at this time and what were some of the—the difficulties in which you personally had putting on the show in which they were giving at that time?

LFH: We had one group at the Flamingo that was much

in demand. And one of the fellows are still one of the great entertainers. I think it was him and his two brothers. The Williams Brothers. Williams? Does that sound—? Andy Williams, sure.

MKR: Oh yes. Andy Williams and his two brothers and they were coached by a very famous woman choreographer. And she was part of their act.

MKR: So Andy Williams, he used to perform with his brothers?

LFH: Oh yes. They had a beautiful act. But our problem was, we had to have the microphones hanging down over their head. And they didn't make a microphone that would hang down and let the sound come up and hit into the diaphragm of the microphone that way. It was this big old bulky—you probably seen them or maybe you forgot 'em, you don't see 'em much anymore, a Shure microphone. Well, in those days, that was one of the best microphones, as far as pick up. It would pick up with so much other distortion around it, no other microphone would, could compete with it. And this was a big old microphone. They made another one that's smaller. But it had to hang from the ceiling. Now that's tough to pick up somebody underneath. So we'd hang three of these microphones down, and I had a hand line, up in the booth—now remember this— this is the lighting booth, is up and in front of the stage. And you're looking down at the stage like this. I'm holding that string that controls those microphones up and down in my teeth. Over my head I've got the old, dimmers, and over here on my left hand, I've got a big seventy amperes spotlight. That was my job.

MKR: So they were—everything was controlled manual back then?

LFH: Yes. Everything practically like that is controlled manually, today. No getting out of it.

MKR: This is the end of side one. Please turn the cassette tape over for side two.

LFH: Time and a little maybe later than that is when Dean Martin and Jerry Lewis came out from their first appearance at the Capital Theatre in New York. But they found out that their type of entertainment was not suited for the vaudeville theatre, theirs was nightclub stuff. And they come out here and they were a big hit right off. But they were young and those were the two I'm always referring back to when I say, you get the young entertainers and they're hard to handle. They just don't understand. But always Dean Martin was the easiest. Jerry Lewis was the hardest man to satisfy. But both wonderful people. I have nothing but good to say about them. However, I had my tongue in the cheek when I said that, because they got drunk on the stage at one night and began to squirt seltzer bottles that they had taken off the tables of their audience, you know, that, this once were the whole audience and the entertainers make a big party right on the stage. They're squirting the seltzer bottles in to my microphones.

MKR: (Laughs)

LFH: Well, the microphones are still working fine and I don't give it another thought until the next night we get ready for a show. You couldn't get a sound out of that microphone.

That seltzer bottle was sullen. The diaphragm on that microphone was just welded in there solid.

MKR: Oh my goodness.

LFH: I never would have forget that. (Laughs)

MKR: Did—did Dean Martin and Jerry Lewis when they first came out here, did they work together back then?

LFH: Oh yes.

MKR: Or worked separately?

LFH: They were a team.

MKR: Oh I see. They—

LFH: They do all of—that's the way they, Dean Martin, Jerry Lewis. Martin and Lewis.

MKR: I see. So they initially started out together.

LFH: Oh yes. Yes. It wasn't until after they got success at the Flamingo and two motion pictures that they split up.

MKR: How were—how'd the pair work together on stage?

LFH: Oh for those days beautiful, they made a beautiful team. Dean more or less the straight man and Jerry the comedian.

MKR: I see.

LFH: And here it was a real good act, for night clubs.

MKR: I see.

LFH: They get pretty raucous at some times. If that word means anything to you. And after we come at that point in show business in Las Vegas, you must remember that such shows as Liberace as appearing at the Last Frontier.

MKR: What date would this be now? What time was this?

LFH: Now we're talking approximately, well, Liberace was coming into the Last Frontier before the Flamingo ever opened.

MKR: I see. Okay.

LFH: And the El Rancho was hanging in there with one of their favorite comedians and the great nightclub entertainer, Joe W. Brown. And you probably never heard of him but one the—

MKR: No. I'm not familiar.

LFH: Corniest comedians that ever come on a stage but the kind that nightclub, making the rounds of the nightclub they—they loved him. Because he would tell these dirty stories, off cover stories, or whatever you want to call them and make you like 'em. He was—he was, in those days, a lot like (unintelligible) that appears at the Flamingo—or at the Sahara.

MKR: Not Rich Little? Or?

LFH: No. A comedian. A round faced guy who's always getting on the people in the audience.

MKR: Not Buddy Hogget?

LFH: Rick, Rick.

MKR: Oh.

LFH: Rick—what's his name? Rickett?

MKR: Don Rickles?

LFH: Don Rickles. Joe W. Brown was a lot like Joe E. Brown—had that same kind of an act. But more suave. He was—oh, he was delightful to hear. Now this is going on at the El Rancho, Liberace is appearing at the Last Frontier and he comes in with this beautiful eleven foot gold grand piano. And in clothes of course that would just knock your eye out.

MKR: So in other words he was more or less, pretty much the same back then as he is today?

LFH: Oh yes.

MKR: In the flashy outfits?

LFH: Oh yes.

MKR: And.

LFH: Those clothes of his were really something and when he wore a mink cape you can bet your life that was the best mink he could buy in this entire world. And nobody had ever seen a man wear such clothes as that.

MKR: How did the people at that time react to his kind of, I guess, innovative dress and style of performing?

LFH: This—I'm not going to say that this interfered with his personality. Because he had the most winning personality of any man you would ever meet. Now some of the other men may not like him at all because they might feel him to be a little effeminate.

MKR: Mm-hmm.

LFH: But when you took and looked at the man the way he dressed, the way he played the piano, and you knew darn well he had to take care of those hands of his, there was no other way.

MKR: Mm-hmm.

LFH: So he was a full man, and if you wore those clothes it was of course to add to his—whatever the word is that they--

MKR: Unique, maybe, or? '

LFH: Cause he would just—he would just lay the women on the floor you know that.

MKR: (Laughs)

LFH: (Laughs) But he—he was the entertainment, and still is, I'm telling you. He would hold up his own with the best of them, today. Then we go back to the Flamingo. The Flamingo begins to bring in such shows as Olson and Johnson, now maybe you don't know what they were.

MKR: No. I'm not familiar with them. Maybe you could elaborate. Were they a singing team or comedian, or?

LFH: Oh no. Olson and Johnson brought in a big variety show.

MKR: I see.

LFH: And it would move so fast that they'd have to have a man in the booth with the spotlight operators calling the spotlight cues at the opening of their show. That's how fast this thing was. The people weren't on the stage. They were out in the audience.

MKR: Hm.

LFH: So with the—the cue master would come into the booth and he'd tell the men, "I'll give you right and left." And he would stand where he could—he could show, out through the port window, about where the person was standing, and the guy running the spotlight was supposed to pick it out, couldn't see a thing, until he popped that light open and it couldn't come sneaking open, it had to pop right open. If you were wrong then you were supposed to move quickly and get right on the person. But the entertainers that were out in that audience, knew your problems as a spotlight operator and they would always move towards the light the instance they saw it come on.

MKR: I see.

LFH: So that always—Nevada was a unison of efforts, you know there that you couldn't beat. Well, now we come to the Last Frontier, which had Liberace and I was telling you about his piano and his costumes. He was an entertainer. With Joe E. Brown and his jokes at the El Rancho and Frankie Lane at the El Rancho, they had beautiful songs like—what did I say that favorite song? Mule Train. Maybe that will bring somebody's ears up and perking right there. And Spike Jones at the Flamingo and his crazy show. In the middle of the year, we would have Spike Jones, at the end of the year we would have Olson and Johnson. In the middle of the year, we would have beautiful Lena Horne. Or—she's on an advertising on television right now—Maria Alberghetti, an opera type singer.

MKR: I see.

LFH: Now—

MKR: Back in these—

LFH: Go ahead.

MKR: Back in these—back in these times is, since initially you mentioned that gambling wasn't in most of the hotels, now since gambling is becoming more popular, and they're more or less structuring their things around gambling. What was the—the atmosphere at that time within the casinos?

LFH: The big gambler, of course, had his way. Anything he wanted, he could have, as long as he paid for it. And that was Ben Siegel (unintelligible). Anything our big gambler guests want, give it to 'em, and we'll make no objections, as long as they pay for it.

MKR: You mean pay for it initially, or by gambling?

LFH: You must understand, that when the man is handing his bill for his room, his meals or whatever, at the hotel, the hotel will either right off his expenses to what he may have lost in the casino. Or if he has won, the management at the casino will say, "Okay, take that guys bill and the hotel will pay for it." We want this guy back next year, or next month, or whenever. You see this is where the casino manager was in complete control and it's by his astute understanding of that particular gambler, he could keep the man coming back and he can keep the hotel casino making money all the time. And the guest is as happy as a (unintelligible).

MKR: So in other words, back then, that the casino managers, they had complete control of the casino itself?

LFH: Oh yes. Yes. You bet.

MKR: What was the relationship between the managers of the hotel casino operations and the entertainers?

LFH: When, the first entertainment started to be a part of the casino hotel operations in Nevada, the entertainment was free to the guest. You could go in their fine dining rooms or their lounges and it wouldn't cost you a thing. You didn't have to buy a drink, you could come see the finest show they ever put on and you wouldn't have to pay ten cents for a coke. And I mean they used to fine twenty-five cents if you wanted a coke, that's all you pay. This gives you some insight as to the change that's been made. But it will also show you the amount of money that was spent in 1947 compared to what is being paid for entertainment in 1980.

MKR: What did a cocktail drink cost back then?

LFH: Bar whisky, as it's called. In those hotels, it was fifty cents a full ounce. Not seven eighths of an ounce, not three quarters of an ounce. And bar whisky meant that, whatever that hotel could buy at the best price, that's what they served. Or—the quality of the bar depended on what kind of whisky they served.

MKR: I see.

LFH: Now a mixed drink, they were generally seventy-five cents. That would be a martini—whatever they are I don't know about. But as they call it, call whisky, that gets when the—that's what you get when the guest says I want (unintelligible) scotch. Or I want some other.

MKR: Yes.

LFH: A name brand. That's—that's when the price went up from fifty cents to seventy-five cents. I see. But I don't know today what they charge. You have to remember that I haven't been out on the Strip to speak of at all since about 1968 or '69.

MKR: I see.

LFH: Now—

MKR: Getting back to—

LFH: I recalled a conversation that I had with Ben Siegel, shortly after the big opening of the Flamingo Hotel, in that there was not any business coming into the room. And of course, our country was rather in a Depression right then. The war stopping and the production out at Henderson, BMI, and it would seem like there was something else going on around here. There was a war production thing. I can't think of it now. Boulder came close to closing up Nellis Air Force Base. All these things had their effect on the economy of Las Vegas. So I asked Mr. Siegel if there was anything that he thought I might do to help improve the attractions on the stage, and he told me, first name basis, he said, "Lea, you just put on as good a show as you can from the entertainment I provide for you. And as long as we've got one man, the right man, in that audience, or in that casino." He says, "We're doing fine. Don't you worry." Well, that is when I learned what this show business is all about. And from that derived another rule of which I passed on to the other members of our union as the hotels begin to build up and our union membership began—today it's over a thousand people. Remember that for those people out in that dining room, this is opening night. I don't care whether the show has been appearing for a year, this is opening night for that audience in that show room. And they will always look at it that way. And you work just as hard as you did on the opening night of that show. And if you will entertain the guest or this gambler, the hotel and the casino is 'gonna do fine. The management is 'gonna be happy. You will always have good jobs. And our production of big shows in Las Vegas will just keep mushrooming, until we're—we used to have two or three men of what we called on stage, we'll have a hundred. That's literally so. A hundred men working on that stage, like the MGM, those huge stages. Now that's some difference in payroll for entertainment. Now you could see where the last entertainment that's coming or the last advertising that's incoming for Siegfried and Roy. It's opening at the Frontier Hotel. They're building a whole show around Siegfried and Roy. Now this now again is 'gonna take a big crew on the stage. This I'd love to see. I want shows in this town—not these dirty little old shows that some of these places put on. I want big lavish productions for the finest talent the world has got to offer—I want in Las Vegas. I forget the title of that one but here was—again they had what was called the Dancing Waters.

MKR: Mm-hmm.

LFH: On the stage, of the Royal Nevada. Now the

Dancing Water is a permanent set, right there in the middle of that stage.

MKR: Mm-hmm.

LFH: And they had to work the scenery and everything over the top of that. Because they just covered it over when they brought in this Broadway show.

MKR: Hm. My goodness.

LFH: And I'll never forget the problems we had to get around, to get that dang show on that stage. But the management was not 'gonna have that Dancing Waters moved. First, because they had signed a contract that that Dancing Waters would be used a certain number of months or weeks or something in every year. So after the tremendous expense of getting it installed, they were not about to have it taken out. Because, under the contract, they'd have to come right back and put it back in again. The fellow on the show MASH, do you remember what his name is?

MKR: Oh, (Unintelligible).

LFH: What's his first name? Allen Alda.

MKR: Yes.

LFH: His father appeared in the lead of this show that was at the Royal Nevada Hotel. Nicely, nicely, was his partner in this gambling racket and here just the other night I saw one of the newer MASH programs, where his father appeared with him. When I saw the man I thought, good heaven's I know that guy. But I hadn't seen the opening upper who was starring or co-starring or whatever. But towards the end, they had built the show around Robert Alda, the father, Robert Alda, the father of—Allen. And it was real clever the way they brought this in. And the father used to be a physician for the Army. A surgeon for the Army. Now here's the boy in MASH doing the same thing, and his father gets back and he was an older man, and it even says so in the show, that he hadn't practiced for so many years but things get so bad that 4077 MASH, that they put him right on the operating table and he passes out. (Laughs) He can't take it anymore. And this is where I wind up finding out who this man was whose face looks so familiar to me.

MKR: Oh yes.

LFH: He carried the lead in that show.

MKR: Brother Hayes in the early development in Las Vegas, how did other people react when they heard the name Las Vegas?

LFH: Well, in those days the minute you mentioned the name, Las Vegas, man, that's like mentioning EF Hutton—everybody listens. (Laughs)

MKR: (Laughs)

LFH: I went to my first convention or reunion in Chicago

in 1946—that was right after the war—1945, and I took my wife along with me to Chicago. I never was able to get her to go to New York. She'd, she went through to Chicago and after that she never wanted to get into a big city again. No way. She was a country girl. Anyway, I took a lot of—what do you call them? Cigarette ashtrays from the various hotels and casinos here in town and a lot of literature and brochures and everything, and I put them out—put them out on the delegates—at the delegates seats.

MKR: Okay.

LFH: In this big convention hall at the Sheraton Hotel. Well, no one ever forgot Lea Hayes or no one ever forgot Las Vegas after that. And it wasn't too many years after that meeting that we had in Chicago that we had the executive board of our union, holding their winter—I guess they call it a quarterly meeting, in Las Vegas.

MKR: Yes.

LFH: And I got some information on that right in here.

MKR: How would you—how do you feel entertainment in our country was—is? Did many parts in the country have entertainment like we did here?

LFH: No place. Not even New York. And that is a fact. Now when I say it I have to put in reservations. Because we're talking about entertainment of any kind. And you couldn't deny that if you were putting on a big hockey game in Madison Square Garden in New York, you're going to have a hell of a crowd of people out there. We had nothing like that. But we tried it out and it didn't work in Las Vegas. We put on a big hockey game over at the convention hall, after it was opened. It wouldn't draw flies because we have all this live entertainment, human beings, beautiful music, and girls. You can't—(Laughs) a hockey game can't compete with that. It's like the guy who built the big racetrack over there, Joe W. Brown, his racetrack wouldn't go either. Because even a (unintelligible) can't compete with a beautiful girl.

MKR: Oh. What led you to go into business for yourself, in the audio sound industry?

LFH: Well, you could not get—you couldn't buy anything, either out of New York, Chicago, or Hollywood, that you wanted here. They invariably would through available, ship out to you, the gift cards, or something that nobody else wanted. Or at least that's the way it appeared to me because I knew what we were supposed to get in first class equipment. We were not getting it. So that's when I decided that I had to go to the extent of starting up a business, whereby we would make these contractors and these architects build and equip the—just so we could put good shows on.

MKR: Brother Hayes, what was one of the—the finest shows in which you could remember, maybe from the mid to the late fifties?

LFH: Now when they come in with a show like the Lido show, the first Lido show, which opened around the fifth to the seventh of July, 1958, in the Stardust Hotel. No one—at least no one that I know of in the United States, had ever seen a show like that. And I kept pretty close of what was going on in show business.

MKR: What were some of the innovations that—that had been put into that stage?

LFH: Well, my son Gordon, he worked very close with the producers of the show from (unintelligible). And he would tell them what we can do and they would tell him what they'd like to have. Now all this was going on during construction. So we're getting the greatest amount of facility out of the stage space that could possibly be done.

MKR: I see, so in other words that stage was more tailored to it before the show itself. Right. Unlike nearly any stage you ever saw, the orchestra was on a big beautiful round platform, probably fourteen or fifteen feet above the people's heads, at ring side area.

MKR: Mm-hmm.

LFH: And another circular stage was on the other side to confirm that this was where the orchestra was. Now the orchestra was such that we would take the sound we wanted out of that orchestra to mix with the sound went out in the room with the entertainer's voice or whatever.

MKR: Mm-hmm.

LFH: Nothing went into that room before unless it went

through to echo chamber. The dining room was made as sound proof or sound resistant, absorbent as you could make it. If you went out there without that sound going through that echo chamber, you would be dead and flat. Because all the walls and the ceiling and everything else was made to absorb that sound. But once you put it through the echo chamber and control the time lag in the echo chamber, that sound was just as lively as though you were out in the mountains or whatever the scene on the stage was supposed to reproduce. It was the first time there'd ever been a three channel stereo system. The guy would start to sing from this—this was over on stage left, the orchestra was on stage right. The guy would start to sing standing up here on this platform opposite the orchestra. And that's where his voice was coming from. He'd come down this beautiful stairway and onto the stage. Then he'd come over here and now the sounds coming right from him, right here in the middle. He goes over there by the orchestra and there's the sound coming from in there.

MKR: In other words the stage, was equipped so that the sound would more or less come from directly wherever he was located?

LFH: Right. Right.

MKR: This is a conclusion of the interview with Brother Leander Fields Hayes. I would like to sincerely thank him for his graciousness and his kindness in offering himself and his home for this interview and for taking the time out of his schedule to be able to discuss his remarks and feelings and thoughts about the early period in Las Vegas.

I am including Lea's Autobiography here so those who didn't know him very well can get a little insight into what an extraordinary life he led.

Remembrances: A collection by Leander Fields Hayes

Born May 23, 1907

Departed February 17, 1983

In Memory of Leander Fields Hayes

(May 23, 1907 to February 17, 1983)

And

Lavenia Emma Casper

(January 21, 1910 to May 16, 1974)

Children:

Gordon Lean Hayes

Gilbert Melvin Hayes

Keith Casper Hayes

Charles Douglas Hayes

George Emmit Hayes

John Leander Hayes

Patrick Wray Hayes

This collection was transcribed from a rough draft penned by Leander Field Hayes. The original context was left as is with the exception of minor spelling and punctuation corrections.

Prepared for the Hayes Family Reunion

June1, 1991

Las Vegas, Nevada

CHILDHOOD MEMORIES

ST. JOSEPH, MISSOURI - 1910

In 1910, my mother and father took me to St. Joseph, Missouri to visit Grandfather and Grandmother Dunn. Grandfather Dunn is in the history of the State of Missouri and can be found in the genealogical library in Salt Lake City. I have read it. He was the Superintendent of Streets and Harbors - a very important job. He had this job for a number of years, and I think he died still having the commission of the job. He lost one son in the Missouri River because they had to get the water to sprinkle the streets out of the river; and the young boy fell off the wagon into the river and drowned.

When we got to St. Joseph, I found out that my Grandfather Dunn was a large man, big. He stood over six foot tall and weighed over 300 lbs. You could understand why he could be boss man of a lot of colored people. I had to stay with him one night in the big house at 418 North 20th Street in St. Joseph, Missouri. He carried me up the stairs to the bedroom and here was this huge canopy bed Grandfather slept in. He laid me down on the bed and I thought, "Boy, this is sure a comfortable bed." Then he crawled into that bed and I found out it was a feather mattress; and the minute he laid down, I flopped right over against him.

It happened to be that my mother and father had gone out to an opera or a show and that was why I was left with Grandfather. We got along just fine. When we got up the next day, snow was all over the ground, about two feet deep.

A day or two after that, I had the opportunity to go and see a show at the Missouri Theater. In the snow, one man was dressed as a woman, and two men sang as they walked up and down the aisles of this theater. There was a movie and vaudeville and singing. The song they sang was "Oh, You Beautiful Doll". This was the first show I remembered attending.

VERNAL, UTAH - 1912

In the spring of 1912, we moved to Vernal, Utah. Dad had the job of getting a big store on a paying basis again. They store was facing bankruptcy and he had been sent by the Intermountain Creditman's Association of Salt Lake City to place the store on a paying basis again. The store was called the Ashley Co-op. The house we lived in was a block north of the store and at the corner was the Unita Freight Lines. The Uinta Freight Lines brought all the parcel post and postage of the department plus all the freight because there were no train lines within miles of Vernal, Utah; and, it is still there in 1977.

In Vernal, I got acquainted with Bishop Davis who lived in the next house down the street by our house and "Mother" Davis as I soon learned to call her. The family consisted of Mamie Davie, George, Karl and Lawrenece. Mr. Davis was the Bishop of the LDS Church and also good friends with the Dr. Martin family. They had two sons, Manfred and dewayne. Right across the street, north of us, was the McAllister's bit white home - still standing there today, as does our old home. Mrs. McAllister was an intelligent, well-read person and she used to be quite a good friend with mother because they loved good books and this set up quite a friendship.

Dr. Earl Douglas, the man who discovered the dinosaurs in the Dinosaur National Monument east of Verna took me and my sister Kathryn, on our first trip out to the area in which they excavated these dinosaurs. A dinosaur is a name for these prehistoric mammals. Some people will call them reptiles. It has been discovered within the last ten years that the dinosaur is a warm blooded animal (Approximately 1967).

Dr. Douglas (receiving his doctorate degree at the University of Utah) set up his camp which consisted of three tents, 10 X14 army type tents situated alongside the Green River, a mile from his camp to dig (excavate). I, Gaylin and my sister, Kathryn, slept in one tent. Mr. and Mrs. Douglas slept in the other; while the third was used for cooking, washing, etc.

We soon found out that Mrs. Douglas was a crack shot with a rifle or shotgun. She would always try to raise a few Black Minorca chickens out there. It seemed odd to see these beautiful chickens, laying big white eggs, running around in that sagebrush. Big hawks and eagles and other predators that lived there were after these chickens all the time. When she would hear the chicken squawk, she would grab the shotgun and run out; and it was too bad if one of those hawks made a dive for one of her chickens because she would sure bring him down. I learned a lot about the world at this age living out at the dig at five or six years of age. I got to use the little chippers, the camel hair brushes. I learned what to look for, what to be careful within searching for the silica. It is the salts of the earth that replaces the bone in exact form and this is what they call petrified replica of the bone.

I remember, vividly on the 4th of July 1914, Dr. Douglas had a mockup made of Stigasaurus which was fifteen feet long and the armor was upright, triangular, bony plates running from the head to the tail and anyone who has studied anything about dinosaurs has certainly seen the pictures of this one. By duplicating this animal, they have been able to prove that the bony armor regulated the body heat and kept it alive. This has been discovered only in the past five years. The burlap covering of the mockup made the dinosaur appear real. Further down along in the parade, rode a King and four kids underneath pushing it down the road. The Diplaudacus measured 80 feet from head to tail. Dr. Douglas captioned this picture "Beauty and the Beast"

ST. JOSEPH, MISSOURI - 1914

I believe we made a trip to St. Joseph about 1914 in the summer aboard a Pullman Train. These trains were fully serviced for dining, sleeping and relaxation. The porters rendered excellent service in a mannerly fashion. My father would spend many hours visiting with cohorts in the mercantile business in the Club Car, also known as the Observation Car. After the porter would make up by berth, I would climb the ladder to the upper berth, close the curtains and the rhythm of the train would lull me to sleep. I became a pet of the porters and waiters since I was often the only small child aboard.

The bathrooms aboard these Pullman Trains were exquisitely done in mahogany woods, genuine silver plated fixtures and beautiful, expensive bevelled-edged mirrors. When you flushed the toilet (only when the train was in progress) it would empty right out on the tracks and you could hear the clackety-clacks flashing by .I travelled for a period of ten to twelve years with my father on these trains which I was so fascinated with. I think, that like me, many others miss these fine, smooth, quiet, fully serviced passenger trains. The meals that were served from their menu are unlikely to be found anywhere else today. They were fantastic! The linen was real and beautiful, and the silverware was real, served with the style of 1912. Everything was fashionable from that era.

WICHITA, KANSAS

We were snowbound in Wichita, Kansas, prior to the 1930's as is recorded in the history books. The snow had almost made the train depot unable to be seen. Food was running out and things were becoming serious. We were stuck there two days before we were able to move out. Just before we left, I remember that I had to put on my cap and coat inside the train to keep warm. I also got into a cyclone in Kansas. I did get the chance to actually see the cyclone approaching before hastening into a cyclone cellar for safety. Except for hearing a heavy wind, I didn't know anything was happening until I emerged from the cellar and saw the damage to the countryside. My Uncle's property was not damaged, luckily.

EARLY SCHOOL YEARS

I had my first schooling in Vernal, Utah beginning in the year of 1911-12 at age six. I had to go to the Willcox Academy. This was a private school because my mother was not going to send me to that Mormon school which was the county school. Well, that was a mistake. A child should never be made to go into a separate place from the friends that he had near his home. They should all go to school together. Evidently, somewhere along the line my mother was told that the Mormons were bad and not to associate with them. She felt they had broken the law when they practiced polygamy; and, that was the worst thing she could think of. My father always admired the LDS people and always got along with them well. And even though the Mormon people knew how my mother felt about them, they liked her. It was wonderful to have them feel that way about her. My mother and father both were buried with services in the Latter-day Saints Church in Menan, Idaho. Beautiful funerals and huge crowds.

Back to the school problem, and it was a problem for me. We lived just across the street, but it street, but it seems I could never get to school on time. I really didn't like that but I guess that was the way my family was, I presume. Maybe I was just too slow in getting dressed or breakfast was difficult to eat that early in the morning and I wasn't able to go until I had eaten some breakfast.

Vernal still remains a small town today, located on the eastern part of Utah, right up against Colorado. There were no freight trains to service Vernal. Freight had to come by these Canastoga Wagons pulled by horses and mules. There would be one driver and helper, carrying a shotgun, because they were carrying the US Mail. These wagons had the seven foot diameter wheels and a four inch wide rim on the wheel. The freight depot was just across the street, west of our house and is still standing today. The freight is delivered by truck today.

My favorite time in Vernal was when we would go on fishing or hunting trips. We traveled by wagons, buggies, or surreys as they were called; and, we would go out to the Diamond Mountains northeast of Vernal to fish and also to hunt. It was practically a community affair with four to twenty families participating. After catching the fish or shooting the sage hens, they would all be dressed out, salted down in crocks, from two to ten gallons in size, for future use. After you got enough of the salt out of it, it was fit to fry and eat. On these hunts, the men would string out across the sagebrush, in a straight line so that there was no danger of getting accidently shot. Trailing along behind would be the children and some of the wagons to pick up the birds. When we would get a wagon load, we would come back into camp and dress out cut across the back end of the bird, grab his wings pulling real hard, causing centrifugal force to throw all of the entrails out. You didn't pick the hen, you skinned it eliminating the hide and feathers. The bird was then salted inside and out and packed into the crocks for storage. Before we had refrigeration, this is one of the ways we preserved our food. Another was smoking it.

In the year 1912, my little brother died of meningitis. It was quite a traumatic thing for my mother. I believe we left Vernal, Utah because of this tragedy. My brother, Douglas was born on January 9, 1914. My father had been running the Ashley Co-op. I guess it was 1916 when we left Vernal and came to Salt Lake. We lived in an apartment house on West Second South about 200 West. It was a nice little apartment and we stayed there a month or two before school was to start and then moved up to an apartment house up on 'H' Street, between Second and Third Avenue. I went to the Longfellow School which was about four or five blocks to walk in Salt Lake City (eight blocks make a mile). The Longfellow School was on Second Avenue which allowed me to take my sleigh with me in the wintertime.

My father had left the store that he was managing in Vernal, the Ashley Co-op and had gone back to the road job selling for a mercantile firm. He liked to do this type of work quite well.

Even as a small boy, I was always out there learning. At the Dinosaur National Monument, I would help excavate with my out chippers and tools, In the 1969's my wife and I watched men work in air conditioned glass rooms and I remember how hard we worked years ago in the early 1900's in the hot weather.

Our hunting and fishing trips were quite a community affair. Every family and to furnish its own tents and food, but when someone forgot to bring something, there was always someone else who had plenty to share. We'd camp in an assembly area and at night there would be a big campfire. Of course, my father would always hold the center position at the campfires because he was known as the best story teller around. He had a famous bear story that was fabulous:

Dad once went deer hunting with a group of men in the fall of 1914. They stopped when it got too dark, up in the Diamond Mountains. They rode horses and each had a pack mule with them. One of the men with the group insisted he knew the way and proceeded through the darkness. Only a minute later they heard the horse scream (as horses do) and the man yelling. So they made a campfire and made torches from branches and proceeded in the same direction; and, sure enough, the horse and rider had gone over a high cliff. There wasn't anything they could do that night. When daylight came, my father and one other man started down the cliff and found the horse and man both dead. They brought the man and his pack back up and went back into

Vernal to report the accident. I was present when the sheriff came to hear my father's testimony. He testified that they were all sober and explained the situation.

In Vernal, the Ute Indians would come off the reservation, all dressed in their custom outfits, performing war dances occasionally. This was always a thrill to me. Unlike some of the stories told of the Ute Indians, these of Vernal were always clean, and kept their clothes always looking clean.

My brother used to make little cars out of spare wheels and axles. Then he would cover them with burlap, after he'd make a frame for it. He even made a special one for me, with a special steering system in it.

All my friends and I were going to take this car out to the 'farther farm' which was the farm that was farther from the house than the other. The Davis' owned them both. The next day when we had planned to go out there, it rained! We were all so determined to go, and since it was my car, they agreed to push while I rode. They pushed all the way out there and turned right around and pushed all the way back in the mud. When we got back, we were all soaking wet.

It seemed like we were always making fun of something or someone. One day at the 4th of July races, we saw a Negro man run a race, running with his head thrown back. It looked like he couldn't see where he was going, but he surely ran fast. So, we'd throw our head back and only think we were running just as fast!

Another night all of my friends came and got me from my house wanting to run races in the dark. Well, it sounded fun to me. So we were all running down in the road and little did I know at the time that the others had slowed down to let me trip over a limb off a tree and fall all over the road. They were always playing tricks like that. But, it's times like those that I remember throughout my life.

At Dr. Douglas' place, I discovered a small valley with his son, Gaywin. It was more like a hole in the sandstone rock, perhaps 150 feet deep and a half-mile across at the bottom. There was no trail down to the valley or out. There was a stream coming out of the rocks on one side, running across this 'hole', and going into some rocks on the other side. I never did get to the bottom of the valley. It's something I would like to do as I am older now.

I once walked over some asphalt with a layer of dirt over it. You never know it was there, but that day was a hot summer day and my feet would sink into it as I'd walk, Then looking back, I could see it in the bottom of my footprint. I'd like to find it again and study it. Also in Vernal, there is the aluminum blue clay.

While I was working and playing, I was learning a lot of geology, mostly from Dr. Douglas. We'd study the layers of the earth and volcanos. We found some interesting sea shells up a big mountain cliff about six or seven thousand feet above sea level. At the time, we didn't know about the great flood and earthquake of the early times. I learned what to look for and how to recognize the things that would have had to happen to create these certain conditions. It's always been interesting to me to climb mountain trails, to walk across the desert and travel to other parts of the country.

I was so fortunate to be able to go to Alaska and see the things that I knew had to be there. When I got there, they were there. The history of man coming from Asia to Alaska, the Indians traveling the country from our western coast to Vernal, Utah and the sedimentary rocks all have interesting histories if you can decipher them.

In the spring of 1919, my father took us to Teton, Idaho from Salt Lake City. That was the bad time of the flu epidemic. Thousands of people were dying and my father thought we'd have a better chance if we were out of Salt Lake City. He would get some work, as our store was going bankrupt and it would help us get back on our feet. We left in March when all the flowers were blooming. We arrived at Sugar City, Idaho. They met us on bob sleighs and horses. We were in Teton almost two weeks when my sister and I came down with the flu. My father kept me down in the basement of the Teton Mercantile and had the doctor come to see me. Here I was so isolated from the rest of the family. Kathryn was in a separate bedroom at the house. Soon after, we both recovered.

From that time on, I learned how to garden, to take care of animals and even raise rabbits! I'd feed our cow and the lamb that was lame and given to me. Over three years in Teton, I accumulated fifty head of sheep. We moved them all down to Menan, Idaho when my father bought the store down there. I stayed there to help my brother, Wallace, run the store.

While in Teton, I also learned to trap. There were all kinds of things for trapping. Minks, muskrats, beavers, ermine and even skunks would occasionally get into your traps. We'd have to take care of them right away. I bought my own traps, boots, coats, and shells. Everything that I put into trapping came out of the money I had made from the pelts. I'd come home with at least two or three muskrats each day!

In June of 1923, I graduated from eighth grade from the Teton Grade School. We had a graduation party in the old Commercial Hall. I had a date with Thora Bright Johnson. I had been working for four to six weeks in Rexburg, Idaho at the Chevrolet Company. They let me use a Buick Roadster to come to Teton to the party. At the party they had sandwiches and soda pop. We danced to the Victrola with not much sound. But we had fun and we were all home by 11:00 pm.

My brother, Wallace, who was married, rented a house so he could run the store in Menan. We sold things like ladies' shoes with high-top buttons. The store was originally opened in 1868. Before June of 1923,my brother made arrangements to buy the house which was next door to the store.

For years I was running motion pictures, stocking shelves, running deliveries, going after merchandise in Idaho Falls and putting up the advertising. We had two motion picture projectors! Two projectors in the same place were rare to find anywhere, even in Pocatello and throughout Idaho.

HIGH SCHOOL YEARS

Later I went to school as a freshman at the Midway High School. It was a school that taught agriculture and home economics. So I learned professionally how to take care of animals and crops. It all helped later on. I graduated with the freshman class in the spring of 1924. All during the summer I helped around the store.

Riverside Garden was the place for the young people to go dancing. It was on the US 191 Highway between Rigby and Thornton, Idaho - straight east of Menan. We'd go there often to dance at night. It seemed like I was always running a show on Wednesday and Saturday nights when they had dances; but sometimes I'd run shows early and dash out to dance at 11:00 pm. I had a souped-up Model T Ford truck.

LEA MEETS EMMA CASPER

When I went back to school as a sophomore, I met Emma Casper. I took an eye to a bigger girl (too big for me) whose name was Marian Green. Marian said one day, "Have you ever met Emma Casper?" I said, "I don't even know her!" Marian pointed her out to me. I thought she was quite a gal! I walked down to her and introduced myself to her. She already knew who I was. I said, "Well, I've never seen you before."

We had a date for October 31, 1924, our first date. We were married December 7, 1927. I graduated from high school in June of 1927. I was running my father's store in Pocatello.

Our first date was a double date. My friend, Ronald Hogge, had a girl from Rigby, Idaho and they went along with us. We went in the old Ford truck which had one seat. We had to drive to Rigby to get Ronald's girl. We went to Idaho Falls to see a movie, then stopped at the Rainbow Cafe and had fried chicken. Afterwards, we drove to Grant, Idaho and went to the Halloween Dance at the church. We danced a few dances and decided to go to Riverside Gardens where there was another Halloween dance, then back to Rigby to get another bite to eat, and drove the girl's home. We had a good time!

There were two other boys that liked Emma. She had one boyfriend who was quite a big fellow. I felt like I had to fight him a few times to get Emma away from him. I suppose that if I would have tried, I would have been thrown in the mud.

The next two years were made up of lots of work. We had school, picnics, dances and Emma was always trying to get me to go to church with her. I just never had the feeling for it. I didn't have anything against the church, I just wanted to do what I wanted to do and I didn't like anyone interfering with the things I like to do.

Emma played the piano and the organ. We worked together putting a quartet together. The seminary teacher of Midway High School had brought out from England an old English Hymn. It was something like 'The Old Rugged Cross'. Our quartet was invited to sing in merely every Ward in that part of the country. A lot of singing. Every Ward enjoyed it very much. We sang all kings of songs and sang at different church activities besides church.

While I was running my father's store in Pocatello, I borrowed my brother-in-law's Pontiac two door sedan to go to Lewisville to visit Emma. As I approached the railroad crossing in Idaho Falls, the train had just passed and a guy came across the tracks in my lane. We had a head-on collision. There were no policemen to take care of things, and we had no such thing as car insurance. So, we both paid for our own expenses for damages done to our vehicles. I had to fix the radiator, the front bumper and grill. It was pretty expensive in those days. After this experience, I never borrowed any cars to go anywhere. This was enough. I was so upset at the time of the accident, once I was at Emma's house we never went anywhere.

I had been running the store for a while when my father bought another little store in Alameda, the name of the township. It was on Wayne Avenue in northeastern Pocatello. The store operated from 7:00 am to 10:00 pm, seven days a week. I was the only one there to operate it. It was with the idea that I would go to the Idaho State University for school. But anyone could see that I alone, couldn't run the store sixteen hours a day and go to school at the same time. I had been appointed to the Navy Academy in Annapolis, Mayland by Senator Borah of Idaho. In July of 1927, I took entrance examinations in Idaho Falls or Pocatello. After my exams, I never heard anything more about it.

I had to do my cooking and cleaning while I ran the store. It wasn't much of a life for a young man. So Emma and I arranged to get married on December 7. On the evening before our wedding, it was 21 degrees below zero at Menan.

After the reception, everyone's automobiles were frozen up and wouldn't start. So, I had to help everyone get them started, drive them home or help push their cars home.

LEA AND EMMA MARRY

The following day, Emma and I were married by Bishop Lee Hart of Menan, in his home. We went to Idaho Falls and stayed in the new Bonneville Hotel. We went to a movie at the Colonial Theater that evening entitled 'Adolph Monjou in Wedding Expenses'. It was quite an appropriate show. The next day we went back to Menan and collected all of our belongings and gifts. We packed them into our car and moved to a two room place in back of the store in Pocatello. It had no bathroom, frontroom, or kitchen facilities. I look back at the place and wonder what kind of a nut I must have been to take a girl into a place like that. But we only stayed there until the following March.

My father bought a store in Victor, Idaho. My brother, Wallace, left Menan and Emma and I moved to Menan and live in Wallace's house. Kathryn and her husband, Reed, took over the store in Pocatello. After Reed passed away, Kathryn kept up the store. Soon after his death, she turned the store into a house. I helped her by doing all the new electrical work. She lived there for fifteen years.

In February of 1928, Emma and I settled into the house next to the store in menan. We had reason to believe we'd have a nice table life there. At that time, we didn't know that October 28, 1929 was coming up.

Wallace and his family - his wife, Maime, and his son, Jack- had moved to Victor, Idaho. So, it was my job to run the store in Menan. It was quite a big business. We had all the comforts a person could want there at the house in Menan. The store lacked toilet facilities or a washroom which made the girls that worked at the store for us use our facilities in the house next door.

GORDON IS BORN

During the summer of 1928, Emma was having a lot of trouble with her pregnancy with Gordon. She went to a rest home in Idaho Falls. She was closer to her doctor that way. In early September, she started having false labor pains. This was when she started staying in the rest home type place. I'd go to Idaho Falls at least once or twice a week to see her. When the time came for her to deliver, I wasn't available. I had gone duck hunting on the 30th of September. To me, it was a case of 'crying wolf' too many times. I've never heard the end of it. I should have been there for our first child's birth.

After he was born, we settled into a quite normal routine. A friend of my mother and father who had once been married to my Aunt Edie (my father's sister) needed a place to stay where he could be taken care of. He was an old man, but Emma and I were elected to provide the place; which is something I never should have stood for. He was able to help me quite a bit and helped to take care of Gordon.

We got away once to go to Yellowstone Park. We had a delivery sedan. It had no windows in the back and had jump seats. It was really handy at that time. We pulled in at the Old Faithful Lodge. It was dark, so we laid down the jump seats and went to sleep. In the morning, I could hear some kind of rumbling going on. I looked out to see bears only thirty feet away. They had come to the fence to be fed by the tourists. There were people all over in tents and some sleeping on the ground. We felt a lot safer in the car.

We took Emma's niece, Ethel Ball, and went to Jackson Hole. We had Gilbert with us. Gordon was left with Ethel's mother. We went on the west side of the Snake River. It was quite a rough trip.

In Victor, I built a little picket fence. It was sixteen or eighteen feet on the sides of the house and the width of the front of the house across the front. It's still standing today. My son, Gordon, could not stand to be fenced into the yard. He'd go up to the door and kick it to get back in.

After the fence was built was the time they were making a Fox film. They would send Brahma bulls in stock cars. When they'd get off the trains, they trailed them right past our house. Now, Gordon wanted to be outside. He'd go and stand out by the fence and to see these bulls going by (bulls that stood seven feet tall at the shoulders) with little Gordon out there was quite a sight for sore eyes. A site to scare anyone to death. I liked Victor and really enjoyed working at the store.

My father came to Menan. We were having problems with the credit accounts at the store. The farmers were scratching for their money and didn't bother much to pay their bills at the store. This was after the Wall Street crash of October 1929 when things started to go to pot. In June of 1930, we moved to Pocotello from Victor. My father was able to get me a job down there. When we moved to Pocatello, it meant living in a basement apartment with two little babies and working from daylight 'till midnight seven days a week. It was a very terrible life then.

GILBERT IS BORN

In April of 1930, the depression had set in real good. Emma and I had moved back to Victor and my father had to take over the store in Menan because of financial troubles all the stores were in. We moved into the old stone house in Victor, where I had built the picket fence. It was a real nice house, quite small but comfortable.

Emma went to the Idaho Falls Hospital to give birth to Gilbert on August 3, 1930. She went to her sister, Nelly's home to stay before confinement.

In October of 1930, we had to move to Pocatello, where I got work in a grocery store Swells United Stores. I earned $25.00 a week working fourteen hours a day, six days a week, and Sundays quite often, for six to eight hours with no overtime. We lived in a basement apartment. The rent was $22.50 a month.

In April or May of 1931, I was sales agent for Shell Oil Company in Bancroft, Idaho. I traded our Chevrolet coupe for a ton and half Chevrolet truck. I spent two years in the oil business.

The economy situation was getting pretty bad. Every month it got worse. I had just received my first commission check which was approximately $10,100.00 from the Shell Oil Company. I deposited it in the bank in Bancroft on a Friday afternoon. The bank never opened up again. I had bills to pay and sent checks for them in the mail, never thinking that the bank would never open up again. I had the loss of the whole check and had to find ways of paying the bills that I thought I had already paid with the checks. This was a very serious blow to us. My little family had a very hard time all through the summer in Bancroft.

SODA SPRINGS

KEITH IS BORN

We moved to Soda Springs and my father sent our cow down from Menan by truck because we had a little pasture and a shed for her at Soda Springs. I was able to get a job at the movie theater, working two nights a week, bringing home $3.00 per week.

Keith was born in our home in Soda Springs, January 11, 1931. Emma was attended by Doctor Kackley and a nurse, Mrs. Smart. Because of the good work of Mrs. Smart, Emma was able to nurse her baby. The lack of proper care in the Idaho Falls Hospital made it so she could not breastfeed Gordon or Gilbert.

With very little sales of Shell products and only $3.00 a week from the theater, we found it almost impossible to live. I borrowed money on my truck to pay for the doctor and the nurse, buy coal, pay for the cow, and feed us. It was a very severe winter.

In the spring of 1931, a tornado came through Soda Springs. It tore up things pretty bad. I was in Bancroft at the time and when I returned to Soda Springs, the buildings were torn apart, the trees blown down across the street, the big wool warehouse was completely destroyed and I had to drive on sidewalks and round about streets to get to my home. One particular big picture window had been blown out. The cow shed was turned upside down and blown over the fence. Emma and the children were safe, luckily; but they did have a close call.

Gordon was playing in the front of the house, when Emma heard him kicking the front door. She dropped the pillows from the big window and ran to get Gordon. Gordon was holding on to the doorknob and the wind was lifting his feet up off the porch. When she had brought him in and closed the door, the big window blew out. Gilbert and Keith were in the north bedroom, in their cribs and safe. The wind had blown some bricks off the chimney and some shingles off the roof. The landlord, Mr. Moore, was quick to repair the damages so we were fortunate that way.

I was appointed Scout Master of the troop of scouts in Soda Springs. I enjoyed teaching and training and taking them on outings for merit badge examinations. A trip that I remember well was into the caverns under Soda Springs. Soda Springs is well known for the different types of water, springing up hot and cold, hot baths and salt baths, and everything you could thing of. As being this type of an area, there are caverns all underneath the crust of Soda Springs. They seemed to lead for miles. We never went back too far because of the danger with the little boys. We enjoyed going in and discovering that the boys had been raised there and never knew the extent of these caverns. It was interesting to see the number of small animals that used the caves for their homes to raise their ones there. We had quite a trip and discovered many fossils. I would like to go back some time.

Gordon had started going with me on the truck when I'd go to Bancroft. It seemed to him that everytime the truck was going, he had to be with it. We had quite some time before he learned that there were times that he could go and times when he couldn't. He was always good about staying with the truck and he was a great joy to me at all times.

Gilbert was my second son. He was a very beautiful baby. I loved him very much and still do.

When Keith came along, he was just as fair. He had blonde hair and very fair skin, though Gilbert was dark with dark hair.

A month or two after the wind storm, the Shell Oil Company took me off the job as their agent. I had no business and I used money to survive on that should have gone to the company. They paid no salary to the agents. I paid them back for the money that I owed them. Because of this incident, I had to return to Menan, Idaho.

BACK TO MENAN, IDAHO

In Menan, it was impossible to make a living. My brother-in-law, Lyman Ball, rented us a home. It was very nice and warm for us. We had a pasture, an orchard, a place for our cow and a chicken coop. We bought two hundred baby chicks. The chicken coop was actually a brooder. The losses were very small.

We raised a lot of eggs which all went primarily to pay off the Shell Oil Company for money I had used. I also helped my father with the store and got myself some work with the truck which I still possessed to haul cement from Inkom which was approximately seventy miles from where I had to deliver the cement. I'd take 100 bags, 90 pounds a bag. I expected the truck to break down along the way, but it kept going. I hauled huge logs out of the Island Park country with it. I bought a trailer to go behind the truck for hauling 40 foot logs. Three was no place in Island Park to eat or sleep - you had to take everything with you. I mostly worked alone. Once in awhile, there would be a tough job to be done and someone would come along with me.

I spent two days loading one big 35 foot log. It was approximately 40 inches in diameter. It was dry so it was not as heavy as it could be if it were green. It took a lot of engineering for one man to get it on the truck. I used a deadman procedure. I took two forked trees, so I could put the forks against the bed so they couldn't roll. Then I dug a hole and put a log in it with a chain around it. I worked the tree up to the truck. As I pulled through Ashton, St. Anthony, Rexburg, and Sugar City, everyone stared at my load of logs.

I'd store the logs in my front yard on the garden spot. I decided that I could buy vegetables we needed fairly cheap from my father and Emma's relatives. I needed our garden spot for the storage of the logs. Many people would come by and buy the logs from me. This way I could get a little cash once in awhile.

In order to raise the chicks, I had to build a fire in the furnace that was at one end of the brooder. We had to keep a fire for four days before they arrived. In order for the furnace to work, you'd have to build a small fire, stick as much wood as would fit into the pit, and seal off the steel cover with mud. This would keep the coop warm for a week. When the floor is warm, you should divide the chicks into small groups so they won't pile on top of each other and smother. I stayed with them all night to see that they knew where to go when they get cold and warm. They'd feed twenty-four hours a day. I couldn't leave them for more than three hours at one time. For the fear of them doing something crazy to each other. When they were older ond on their own. It begins to be a busy place with a lot of noise. It was very interesting and exciting for me. In those days, accomplishing something was a pleasure whether you were paid for it or not.

One fall, I got a job from Mr. John Poole hauling hay. I had to get a man to help me to get the hay out of the stacks and loaded. I learned. Boy did I learn. After I hauled two or three stacks of hay, I had $80.00. After I paid the man for his help and the gas and oil for my truck, I had $15.00 for myself.

While we were living there in Menan, Emma became acquainted with Dee Cherry and his wife who now live in Lima, Montana. They became very close friends to us. They lived right across the fence southwest of us. I've tried to keep in touch with them. Our children played together, and it's a great comfort to know that they are real friends.

Dee and I used to go fishing. We used to do a little 'poaching' in the spring when the trout would come up into the Menan sloughts to lay their eggs. They would lay them at night and we'd catch them with a pitchfork. We knew it was the wrong thing to do but in those days to get something to eat you'd sometimes have to break a law.

OFF TO LOGAN, UTAH - 1933

The following year in 1933, I received a request to go to Logan, Utah to work in a theater as a projectionist on a trial basis. I borrowed some money from my father and scraped up what we had and went to Logan. We stayed in a hotel while I was getting acquainted with the job. I stayed there for a week or ten days. Mr. Thatcher let me know that he wouldn't need me anymore and would hold a place for me later. He told me I needed to brush up on my projection skills. I was a little sloppy since working in the Edahah Theater in Soda Springs.

Before I left for Logan to run the projectors, I had lost the business with the Shell Oil Company which was a mighty good thing for my sake. My father came to Soda Springs to take Emma and our three children, along with all of the personal belongings he could haul in the sedan delivery truck to Emma's mother's place on their farm which was south of Lewisville, Idaho. Within the two or three week period, I had loaded up the truck with all of our furniture, carpet and such items and taken them to Menan. We stored them in my father's warehouse in back of the store. I made a second trip back to Soda Springs for our cow and more furniture.

In the winter of 1932, we spent at Grandpa and Grandma Casper's farm. Everybody got fat, we were fed well. We didn't have much, but we were happy to have something to eat and shelter. No one got sick during this time, thank goodness. I hope we didn't cause Emma's parents too much inconvenience. I helped out in every way that I could. However, I was not a farmhand. I can still hear Emma laughing when I first rode a horse bareback.

We hauled coal from the mine. The coal from eastern Idaho was very soft. It had never been put under high pressures. This is called surface mining. The coal gave us plenty of heat and many ashes. You could get about as many ashes out as you put coals in. I'd have timber and willows, mostly anything to keep the house warm because now we needed another stove in the bedroom at the Casper's home. To keep the children out from under their feet, we all (more or less) lived in this big bedroom. Therefore, we had to have a fire going in there.

During this time was the only time in my life that I really got to enjoy the children. There was no work to do, so I just did the work that needed to be done, and lived in the house through the cold winter with my children and my wife. As

I wasn't a person who could sit back and take whatever the world dishes out to him, I was quite unhappy that winter.

BACK TO MENAN, IDAHO

The following spring we moved into the house of Emma's sister, Nelly Ball, in Menan. It was a nice little brick house with two bedrooms, a kitchen, living room and a bathroom. Yes, it even had a bath and a basement. We were quite comfortable there. We had enough furniture to fit it up. Emma really enjoyed having a cow and chickens around.

Here I had my first opportunity of slaughtering hogs and beef. Although I never did it a second time, I could say to myself "If I every have to do it again, I could." It was nerve-wracking the first time around.

I should explain the process of killing and dressing out a hog. You have to have a black iron 50 gallon barrel that can be sat on bricks or rocks to build a fire under it and around it, filling the barrel halfway full of clean water. Bring the water almost to a boil; but definitely do not boil it. I have been around when men had shot the pig or beef and then cut their throats to bleed them. I had always been told that this process was not as good as when you cut the throat that then let them stand up. After the water is hot and you've got a rope on the hind legs of the hogs and have gotten the tripod set up with a block and fall on it, you are ready to trip the hog up and cut its throat. This hog weighed about 300 pounds and having it around, it grew to be quite a pet. You've got to get the jugular vein without getting the heart. In a hot, the jugular vein in quite deep. You should know how deep the heart is. The safest thing to do is to have a knife with not over a 4 inch blade. Just thrust the knife in, pull it across and pull it out. Then let the hot get up. The poor old thing stood there pumping its blood out and pretty soon the slop is over.

When the hog is dead, cut the tendons out of the hind legs, put in the separator made of 2 X 4's and cut down the ends to hold the legs apart. Hook the center of it into the block and tackle; hoist him up. Afterwards, roll the barrel of hot water underneath, lower the hot down in, set up the table that he'll be scraped on; 2-2 X 4's and 3-2 X 12's. Start immediately scraping the head. You have to work fast and be arranged to put the hog back into the water before he's completed. The women can help scrape it. It's pretty simple. After it's all scraped, put it back on the block and tackle, cut him open and get all the inners out.

I never thought I would have to do this, but I did. I'm glad that I was able to say according to the people who saw the meat and saw my butchering operations that there wasn't a thing wrong with it. There is the heart and the liver that has to be taken care of. You should hope that the evening and night of the day that the butchering is done will be cold so that the meat will set up firm and it will drain good. Because the following day it has to be cut up; therefore, at this time you must start making the sausage, curing the hams, shoulders and bacon and the good pork chops.

Of course, this little family of mine - Gordon, Gilbert, Keth and Emma and I ate good during the summer and winter in the house of Lyman Ball.

After working all summer on odd jobs with everything I could with the truck, I got to put in a full day on the WPA Project. They paid me only $3.00 for the whole day, and, I didn't like that, so that was the end of that. I've never seen so much gold bricking in all my life, and never want to have to see it again.

CHARLES IS BORN

Emma was pregnant again it seemed to me that that time came on right after another every year. The following spring in 1934, Charlie was born. Charlie was the first child born that I was able to see his birth, the only child. It was quite a thrill to me to be handed my son, so wiggly and warm. I was supposed to take him into the other room and place him by the stove. Well, I did; but there was not fire in the stove. Emma said later that she had never seen me so mixed up in all her life than at that time. I had really gone bizerk. It was enough to shake me up alright. This was on April 12, 1934 when Charles was born in Menan, Idaho. Emma was able to handle the birth quite well and recovered very quickly. I suppose that being happy and comfortable has a lot to do with whatever the woman has to go through during childbirth.

BACK TO LOGAN, UTAH

I was called back to Logan, Utah to work as a motion picture projectionist at the Lyric Theater about May 15, 1934. Our son, Charles, was about one month old and Emma had four sons to take care of. We had no ready cash at anytime because of the indebtedness to the Shell Oil Company. Somehow I got a bus fare and enough for a little food and a room. I arrived late at nite and was to report to work at 12:30 pm the following day. I was so nervous that I could not sleep and was on the street at 7:00 am.

After being without a job for two years and now going into professional work, I had reason to be nervous. After a week of work, I found an apartment on 3rd East and 4th North. This was after Mr. Thatcher had assured me that my work was satisfactory, and I had the job. It was a basement apartment. We soon learned that it wasn't a healthy place for the children - that the moisture from the lawns settled in at night. There was no fenced in area for the children to play in and my work was ten hours a day, seven days week for $18.00. So, I couldn't help Emma much with the children.

Little Keith wandered away from the apartment only a few days after they arrived in Logan. It was almost two hours before we found him approximately two blocks away. A nice lady had taken him in and saved me a lot of hunting.

After a month in Logan, we moved to a house on West Center Street. We didn't have a fenced here, but we didn't have to sleep in a damp basement and Gordon and Gilbert were soon over their colds. We spent the summer and winter in that house, nearly freezing in the winter.

In the following early summer, Keith was struck by a car in front of the house and nearly killed. The people who hit him drove away and I had to find someone to take myself and the baby to Budge Hospital. Keith had a double compound fracture of the lower jaw. The poor little fellow suffered great agony for a week in the hospital. Emma would walk eight or ten blocks to the hospital to stay with him in the late afternoon until 11:00 pm; and I would get there from the theater as soon as I could. We had no car, so we walked each way.

GEORGE'S BIRTH AND DEATH

Emma was pregnant at the time with George Emit. He died less than 24 hours after birth. Colin Sweeten (Emma's sister Mary's husband from Malad, Idaho) drove me and the baby to Lewisville, Idaho for burial in the Casper plot. Emma is buried in the same plot.

I don't think I could convey to my children the stress that I endure now just by telling of these events. The times and conditions by which their mother endured trying to be a good wife and homemaker with the very little I could provide, caused me so much heartache that I can hardly stand it.

THE MOVE TO WESTFIELD

Emma located a little house on two and half acres of land in the area west of Logan known as Westfield. A very old couple owned it and agreed to sell it at $1,000.00 - $100.00 down and $100.00 per year, no interest. It is hard to believe now that you could have ever purchased good land with irrigation water rights and an artesian well for that kind of money.

Naturally, I didn't have that kind of money. Emma arranged to borrow it from Lyman Ball, her sister Nelly's husband from Rigby. With a cash gift from Aunt Edie Jones of Mt. Dora, New Mexico (my father's sister), we got the house refinished on the outside by a contractor who did a fine job. Also, a new roof with a total cost of $900.00. At the purchase of this property is where I had my confrontation with lawyers and the establishment that hold all people slaves to the laws that lawyers have designed to perpetuate and endow them with the riches and the more mpower at the expense of the small landowner and the tax payers. The large tax payer can generally make the lawyer take a second appraisal of his actions.

It was the title search in a place like Logan and on the old piece of property where the small two and a half acres that we bought was all that was left of an original land patented of one hundred sixty acres. There was no such thing as title insurance in Utah and may not be to this day. That dirty little lawyer had a field day with that, and his charges were $140.00 under title insurance as it was when Emma and I bought our home in Las Vegas, (the guarantee to a clear title was $2.00).

Our having this home (although it had no sanitary facilities, was fairly warm and definitely dry) gave us the protection that was badly needed when I decided to join the union and with three or four other men struck the Capital and Lyric Theaters in Logan, Utah inMarch 1938. This was a very historic occasion. Never before in the history of men, had the law protected a citizen and given him the right to be heard. Not in an established court of law where lawyers and judges who are members of the same establishment set the rules; but in a labor law court where a man had the right to say what he thought, and in his own way. He judged thought and in the way he judged would be to his benefit, no attorney had the right to object. This labor court file copy would be interesting reading to a labor lawyer today.

With our garden, chickens, cow and pigs we managed very well. I piped the flowing well into the kitchen and with the kitchen sink and drain out to the canal in front of our house so we always had water in the house. It ran continuously which is necessary in order to keep the artesian well open.

The law required that we do not block the free passage of people along the sidewalk and not talk or be interviewed by carrying a picket sign. I had the wife of a Thatcher nephew try to force her small daughter into contact with me, but I was too quick for her. I had to ask the principal of the school where my sons were going to call a new meeting of all the teachers; so I could explain our position in the labor trouble, and ask the teachers to explain it to their classes so that my children would not be set upon by the children who were not informed about the truths that were being labeled as Communists.

My children and wife were suffering indignities that were caused by lawyers and who could see what the Wagner Act was doing in Logan to organize law enforcement and to the common people who had no idea what benefits that labor controversy would prove to be to them. I do not know if the teachers and principal stopped the harassment of my children, or if my children failed to report it to me.

We, the strikers, were awarded the unemployment benefits of the law from the State. We didn't get any money until long after the pay period had ended. Then, they all came in one envelope; twelve checks for $16.00 each. This was another move by lawyers to harass and discourage where they did not win a case. Local unions of our international organization and other craft unions, even the CIO which was not then a part of the AFL, contributed pickets and money to help.

For many months, people attended the two theaters; not that they liked the shows, but they just wanted to try to discourage us. After eleven or twelve months, these people could see that we were determined to win and that they could not face us any longer. After thirteen months and thirteen days, the strike ended; but for two or three weeks that I worked and a powderman and driller on the railroad project in Logan Canyon, I was on the picket line in front of either the Lyric or Capital Theater.

Soon we were back working in the theaters under a union contract. For myself, it was a re-establishment of my faith in America and a determination to try to change the lives of as many people as I could by showing how to do good honest work for an honorable wage. I received more than twice the money for less than half the time.

JOHN IS BORN

On December 9, 1938, our son, John, was born in our home in Logan. Dr. Wilford Hale and his wife attended. "Such a beautiful baby," Dr. Hale said. And he really was.

Not being employed, I was able to take care of mother and baby. The relief society teachers were there one day to see how we were getting along. I gave the baby a bath and dressed him while he was still wearing his navel bandage. The two teachers told me later that they were really impressed.

Between working on the picket line and caring for a family, I kept pretty busy. All of my sons were good to help and had each his special way of showing love for his mother and father. We had plenty to eat and all stayed well during the winter. And, spring would soon be here!

In May of 1939, the strike was over. The preparedness program was starting to prepare for war. I had the opportunity to attend a wood pattern makers class at Utah State University. Also, on nights that I didn't work in the projection room, I took a class of aircraft mechanics. I didn't have the time to train and make a passing grade. As soon as I passed the pattern making class. I was employed by the Ogden Iron Works - five and a half days from 7:30 am to 5:00 pm. Then I drove to Preston, Idaho for a one night's work and one night's work in Ogden. On Saturday nights and Sunday afternoons, I worked in the theaters in the theaters in Logan. So, I was making approximately $85.00 a week net.

OFF TO LAS VEGAS

In December of 1941 after Pearl Harbor, our union had a call to go to Las Vegas, Nevada to do relief work for four or five men in Local 720 who had not had a day off since a year ago. I was chosen to go and left my family, traveling by bus to Las Vegas. I arrived there at 10:30 pm on December 21, 1941.

It was rather a dismal town in those days. The signs were all turned off and the windows were all blacked out. Boulder Dam was a prime target and it had to be dark. Submarines had been spotted off the California coast. Living facilities were nearly impossible to come by. I had to stand in line at a cafe to get something to eat. You might get a room for the night, but that was all. You were to understand that you were to vacate by 11: 00 am the following day. I found the El Portal Theater and went up to the booth to report to the business agent, Barney Duessen and plan the relief work.

After the show was over, Barney took me over to meet with Art Lush at the Palace Theater. I soon discovered why these men wanted off for a week or so. Their show started at 1:00 pm which was one show - a matinee. Saturdays and Sundays were a continuous ten hours. The salary was about $70.00.this was not exactly what I was let to believe. In Logan, we worked a five and a half hours shift, five days each week for about $35.00. Here in Las Vegas you worked six hours for five days and ten hours for two days. It required seventy hours of your time each week to accomplish this for $70.00. I was not too happy about it; but, since I had agreed to do it, I would.

After two weeks in Las Vegas and seeing the New Year end with Art Lush and the El Rancho Vegas HOtel (which was the only hotel on the Strip at that time), I was convinced that Las Vegas had a future and I wanted to be a part of it. I was promised by the business agent that I could have the job at the new theater which was to be built in Henderson. After leaving the Boulder Theater (where I relieved Wally Roper), I took the bus to Victorville and worked for a week for Bill Jones. In Barstow, I worked for Rudy Trotter, who was the secretary of Local 720 of Las Vegas. In those days, Locas 720's jurisdiction consisted of Kanab and St. George, Utah; Las vegas; Henderson; Bounder CIty; Kingman, Arizona; and Needles, Barstow, Victorville and Mohave, California. In Mojave, I worked for Fred Jones. He and his wife let me stay at their house while they were away. I then went to Visalia and worked there for a couple of days. I also went to Handford. From Hadford, I went to San Francisco and worked two days. I returned to Logan, going through Los Angeles and Las Vegas.

The construction headquarters of the Basic Magnesium Plant had burned to the ground the day before I arrived. I noticed the smoke from the train and recognized the destruction. I learned later that within twenty-four hours, new construction had begun and never stopped. Copper was in short supply and when it came to supplying bus bars for the magnesium circuits, the U. S. Treasury Department sent several million dollars of silver ingots to Henderson. The silver was then shaped into bus bars for the electric circuits; so necessary in the production of magnesium. When the plant closed and the silver was returned to the Treasury Department, every once was accounted for and the Treasury guards were terminated.

Upon my return to Logan, after the trip to Las Vegas and California, I contacted my friend at the Ogden Iron Works and was told that there were pattern making jobs coming up if I qualified. At this time, I applied for admission at the Utah State Agricultural College for training in wood-pattern making.

Although there was not much work at the Local 720, we managed but I was restless. I knew what was going on in

Las Vegas. I knew there was money to be made there; and, I became very unsatisfied with Logan, but I had to carry on. I went to school, receiving my training and went to work at the Ogden Iron Works.

PATRICK IS BORN

The medical problems and Emma's pregnancy, along with many other things at this time, were just about more than a man could handle. A man doesn't always do what he would under normal conditions, but he does what he is forced to do and reacts sometimes violently. After all the work in Ogden, Preston and Logan, I was tired to death and dissatisfied with everything.

In July of 1943, I received the call to Las Vegas for a job that would be opening around the first of August. Emma and I traveled to Las Vegas, after Pat was born (January 27, 1943); and she and I looked over the town. I worked for several weeks before the theater opened. Wally Roper and I did most of the installation of the nice equipment in the beautiful projection room. I had never been in a theater to equal the theater in Henderson.

THE FAMILY MOVES TO LAS VEGAS

In August, we arranged to bring our family down to Las Vegas. We hired a van to bring the few things down that we had coming. In order to get the house, we had to qualify as defense personnel, which was something I could do as an entertainment worker or motion picture operator. We got the house that was vacated by one of the superintendents of the Magnesium construction. I bought the furniture that was already in the house, so we didn't have to bring too much down. The children came down and went to school in the latter part of August. We spent the winter in Henderson. I'll never forget a windstorm we had there. I thought the wind was going to blow the roof right off the house.

THE FAMILY RETURNS TO LOGAN AND LEA REMAINS IN LAS VEGAS

After the first year, the word came out that they were shutting down the Magnesium plant. The war in Europe looked like it was going to be over real shortly. Emma's brother, Charles, came down and we loaded everything up in his truck and sent them home while I remained in Las Vegas.

This was a rough time for me. The theater went down to a matinee on Wednesday, Saturday; and Sunday operating the whole day and evenings every night. My pay was cut to two-thirds of what it had been. I began to wonder if I had made the right decision. I couldn't help to believe that there was more work to done in Las Vegas and I had to hang in there. I was watching things very close on the strip. The Last Frontier Hotel had been built since the last time I had left Las Vegas in 1942 and returned in 1943. The Frontier was putting on pretty big shows considering that they had very little facilities. A roadshow was coming there, 'The Earl Carol Show'. They had a yellow card that showed that a union man worked the show. Barney Duessen wouldn't do anything as a business agent to force this big casino to hire other union men.

Barney said, "Lea, you go do it." I said, "I can't do it, I'm not the business agent." He said, "Well, why don't you take over the job of business agent?" I said, "Well, it's a job that has to be appointed by the President and voted by the members of the Union." He said, "Well, you know how spread out we are and we can't do that. We've got a job that needs to be covered so why don't you go and do it and I'll notify the union officials that that's the decision I had to make a business agent.' I said, "Okay, Barney. Just don't get me in a jam."

I went to see Bill Moore who was the general manager for the Last Frontier Hotel and Casino. I told him what the yellow card meant and that we would cause him a lot of trouble if he didn't employ some union people with the show coming in. The people in that show expected the type of craftsmen that you find only in the theatrical union. After quite a lot of arguing with them the Hotel, Bill Moore and his associates agreed that one man would go on and replace the man they regularly had as an electrician and sound man. I agreed to that. At least we had an opening and a start.

Incidentally, Mr. Teal who was the pro of the Desert Inn Golf Course was the spotlight operator, stage electrician and sound man who had to come off the show. I assigned Ralph Hamilton, the brother of Kelly Hamilton to the job. I thought everything was going alright. Two or three days later, I stopped Ralph Hamilton on the street and asked him how things were coming along with the Last Frontier Hotel. He said that they had fired him because he couldn't do the work that they expected to be done.

Now it was my duty to go to the hotel and take over for the Earl Carol show. Following the show, I began to get my teeth into this business. The contracts were coming to the projection room and at the same time the other members of California didn't like me coming in and taking over Barney's job. They were getting 'whiplash and crack' from other Locals that I had forced Earl Carol's show into almost no show the first night because I couldn't get someone to cover the job.

These things were slightly true but not totally my fault. I was almost kicked out of the Local 720 jurisdiction. We found out that I couldn't be active as the business agent since I was not a member of the Local. It's hard to say how all these things have affected me later in life. It is necessary to realize that I had gone through periods of life with no money, no job, and I had the ability and energy to work. And now I'm in a town where they need my capabilities. The first thing I knew, they began to see that I did have capabilities.

EMMA AND THE BOYS JOIN LEA

IN LAS VEGAS ONCE AGAIN

It wasn't until 1945 that I got my family down to Las Vegas on August 12. My wife and children told me how they came through towns that were celebrating the end of World War II.

The construction of the Flamingo Hotel had gone on all this time during the war. I'll never understand where they got the materials. The whole thing was built of steel with plenty of copper and lighting and everything.

On December 26, 1946, the Flamingo Hotel opened and stayed open until about the 10th or 15th day of January, 1947 when it closed because of the murder of Ben Seegal. The closing lasted for only a week until some new people took it over - Ben Greenbaum and that association. I had been working there along with Kelly Hamilton as a sound man until 1950.

This is the show business that I had hoped for and it took an awfully lot of work to make the gamblers understand that their key to gambling was show business. In my later years, the idea did get across. However, we have had a cutback in the entertainment in Las Vegas when they began to shut down the lounge entertainment. It's beginning to pick up again and the casino people are beginning to understand how to run the show business. They wouldn't listen to me or would come in and talk so big that they'd 'bull them over'. There was too much production and too many costs; the casino just couldn't stand it.

UNION ACTIVITIES HEAT UP

Between the time that the Flamingo opened, there was a lot of changes being made in the union Local 720. We had a fight with the International concerning the jurisdiction of Kanab after a trip to the convention in Minneapolis, where I met with the business agent of Stagehands' Local 150 in Salt Lake and the International president, Richard Walsh. I thought it was understood that Local 720 would manage the Kanab movie location and that members of Local 720 would be given half of the work that was there. When the convention was over and the reports were made and we had received the letters from the International Union - no matter how many more production people there were in television, radio or motion picture operators, the Stagehands were still bossing the movements of the IATSE.

It was much to my dismay to find out that we had to take second fiddle to Salt Lake. There is a mixed Local in Provo, Utah and Local 720 in Las Vegas is a mixed Local but Salt Lake has a Stagehands' Local which has been there a long time: Local 99, a motion picture operator's Local. There's a mixed Local in Ogden and another in Logan, Utah which was where I had my first membership in the IA Local 508.

We were in a bind in Kanab because there were a few men who were going to be members of Local 720. The members of Local 720 in the California district or the California heart of Local 720's jurisdictions were very unhappy with the way I was running things. So we were granted permission from the International to split off the part down in California and from another local down there - Local 730. Local 720 in Las Vegas was able to take care of their business better, not upsetting good members in the California district who felt that they could not compete and not get their vote of control as to what Local 720 in Las Vegas was doing.

When Local 720 began to grow, there were more problems for me. In those days, in order to become a member of Local 720 or any other IA Local, you had to get two-thirds majority of the membership in attendance. This made it such that I could not get the membership that was needed in the growing Local.

The Thunderbird Hotel was built right after the Flamingo, then the Sahara and Desert Inn. In 1955, there was to be five hotels opening within two or three months and I needed manpower. It was necessary for me to get this manpower, if we were going to continue to serve these hotels and show them that we had the men. Some dirty little rascal from the Local had told the International that I was breaking the rules of the International by hiring men without union cards. I hired the men that I thought could do the job; card or no card. The men who were qualified to do the job should be qualified to join Local 720. Since Local 720's membership didn't want to take in any more members, then you must realize the position I was in. However, it seems that the information never got back to the International or the International never recognized.

The International took me off the job of business agent and assigned an outsider to run the Local's business. That was a force if ever I saw one in my life. At that time, I threw my hands in the air and cut loose from Local 720.

To name the hotels and the number of men required: There was the Moulin Rouge which was built by Joe Lewis (the boxer); the Royal Nevada which is now a part of the Stardust Hotel; the Dunes Hotel; the Riviera Hotel; and , the Hacienda Hotel.

Hacienda Hotel = 5 men

Riviera Hotel = 7men

Dunes Hotel = 5 men

Royal Nevada Hotel = 7 men

Moulin Rouge Hotel = 5 men

The total membership of Local 720 was twenty-nine men at that time. Today, there are one thousand men. Today if those members who could not approve more members could look back, they ought to come to me and bow their heads and ask my forgiveness. That's the only way I can put it.

THE FAMILY BUSINESS BEGINS

The necessity for someone to supply these hotels and stages became very evident. I, with the encouragement of Fred Jones and Jim Harford, started the business of supplying lighting and sound equipment and some stage products. My family and I decided it should be called the STAGE, SOUND AND EQUIPMENT COMPANY. We started out just taking part in the space, any place we could. In town, the rent was very little - $25 to $35 per month- and we didn't have enough stuff to fill up a small corner of a building; but it was a beginning and I had no money to invest in a business. It's impossible to get your own business going. That's one of the terrible things about the tax laws. It was a terrible thing when I was trying to start a business.

This went on with the help of my sons, Gordon, Gilbert, Keith, Charles, John, and Pat. We got it going and held it together; building it all the time. I was working almost every night in the theater business and then running our own business during the day. With the encouragement of Emma, we took the building that belonged to Dan Plunkett on Wall Street, on the west side of the railroad tracks in Las Vegas. We paid him $100 a month for two or three months and with the right to extend it and having to pay $125 if things went the way we hoped. I asked Dan to give me a break because I had never had to pay that much money for rent. I didn't know we could make a profit while paying that kind of rent.

It was a very hard struggle for the next ten years. Finally, I quit working in the theatrical business as soundman or spot director to put all of my time in at the STAGE, SOUND AND EQUIPMENT INC. It began to grow by leaps and bound. We began to get additional space and more employees. We had video and audio engineers, a designing room, an engineering department and hundreds of thousands of dollars invested in equipment. As I have a copy of the purchase order from Sylvania Electric for over 1.6 million dollars for doing a video closed-circuit camera job at the Landmark Hotel. We had a big business.

LEA RECOGNIZES HIS HEALTH PROBLEMS

After all of these years, it dawned on me that I had bad trouble. I had stomach trouble which was caused by irritation of the hips upsetting my stomach. After many doctors and xrays, i was still looking for someone to help me with my hips. The hip problem had gotten so bad that when the doctors would examine me, they couldn't see anything wrong. They knew I was in pain, so they'd give me some drugs. The law said that they could fibe drugs to me for only so long and then they'd have to take it away from me. When this happened, I turned to alcohol. I became an alcoholic, although I was not one to go around to parties or anything else. I just wanted to use the alcohol to get rid of the pain and get some rest so I could do another day's work.

In the last few days before I sold the business, I was under this kind of physical pressure. It was necessary for me to work six hours a day, and my hips got so sore that I dared not to walk down to the shop. They felt like they'd slip out of place or something and I'd nearly fall on my face. One particular time both hips went out and I received some terrible cuts and abrasions from falling that way.

THE FAMILY BUSINESS GETS SOLD

After trying to find someone to buy the business, and failing to get someone, Ron Brako who was a young man I brought up in the business made a proposition to me to take over the business himself. He made a mistake by getting a lawyer to come and see me, although he knew how I felt about lawyers. The lawyer came in and began to tell me what I had to do to make the business acceptable to this young man. I certainly didn't need this type of lecture in my physical and mental condition; but I did go to see a lawyer myself. After all of the talking we did with him, he presented us a bill of $150.00. About this time, there was a fellow coming in from Texas to take over the business so we made everything look the best for him. He was supposed to be a big electronics businessman who was President of the Video Data Corporation of Houston, Texas.

When he got here, it didn't take me long to give it to him. My son, Keith and my wife were so upset at me for this. They just couldn't believe it. I checked with my bank and the President of the First National Bank and his two Vice-Presidents. He called the bank's consultants. We sat there and talked awhile, while they looked up the Video Data Corporation. Pretty Soon, the phone rang. After the President talked for awhile, he said, "It looks like we've got a millionaire in Las Vegas." He said that Video Data is selling for 6 ½ a share and they are asking 7 ½ a share. So, in effect with the stock certificates that I would receive in return for the stock certificates for STAGE, SOUND AND EQUIPMENT, it would put me over a million dollars.

Emma and I planned a trip to New Zealand. She had wanted this for a number of years. It was the one place she wanted to see in the world. From the promise I had made to her in 1966 when we went to Alaska, she went along with me. The sailing for the trip would start March 31 1969.

I had sold the business on December 10, 1968 to the Video Data Corporation and I was to stay on there to assist in the business. It wasn't long until I was asked to leave, which I was glad to do because I couldn't understand what they were trying to do there in running that business.

As the work started on the International Hotel (which was under construction then), we have a $750,000 contract for all the video and audio work to be done in the Hotel, including the casinos, showrooms, wired music and video to all the rooms. It was a big job, but we had all the materials coming in. In fact, we had a $210,000 in accounts receivable at the first of the year against $165,000 in accounts payable. I turned these over to the Video Data Corporation. The difference was that all the materials were coming in for the construction of the International Hotel which is now the Hilton Hotel.

LEA AND EMMA TAKE THEIR DREAM VACATION

I kept in touch with Ron Brako. They got a trailer to put on the job. Ron was working in the trailer, the men were working on the job. Then came April when Emma and I went to San Pedro, California by air. We went to the Orange County Airport. It was in Long Beach, California where we got the luxury liner, the Monterrey. We sailed out of the harbor at 11:00 pm from Long Beach. Charlie and Lois and their two little girls came to see us off. We entertained them in our nice stateroom. They had come over one hundred miles to come see us off on our trip. It was seventeen days of sailing to Auckland, New Zealand. We stopped at the island of Bora Bora, went ashore and enjoyed it very much. Emma was very happy being able to travel and not worry about the boys at home. She thoroughly enjoyed herself.

We stopped at Tahiti and went through the town of Papiete and saw the new hotel being built there. It was quite unusual to see the French flags. It shook me up when they took down the stars and stripes and run up the tri-color above the stars and stripes. The natives of Morea cooked us up a fantastic native dinner. This was a fine American built hotel where we stayed with bathrooms, tubs, toilets, and the whole works. The architecture of the cabins was native with the patched roof. They seemed small, but once you were inside, you noticed you had two or three rooms plus the bathroom. We stayed here until that evening when the launch took us back to our shop, the Monterrey. The natives sang and waved farewell.

The night we got underway again, we ran into some real rough weather and heavy storms. We were in the middle of the ship, so we didn't get shook up too much. At 2:00 or 3:00 in the morning, we arrived at Auckland. The big Monterrey had to stand by until the harbor pilot came out and boarded us to take us to the docks. It was quite an exciting night. At this point, the people who were making the big loop trip on the Monterrey would stay a few days, then go back through the islands. There were a lot of good-byes to the other passengers we had met at this point.

We stayed at the Intercontinental Hotel in Auckland. I believe it was built and owned by the Pan American Airways. We thoroughly enjoyed our visit in Auckland. We went around visiting some of the boat races on the harbor, seeing their horse racing facilities, their university, museums, and even the sheep ranches. There were some beautiful green pastures there. This was in the month of April, so everything was green.

We bought some gifts there for our children and some for ourselves. The next part of our trip, we took a bus to Rotorua. We contacted a guide and went fishing there at Lake Rotorua. Emma caught the first fish of her life there.

She'd never thrown a hook in the water before. She caught the only fish of the day. We were out there before daylight while the fish were still biting. When the sun came up, the wind came up and we headed back to our cabin. When we got to our cabin, Emma had her big fish with her; so I took a picture of her holding the fish. You could not keep any fish out of the New Zealand waters unless it was seventeen inches or longer. This seemed so unusual to me. I found out later that there were rainbow trout planted in that lake many years ago. They had an oxygen plant in the lake that provided oxygen in the water that the fish needed. This was one of the reasons why the fish grew so fast. Also, in New Zealand they have no predatory animals. The English brought the red deer into that country. Today, there are no closed seasons on the deer. Many American people would come to New Zealand just to shoot deer; but they were happy to have you kill them off.

I got the chef at the restaurant in Rotorua to prepare the fish for $3.00 with a lot of vegetables with it. We didn't stay in a hotel; we stayed in a motel. We went to the restaurant which was part of the motel assembly. I invited some young men who were in the dining area to join us to eat the fish. I didn't like the fish myself. It had a sulfur taste to it - if you could imagine such a thing.

The next day, the bus stopped for us to see the Thermal Plant. From then on down, we were seeing the south end of the north island of New Zealand. It was beautiful country. We came out on the west coast of this island. We drove clear down to the capital of New Zealand - Wellington. That night, we had a quiet walk to the ferryboat. We took a ferryboat to a little town close to Christchurch on the South island of New Zealand. Emma was so tired and we were so cramped in this little stateroom. There was barely room for us, our luggage and the bunk beds. Emma settled right down while I went out. We got a good night's sleep. By morning, the water was getting quite rough.

We were off the ferryboat by daylight and were transferred to a train that took us from the dock to Christchurch. At Christchurch, we got into the oldest hotel we had ever seen in our lives. It was funny. It was a beautiful place and this was where we noticed how quiet the people were. We were ordering our dinner, and I had to ask the waitress to speak up a little more. Of course, my voice could be heard throughout the restaurant. Everyone's head was turning. I was embarrassed as heck. There was nothing else we could do. We were amazed at how much American business there was in New Zealand.

We took a trip with a young man from Australia. He was a salesman. He was interested in us since we had come from Las Vegas. He offered to take us out in his car and show us the surrounding country. We went with him and he really did show us the country around Christchurch. He asked us all kinds of questions about Las Vegas which I was happy to answer.

After we left Christchurch, we left by airplane to the Hermitage. This was a ski resort, a winter and summer resort in the Southern Alps. I was amazed to see the huge mountains in this area - glaciers with snow all over them. We stopped and spent a couple of days at the Hermitage. This was delightful, too.

Emma didn't want to go with me in the little plane up onto the big glacier. It comes down the side of Mt. Cook which is the highest peak on the Southern Alps. As we were coming in to land on this glacier, I noticed that a skier had already been down that snow and ice. I mentioned to the pilot who was sitting beside me that the skier had got out early. He said that it was his landing skis of his plane from his trip before this one. I was so amazed. When we landed, the pilot let us out. We were up to our ankles in snow, under the thousands of feet of ice. The pilot took a picture of me in front of the plane. That's the record we have.

We took off and went back to the Hermitage. I walked up one of the trails which was used in the summer for those who wished to climb through those mountain peaks and beautiful trails. At this time, it was autumn New Zealand and it was cool with frost on the ground. I walked up through there with my camera, alone, and took a lot of pictures as such things as signs saying "Beware of Snow Slides', 'Do Not Make Intentional Noise that Would Trigger a Snow Slide". It kind of shook me up a bit; but we had a good time and good food.

The first night we went up to the top of the Inn. There was a nice dining room and orchestra up there. We danced a little bit and had a little bite to eat. When we finally located the restaurant in the Intercontinental Hotel in Auckland, the orchestra played the song from Doctor Zhivago: The theme song titled Laura's Theme. The second time after we asked the orchestra to play it for us, we came in the second night and they began to play that music the minute we walked in the room. Emma thought that was just great because it was tune we both loved.

When we left the Hermitage, we flew to Queenstown. Queenstown was the sportsman center for the New Zealand islands. This was where they got the deer, fish, and such animals. During our stay there, we were able to see the gold mining country of New Zealand. I have movies and pictures of that trip that would scare you to death; because of the narrow road we had to travel on to see it. We stayed in a motel there. Tea was brought to us every morning in New Zealand. I wanted to make a trip to the tip end of the south island. We went on a boat, as it was a sight seeing yacht. They took us to where the whalers would come in. the people remarked that for years there were the thickest flies in that dock area. The Melford Sound was really a sight to see. I have pictures of this place.

I noticed that from Melford Sound to the South Pole and from Point Barrow to the North Pole there wasn't much difference. Emma and I were as close as civilians could get to both the North Pole and the South Pole. We hadn't been around the world, but if we would have straightened things out in one long line, we would have gotten around it at the equator.

When we were through with our trip at Milford Sound, we went back to Auckland to the Intercontinental Hotel for a night or two and prepared to fly to Australia. This was the longest trip we made which was over 4,000 miles from New Zealand to Sidney, Australia over the Indian Ocean.

In Sidney, we were put into another one of the oldest hotels where it was so noisy we couldn't stand it. The stay in Sidney was enjoyable anyways. We saw their museums, universities, their race tracks where there were a lot of horse races in that country and some of the beautiful homes with beautiful furniture. Some of them are hard to believe.

We went to Botany Bay, to the capital, then I made a trip alone to Alice springs which is in the middle of nowhere. No one knows where it came from. Their desert isn't like our Nevada and California. They don't have any mountains at all. There are miles and miles of nothing but miles and miles of desert.

LEA AND EMMA RETURN HOME

Suddenly we were worried of the business going bankrupt, so we got on a plane instead of finishing our trip there (which would have taken us to Taiwan, Hong Kong, Japan and Anchorage, Alaska before we returned to Las Vegas). I hope I didn't leave out too much detail. It was an enjoyable trip. Emma and I took off from Sidney on Pan Am Airlines. I believe it was a DC 8. We flew first-class so we had plenty of room and were served a fantastic meal. I still have the menu of that dinner. It was 4:00 in the afternoon when we left Australia. We flew continuously until 2:00 the following afternoon to reach Honolulu, Hawaii. We were then allowed to get off the plane while it took two or three hours to re-service the plane. This was the first time we had been in the new airport in Honolulu, so we had a good time looking around there. Our next flight from Honolulu to Los Angeles was so large that my ankles started to swell and it was very painful with any hip problem, also. Coming in over the lovely blue ocean and having to land in the dirty smog of Los Angeles, I couldn't imagine how people could live there. The sun was so bright in the thin air, it almost blinded us looking out that window.

Shortly after we landed in Los Angeles, we got a Western flight to Las Vegas; arriving there on my birthday, May 23, 1969 at 11:30 in the morning. By 2:00 that afternoon, l had received a phone call from Richard Brown, who was the man who supposedly bought the business. He told me that he was sending $5,000 by western union which was all the money he had. He apologized for what had happened to the business and that there was nothing more that he could do.

There I was, back in town with all the problems of a bankrupt business over my head (which was none of my doing at all) . The law says that under the conditions that I sold the business, I was the party responsible for everyone not getting their money. This upsets me to hear that type of thinking from who you would think were normally intelligent people. Lawyers, I have my opinion of them.

It wasn't long until there was a meeting of the bankruptcy which was calIed an involuntary bankruptcy. This was some of the gobbledygook the lawyers put out. The fact that the man who took over my business was given all of the assets, then all of the liabilities should have been hung around his neck. If he wanted to do it; fine. Then, if he signed with me for a transfer of assets and liabilities, that's what he took over - not to be hung on me. According to the law from what Keith told me, they don't look at it that way.

All of these things upset me terribly. The bank loans hadn't been paid off. The money that should have gone to the creditors was dissipated. There is one question in my mind since I have a copy now of a purchase order from Sylvania Electric for over a million dollars. I wonder what became of the money - the one million dollars. Because there is no record of it anywhere and yet a purchase order is in effect; a bank draft. This is how the business world operates. If you're paying a bill, you pay only by the purchase order which you issued to get the material that makes the bill possible. That's the way all businesses operate. The invoice that I might send to Sylvania covering this purchase order was not really what Sylvania was paying. Sylvania was issuing a draft to cover that purchase order from their company.

The fact that there was no mentioning of this or any record of this kind of money and since the people who were connected with Sylvania are involved in many ways with the conduct of this business leads me to believe that there was a conspiracy somewhere along the line to destroy that business of mine.

I think that everyone made money on it except me. Not everyone. But the people at Sylvania and the Video Data Corporation did.

Made in the USA
Middletown, DE
30 October 2021

50831583R00195